ROGET'S
THESAURUS OF PHRASES

ROGET'S

THESAURUS OF PHRASES

BARBARA ANN KIPFER, PH.D.

WRITER'S DIGEST BOOKS
Cincinnati, Ohio
www.writersdigest.com

 Published by Writer's Digest Books, an imprint of F&W Publications, Inc., 1507 Dana Avenue, Cincinnati, Ohio 45207. (800) 289-0963. First edition.

05 04 03 02 01 5 4 3 2 1

Library of Congress Cataloging-in-Publication Data

Kipfer, Barbara Ann

Roget's thesaurus of phrases / by Barbara Ann Kipfer.

p. cm.

ISBN 0-89879-999-6 (alk. paper)

1. English language—Terms and phrases. 2. English language—Synonyms and antonyms. I. Title: Thesaurus of phrases. II. Title.

PE1689.K47 2001

423'.1—dc21 2001026124

CIP

Edited by Meg Leder

Designed by Angela Wilcox

Cover by Sandy Weinstein; Tin Box Studio; Cincinnati, OH

Production coordinated by John Peavler

ACKNOWLEDGMENTS

This book, as the other books I have written in the past ten years, would not have come to fruition without the assistance of my husband, Paul Magoulas. He tirelessly helped research and organize *Roget's Thesaurus of Phrases*. His hard work and enthusiasm make all the difference.

I would also like to thank the best programmer in the world, Mark Dinan—who can "do it all" with data.

I'd also like to acknowledge my cherubs, Kyle and Keir, who make everything I do a worthwhile challenge.

—Barbara Ann Kipfer

ABOUT THE AUTHOR

Dr. Barbara Ann Kipfer is Head Lexicographer for Cymfony, a leader in information extraction, text mining, and question answering. Previously, she worked for Ask Jeeves, Answers .com, CitySearch, GoTo.com, Mindmaker, TextWise, General Electric Research, Bellcore (now Telcordia), IBM Research, and Knowledge Adventure.

Dr. Kipfer is the author of more than twenty books, including the *Writer's Digest Flip Dictionary*, the best-selling *14,000 things to be happy about* (Workman) and Page-a-Day calendars based on it. She has also authored *the wish list*, *1,400 things for kids to be happy about*, and *8,789 Words of Wisdom* for Workman; *Roget's 21st Century Thesaurus*, *21st Century Spelling Dictionary*, *21st Century Manual of Style* (Dell/Laurel), *The Order of Things* (Random House), *Dictionary of American Slang*, third edition (with R. Chapman; HarperCollins), *Sisson's Word and Expression Locater* (Prentice-Hall), *Encyclopedic Dictionary of Archaeology* (Kluwer Plenum), and *Something to Talk About* (iUniverse.com). She is the editor for the sixth edition of *Roget's International Thesaurus* (HarperResource).

She has done lexicographic work for clients in artificial intelligence, information retrieval, natural language processing, publishing, book packaging, and multimedia. Clients have included HarperReference, Wang, Random House Reference, Dorling Kindersley, Fitzhenry & Whiteside, Macmillan, Longman, Grolier, Columbia University Press, BellSouth Publishing, Ameritech Publishing, and Funk & Wagnalls.

Barbara holds a Ph.D. in linguistics (University of Exeter), a Ph.D. in archaeology (Greenwich University), a Master's in linguistics (Exeter), and a Bachelor's in physical education (Valparaiso University). She is working on a Ph.D. in Buddhist Studies with Greenwich University.

INTRODUCTION

Nonexistent in the wide world of reference books until now: a book devoted entirely to the synonyms of phrases, a thesaurus of phrases. Thesauri are well over 75 percent devoted to offering synonyms for single words, and in many thesauri all the headwords are single words. Hidden amongst the millions of words are some phrases. At best, a smattering of phrases are offered as headwords. This new book, *Roget's Thesaurus of Phrases*, is for that neglected but very, very large part of our vocabulary—the multiword combination.

Roget's Thesaurus of Phrases is a book for the twenty-first century, for all of us trying to look things up on the Internet. We need to know alternate phrasings so that we can find what we are looking for. Anyone who has tried to access these resources knows that the keywords and phrases picked out will drive what information will be retrieved. *Roget's Thesaurus of Phrases* will help you broaden or narrow your searches. It is a tool to help you make the most of your vocabulary in a time when how you word things has become ever more important.

It is not so difficult to find synonyms for phrases like "birth control," but how about "crowning achievement" or "peace treaty"? Think of the power *Roget's Thesaurus of Phrases* puts into your hands; with alternate phrasings, it makes finding information so much easier. *Roget's Thesaurus of Phrases* is also the equivalent of the standard thesaurus—but for phrases. It's a resource for finding another way of saying what you mean. Just as you need alternate ways of saying things when writing single words, you also need other ways of expressing phrases.

The main difference between having a copy of *Roget's Thesaurus of Phrases* and having a copy of a thesaurus that includes phrases as synonyms for single words is accessibility. You cannot look up close synonyms for phrases in a regular thesaurus. You can get to the synonyms for phrases only by locating an entry for a single word first. For example, "flower arrangement" has the close synonym of "floral decoration," but it cannot be found through the index of a thesaurus. It is listed under "arrangement" in the category "ornamentation." *Roget's Thesaurus of Phrases* will make finding synonyms for phrases much simpler.

Think of all the collocations—words that are commonly used together—that you cannot look up in standard reference books. Think of "consumer credit" and "flight path." Think of "sports arena" and "buffer zone." Where can you go to find another way of saying these phrases? Collocations and other types of phrases are very important in our language, and they are the keystone to looking things up electronically.

Roget's Thesaurus of Phrases is also useful for crossword fans. Many crosswords have multiple-word clues. Many of these phrases are included in this book. Multiple-word clues are also not the basis for any of the crossword puzzle dictionaries out there—even though the puzzles are built of multiple-word clues.

Roget's Thesaurus of Phrases works as a reverse dictionary, too. It will help get you from an idea to the phrase or word you want to use. In many cases, you might be starting with a phrase that expresses your idea, but not in the specific way you desire. *Roget's Thesaurus of Phrases* reverses the lookup to get you to the right phrase or word.

Roget's Thesaurus of Phrases is not restricted to providing only phrasal synonyms for phrases; if a single word is a synonym for a phrase, it is certainly included.

This book is for businesspeople, journalists, authors, crossword puzzlers, information retrievers, students and word lovers. Phrases have been left out long enough. Now they have a place: *Roget's Thesaurus of Phrases*.

Everyone has experienced the frustration of not being able to rephrase something or find the word or phrase they want. Another phrasing or the right word can enable you to do so much more, and *Roget's Thesaurus of Phrases* will help you find it.

—*Barbara Ann Kipfer, Ph.D.*

Aa

abdominal muscle abdominals, celiac muscle, intestinal muscle, peritoneum, stomachal muscle, stomachic muscle, stomach muscle, tummy muscle, viscera

abject fear cowardice, fear

abject slavery involuntary servitude, servitude, slavery

able seaman AB, able-bodied seaman

abominable snowman yeti

abortion pill French abortion pill, mifepristone, RU 486

abortive attempt failure, futile effort, vain attempt

about-face change, 180-degree turn, overturning, policy change, repeal, retraction, reversal, switch, turnabout, turnaround, U-turn, volte-face

above all chiefly, especially, importantly, in particular, mainly, most importantly, mostly, most of all, primarily, principally, supremely

above suspicion chaste, incorrupt, inculpable, inerrable, innocent, irreproachable, irreprovable, pure, reproachless, scrupulous, unblamable, unblameworthy, unimpeachable, unindictable

Abraham's bosom blessed state, bosom of Abraham, eternal home, eternal rest, happiness and rest, happy home, happy hunting ground, heaven. in sinu Abraham, kingdom of God, nirvana, paradise

absence of dust cleanness, freedom from dirt, immaculateness

absentee vote absentee ballot, mail-in vote, proxy

absent without leave absent from duty, absent without permission, AWOL, desertion, French leave, hooky, truancy, unauthorized absence

absolute certainty apodictic, categorical, moral certainty, positive, unequivocal

absolutely nothing nil, nothing, zero, zilch, zip

absolute power absolutism, autarchy, autocracy, despotism, dictatorship, tyranny

absolute ruler absolute monarch, autocrat

absolute sovereignty autarchy, self-government, self-rule

absolute temperature thermodynamic temperature

absolute value numerical value

absolute zero absence of heat, lowest temperature, -459.67 degrees F, -459.67 Fahrenheit, -273.15 Celsius, -273.15 degrees C, 0 degrees Kelvin, zero degrees Kelvin, zero kelvins

abstract thought logical thinking, reasoning, systematic thought

abusive language bad language, invective, profane language, vituperation

academic degree associate's, associate's degree, bachelor's, bachelor's degree, degree, graduate degree, master's, master's degree, Ph.D., undergraduate degree

academic freedom freedom to learn, freedom to teach, right to education

academic gown academic costume, academic dress, academic robe, cap and gown, judge's robe

academic press university press, university publishing house

academic world academic affairs, academic realm, academic setting, college world, educational realm, educational setting, educational world, scholastic world, university world

academic year academic grade, academic term, academic track, college year, collegiate year, scholastic year, school term, school year, session, term, university year

Academy Awards Oscars

a cappella choral, without accompaniment, without instruments

acaroid resin accroides gum, gum accroides

acceleration lane fast lane, passing lane

acceleration principle accelerator principle, principle of acceleration

accelerator card accelerator board

accepted meaning acceptance, practice, usage

access provider IAP, Internet access provider, Internet service provider, ISP, service provider

accessory apartment granny flat, in-law apartment, in-law rental

accessory cell subsidiary cell

accessory fruit false fruit, pome, pseudocarp

access road feeder road, frontage road, slip road

accommodation ladder boarding ladder, companion ladder, gangway ladder, side-mount ladder, stern ladder

accomplished fact fait accompli, matter of fact

according to Hoyle according to regulation, according to rule, according to the highest authority, as it should be, by the book, by the numbers, gospel, indisputable, proper, up to par

account book balance sheet, blank book, book of account, daybook, journal, ledger, logbook, record book, register

account executive account representative, associated person, customer's broker, registered customer support person, registered representative

account payable balance due, bill, debt, invoice, liability, outstanding account, tab, unpaid bill

account receivable amount owing, balance due, bill, debt, invoice, receivable

accumulated arrears debt, overdue payment

accurate knowledge scientific knowledge, verified knowledge

accused person culprit, defendant, litigant, prisoner, suspect

Ace™ bandage elastic bandage, elastic support bandage, stretchable bandage

ace in the hole ace up one's sleeve, card up one's sleeve, decisive argument, decisive resource, hidden advantage, reserve, secret advantage, secret weapon, sure advantage, trump card

acetylene lamp carbide lamp, miner's lamp

Achilles' heel chink in the armor, damaging weakness, defect, failing, flaw, foible, forlorn hope, frailty, handicap, heel of Achilles, susceptibility, tender spot, vulnerability, vulnerable point, weak link, weakness, weak spot

aching heart broken heart, heavy heart, sorrow, weariness

aching muscles fatigue, physical fatigue

acid rain acid deposition, acid precipitation

acid rock drug-experience music, psychedelic rock, repetitive rock music

acid test analysis, conclusive test, critical test, crucial test, decisive test, definitive test, experiment, proof, proving ground, substantiation, sure test, trial, verification

acid trip bad trip, drug trip, head trip, LSD trip, trip

acknowledgment of payment receipt, voucher

aclinic line magnetic equator

acorn nut cap nut, wing nut

acoustic nerve auditory nerve

acquaintance rape date rape

acquired character acquired characteristic

acquired immune deficiency syndrome acquired immunodeficiency syndrome, AIDS, HIV-positive, immune failure, SIDA, Sindroma de Inmunidad Deficiente Adquerido

acquired knowledge erudition, learning

acquired taste connoisseurship

across-the-board all-embracing, all-encompassing, all-inclusive, blanket, broad, broad in content, broad in scope, complete, comprehensive, encompassing, extensive, global, including all categories, including all members, panoptic, sweeping, total, wide, widespread

across the sea over the water, oversea, transatlantic, transmarine

action painting abstract painting, dribbled painting, smear painting, splash painting

active capital active wealth, convertible property, ready money

active cell current cell, selected cell

active duty active service, AD, full-time military service, mobilization

act of courage chivalry, gallant act, heroic achievement, heroism, knightly deed, soldierly conduct

act of courtesy common courtesy, courteous act, graceful gesture, polite act

act of God accident, circumstances beyond one's control, divine act, force majeure, freak accident, inevitable accident, marvel, natural disaster, phenomenon, supernatural event, unavoidable casualty, unforeseen event; miracle, vis major, wonder

act of legislature decree, law, regulation, rule, statute

act on act upon, follow, follow up on, motivate, pursue, take action

act the fool horse around, make a fool of oneself, play the fool

act up (malfunction) break, break down, conk out, fail, function improperly, go on the blink, jam, malfunction, not work, stall, stop running

act up (misbehave) act out, be bad, behave badly, be out of line, carry on, fool around, horseplay, make trouble, misbehave, rebel, set a bad example, show off

acute pain darting pain, sharp pain, shooting pain, smart, sting

Adam's apple thyroid cartilage

ad card card page

adding machine abacus, calculating machine, calculator, computer, pocket calculator, totaliser, totalizer

adding up addition, counting up, summation, tally, totaling

add insult to injury add fuel to the fire, aggravate, exacerbate, heighten, make worse, provoke, rub salt in the wound, slap in the face, twist the knife, worsen

address book agenda, agenda book, calendar, electronic organizer, Filofax™, handheld organizer, personal digital assistant

add up to amount to, boil down to, spell

adhesive tape adhesive bandage, Band-Aid™, Scotch™ tape, sticky tape, tape

ad hoc (formed for a specific purpose) for one specific case, for this purpose only, special, specific, specified

ad hoc impromptu, improvised, spontaneous

ad hominem to the person

ad infinitum at length, continuously, endlessly, forever, having no end, interminably, never-ending, on and on, perpetually, relentlessly, to infinity, unlimitedly, without end, without limit

adjustable rate mortgage ARM, variable rate mortgage

adjutant general brigadier general, chief administrative assistant, chief administrative officer, general's adjutant, major general

ad-lib deliver extemporaneously, deliver spontaneously, extemporize, improvise, play it by ear, wing it

ad lib according to pleasure, ad libitum, as one thinks best, as one wishes, at pleasure, at will, extemporaneous, freely, impromptu, improvised, impulsive, made-up, offhand, off-the-cuff, spontaneously, unrehearsed, without restraint

ad libitum according to pleasure, ad lib, as one thinks best, as one wishes, at pleasure, at will, extemporaneous, freely, impromptu, improvised, impulsive, made-up, offhand, off-the-cuff, spontaneously, unrehearsed, without restraint

administrative segregation solitary confinement

admitted guilt confessed guilt, confession

ad nauseam at length, boringly, endlessly, in detail, lengthily, long-windedly, more than one can stomach, repeatedly, repetitively, to an excessive degree, to a sickening degree, to nauseating extremes, too much, to the point of queasiness

adrenal gland adrenal, endocrine gland, suprarenal gland

adrenocorticotropic hormone ACTH, adrenocorticotrophin, adrenocorticotropin, corticotrophin, corticotropin

adult education continuing education, night school

adult movie blue movie, porn film, porn flick, porn movie, porno film, porno flick, pornographic film, pornographic flick, pornographic movie, porno movie, skin flick

ad valorem according to the value, ad val

advanced studies graduate studies

advance man advance agent, arranger, press agent, press officer, publicist

advance notice announcement, warning

adventure story heroic tale

advertising agency ad agency, ad company, advertising company

advertising campaign ad blitz, ad campaign, advertising blitz, dog and pony show

advisory board advisory body, board of advisers, consultants, consultative body, planning board

aerosol can aerosol bomb, aerosol container, aerosol dispenser, atomizer, propellant, spray can

aerospace medicine aeromedicine, aviation medicine

aerospace science rocket science, space science

affair of honor affaire d'honneur, duel

affinity card credit card, custom credit card, gold card, membership card, platinum card

affinity group PAC, political action committee, pressure group, single-issue group, special interest group, special interests

affirmative action antidiscrimination program, equal opportunity, even break, fair hiring practices, fair shake, fair treatment, limited choice, nondiscrimination, positive discrimination, quota system, reverse discrimination

a fortiori all the more, all the more so, from the stronger, more than ever, still more, with greater reason, with more reason

African swine fever hog cholera

after-dinner drink dessert wine, digestif, nightcap

afternoon tea cream tea, five-o'clock tea, high tea, light supper, tea, teatime

against the law banned, criminal, illegal, illicit, unconstitutional, unlawful

Agent Orange Agent Blue, Agent Purple, Agent White, defoliant, herbicide

agent provocateur agitator, firebrand, goad, incendiary, instigator, intelligence agent, noncooperator, operative, provocateur, provocative agent, provoker, rabble-rouser, radical, ringleader, secret agent, spark, spy, troublemaker

age of consent adulthood, legal age, manhood, marriageable age, maturity, womanhood

Age of Reason Enlightenment, the Enlightenment

agricultural college college of agriculture, cow college, cow tech, farming college, school of agriculture

agricultural worker agricultural laborer, farmer, farmhand, farm laborer, migrant worker

ahead of time before, beforehand, early, too soon

aid and abet abet, collude, countenance, foster, keep in countenance

aide-de-camp ADC, adjutant, aide, assistant, girl Friday, helper, man Friday, number two, right-hand man, right-hand woman, secretary

aide-mémoire position paper

AIDS test ELISA test, HIV test, Western blot test

air bag side air bag

air base air station, aircraft base, military aircraft base, military aircraft center, military airport

air bladder air vesicle, float, swim bladder

air campaign aerial bombardment, air attack, air raid, air strike, bombing, surgical air strike

air cargo airfreight, payload

air-conditioning A/C, AC, air cooling, C/A, central air, central air-conditioning, climate control, climatization

aircraft carrier attack aircraft carrier, carrier, flattop, warship

air-cushion vehicle ACV, captured-air vehicle, cushioncraft, flarecraft, GEM, ground-effect machine, hovercraft, surface-effect ship

air gun air rifle, BB gun, pellet gun, popgun, toy rifle, windgun

air hunger dyspnea

airing out airing, fumigation, ventilation

air lane airway, flight path

air letter aerogram, aerogramme, airgraph, airmail letter

air mattress blow-up mattress, inflatable bed, inflatable mattress

air pipe air passage, air shaft, airway, ventilating pipe

air piracy aircraft piracy, airplane hijacking, high-jacking, hijacking, skyjacking

air plant aerophyte, epiphyte, epiphytic plant

air pocket air bump, air hole

air potato aerial yam, potato yam

air power air military strength, aviation, aviation strength

air pump bicycle pump

air raid aerial bombardment, air assault, air attack, air campaign, air strike, bombing mission, bombing raid, bombing run, fire raid, saturation raid, shuttle raid, strafing

air route air corridor, air lane, corridor, flight lane, flight path, skyway

air sac air cell, alveolus

air shaft air duct, air hole, air pipe, air tube, air well

airsickness bag barf bag

air sock wind cone, wind sleeve, wind sock

air taxi shuttle plane

air terrorism air terror

air traffic control air traffic control service, ATC, flight control

à la carte from the menu, separately

à la mode served with ice cream, topped with ice cream, with ice cream

alarm bell burglar alarm, danger signal, fire alarm, tocsin, warning bell

alarm clock alarm, alarm watch, clock radio, travel alarm

Alaska Highway Alcan Highway

Alaska pipeline Alaskan pipeline, TAPS, Trans-Alaska Pipeline System

alcohol abuse alcohol addiction, alcoholic abuse, alcoholism, dipsomania, drinking, hitting the bottle, substance abuse

alcoholic beverage alcohol, alcoholic drink, beer, booze, cocktail, drink, hard drink, hard liquor, inebriant, intoxicant, liqueur, liquor, mixed drink, spirits, wine

Alcoholics Anonymous AA, Twelve Steps

al dente firm, medium

al fresco in the open air, open-air, outdoors, out-of-doors, outside

A-list aristocracy, beau monde, beautiful people, cream of society, crème de la crème, cultured class, elite, haut monde, high life, high society, in group, jet set, privileged class, smart set, society, the Four Hundred, the privileged, upper class, upper crust, upper echelon

all clear clearance, go-ahead, green light

Allen™ wrench Allen key, hex key, hex wrench

allergic reaction allergy, anaphylactic shock, anaphylaxis, shock

alley cat homeless cat, stray cat

All Fools' Day April 1, April first, April Fools', April Fools' Day

all fours hands and knees

all hands everybody, every man, everyone, one and all

alligator pear avocado, avocado pear, midshipman's-butter

all-or-nothing adamant, firm, hard-line, inflexible, unbending, uncompromising, unyielding

all-points bulletin APB, dragnet, manhunt

all possible precautions caution, nothing left to chance

All Saints' Day Allhallowmass, Allhallows, Hallowmas, Hallowmass, November 1

all shapes and sizes all sorts and conditions, hodgepodge, mishmash, mixed bag

all-terrain bicycle all-terrain bike, ATB, mountain bicycle, mountain bike, MTB, off-road bicycle, off-road bike, off-roader

all-terrain vehicle ATV, jeep, off-road vehicle

all the time in the world ample time, no hurry, time on one's hands, time to spare

all-time low lowest level, lowest point, record low, rock bottom, the bottom

Almighty, the Allah, Creator, Father in Heaven, God, Heavenly Father, Jehovah, King of Kings, Lord of Lords, Supreme Being, the All-Powerful, the all-powerful, Yahweh

almost all chief part, main part, nearly all, principal part

alpha and omega A to Z, be-all and end-all, beginning and end, entirety, first and last, totality, whole; crucial part, main element, most important part, principal element

alphabet soup hodgepodge, potpourri, salmagundi

alpha ray alpha radiation

alpha wave alpha rhythm

alpine glacier cirque glacier, mountain glacier, valley glacier

also known as aka, alias

also-ran defeated player, failure, loser, nonstarter, unsuccessful candidate, unsuccessful challenger, unsuccessful person

altar boy acolyte, acolytus, altar attendant

alter ego ally, alternate, backup, body double, buddy, chum, confidant, counterpart, friend, mate, other personality, other self, pal, pinch hitter, private side, second self, soul mate, stand-in, supporter, surrogate, trusted friend, understudy

alternating current AC, free alternating current, single-phase alternating current, three-phase alternating current

alternative medicine complementary medicine, faith healing, folk medicine, holistic medicine, natural medicine, unconventional medicine, unorthodox medicine

alternative route detour, deviation

alternative school alternate school, nontraditional school

altitude sickness high-altitude sickness, mountain sickness

aluminum foil foil, tin foil

Alzheimer's disease Alzheimer's, senility

amateur night talent night

ambulance chaser attorney, lawyer, legal eagle, pettifogger, shyster, unethical attorney, unethical lawyer

amende honorable atonement, full apology, making amends, public apology

American dream material wealth

American flag American Stars and Stripes; Old Glory; red, white and blue; Stars and Bars; Stars and Stripes; Star-Spangled Banner

American plan AP, full American plan

amicus curiae adviser to the court, friend at court, friend in court, friend of the court

amino acid aminoalkanoic acid

ammunition chest caisson

ammunition dump armory, arsenal, magazine, munitions dump

amorous glance come-hither look, fond look, ogle, sheep's eyes, wink

amour propre conceit, good opinion of oneself, self-esteem, self-love, vanity

amplitude modulation AM

amusement park amusement center, carnival, funfair, pleasure ground, safari park, theme park, Tivoli, water park

anabolic steroid muscle pill, steroid

analog computer analogue computer, computer

anal personality anal, anal character, anal retentive personality, compulsive character, perfectionist, precisionist

anal sex anal copulation, anal intercourse, buggery, sodomy

analytic geometry analytical geometry, Cartesian geometry, coordinate geometry

analytic philosophy philosophical analysis

anaphylactic shock anaphylaxis

anatomically correct biologically correct, structurally correct

ancestor worship necrolatry

ancien régime ancient regime, ancient times

ancient history ancient times, antiquity, bygone days, distance of time, distant past, early history, prehistory, protohistory, remote past, the past, time immemorial, way back when

Ancient Mariner Captain Ahab, Flying Dutchman

angel dust animal trank, animal tranquilizer, cycline, DOA, dummy dust, dust, dust of angels, elephant tranquilizer, gorilla biscuit, green tea, hog, horse tranquilizer, mad dog, magic dust, monkey dust, PCP, peace pill, phencyclidine, purple rain, rocket fuel, STP, supergrass, superweed, worm, yellow fever, zoom

angel of mercy caregiver, Florence Nightingale, lady with the lamp, nurse

angle iron angle bar, angle bracket, angle section

angle of incidence incidence, incidence angle

angry young man complainer, dissatisfied customer, dissatisfied person

animal cracker animal cookie

animal doctor vet, veterinarian

animal heat blood heat, body heat

animal husbandry animal culture, animal raising, animal rearing, farming, livestock farming, pasturage, ranching, stock raising

animal kingdom animal group, Animalia, animality, animal life, animals, animal world, brute creation, fauna, kingdom Animalia

animal magnetism attractiveness, aura, beguilement, bewitchery, charisma, charm, hypnotic attraction, it, magnetism, mesmerism, od, odyl, odylic force, personal appeal, pizzazz, sex appeal, sexiness, sexual attraction

animal spirits bounce, energy, exuberance, frolicsomeness, life, liveliness, nervous spirits, sportiveness, spriteliness, vitality, vivacity, zing

animated cartoon animated movie, animation, cartoon, cell animation, Claymation™, comic, comic strip, drawing

ankle sock anklet, bobby sock, crew sock

Annie Oakley comp, complimentary pass, complimentary ticket, free admission, free pass, free ticket, guest pass, guest ticket, pass

anno Domini AD, CE, in the Christian Era, in the Common

Era, in the year of our Lord, since the birth of Jesus Christ, year of our Lord

annus mirabilis amazing thing, marvelment, nine days' wonder, notable year, remarkable year, wonderful thing, wonderful year, wonderment

anointing of the sick extreme unction, last rights

anonymous person anonym, anonymous, unnamed person

anorexia nervosa anorexia, dieting disorder, eating disorder, food aversion

answering machine voice mail

answering service message center, message service, telephone service

answer the call enlist, join up, sign on, volunteer

antiballistic missile ABM, antimissile missile, defensive missile

antidiuretic hormone ADH, arginine vasopressin, vasopressin

antigenic determinant determinant, epitope

antihemophilic factor antihemophilic globulin, factor VIII

antilock brake ABS, antilock braking system, nonskid brake

antimalarial pill quinine

antique dealer antiquarian, antiquary, antique collector

anti-roll bar anti-sway bar, roll bar, stabilizer bar, sway bar

ants in one's pants fidgetiness, fidgets, heebie-jeebies, itching, restlessness

anxious seat anxious bench, mourners' bench, on tenterhooks, shpilkes

any which way carelessly, indifferently

apartment building apartment complex, co-op, cooperative apartment house, flat house, flats, high-rise apartment, tenement, tower block

a posteriori analytical, empirical, experimental, from the latter, inducible, inductive, logical, practical

apostolic faith old-time religion, primitive faith, the faith, true faith

Apostolic see papacy, papality, see of Rome, the Church, Vatican

apothecaries' measure apothecaries' liquid measure

apothecaries' weight apothecaries' system, apothecaries' unit

apple of one's eye angel, beloved, cherished one, darling, dearest, fair-haired boy, favorite, honey, light of one's life, loved one, object of one's affections, pet, sweetheart, treasure

apple-pie order fine fettle, good shape, just so, neatness, orderly, perfect arrangement, perfect order, precise order, shipshape, tidiness

apple-polisher ass-kisser, bootlicker, brownnoser, fawner, flatterer, flunky, groveler, lackey, lickspittle, sycophant, toady, truckler, yes-man, yes-woman

applied art commercial art, industrial art

approach lights flare path, guide lights, runway lights, sequence flashers

après-ski after skiing

April Fools' Day All Fools' Day, April 1, April First, April Fools'

a priori based on theory, deductive, derivable, presumptive, rational, reasoned, supposed, theoretical

apron strings leash, swaddling clothes

apropos of apropos, concerning, in connection with, speaking of, with reference to, with regard to

Arabian Nights Thousand and One Nights

Arabic numeral Arabic figure

archaeological site archaeological remains, archaeological ruins, historical site, ruins

Archimedes' screw Archimedean screw

Arctic region Arctic, Arctic Circle, Arctic Ocean, North Pole, polar region

ardent spirits alcohol, alcoholic liquor, aqua vitae, booze, hard liquor, intoxicant, liquor, spirits, strong waters

area code telephone area

area rug scatter rug, throw rug

Aristotelian logic Aristotelianism, Aristotelian philosophy, formal logic, syllogism, traditional logic

arithmetic mean average, expectation, expected value, first moment, mean, sample mean, simple average

arithmetic progression arithmetic sequence, arithmetic series

Ark of the Covenant Ark

Arkansas toothpick bowie knife, hunting knife, Missouri toothpick

armed aggression armed conflict, armed fighting, armed hostilities, battle, combat, engagement, fight, war, warfare

armed forces armament, armed services, defense forces, fighting machine, military, military forces, military service, service, troops

Armistice Day Remembrance Day, Veterans' Day

armored vehicle armored car, armored personnel carrier, armored truck, tank

armor plate armor, armor plating, plate armor

arms control arms limitation, arms reduction, defense cuts, nonproliferation, weapons reduction

arm's length at a distance, distant, remote

arm wrestling Indian wrestling

army brat air force brat, marine brat, military brat, navy brat

arrogant strut confident walk, pompous gait, prance, swagger

Art Deco Art Moderne

artesian well cistern, deep well, flowing well

art exhibit art display, art show, display, exhibit, showing

art film art movie, avant-garde film, experimental film, representational film

art form genre

Artful Dodger crafty fellow, crafty rascal, dodger, opportunist, smoothie

articles of faith articles of religion, creedal statement, doctrinal statement, formulated belief, stated belief

artificial horizon attitude gyro, attitude indicator, flight indicator, gyro horizon

artificial insemination AI, intracervical insemination, intratubal insemination, intrauterine insemination

artificial intelligence AI, expert systems, intelligent retrieval, knowledge engineering, machine learning, natural language processing, neural networks

artificial kidney dialysis machine, hemodialyzer

artificial language American Sign Language, Ameslan, Esperanto, sign, sign language

artificial life AL, A-life

artificial limb artificial arm, artificial leg, fake limb, pegleg, prosthesis, prosthetic device, wooden leg

artificial lung inhalator, iron lung, respirator

artificial reality artificial environment, computer-generated environment, computerized simulation, virtual reality, VR

artificial respiration kiss of life, mouth-to-mouth resuscitation, mouth-to-nose resuscitation

artificial sweetener aspartame, calcium cyclamate, cyclamates, Equal™, NutraSweet™, saccharin, sodium cyclamate, sucralose, sugar substitute, sweetening agent, Sweet'n Low™

artistic license artistic freedom, license, poetic freedom, poetic license

ascending order A to Z {compare *descending order*}

Ascension Day Ascension, Ascension of the Lord, Holy Thursday

ASCII American Standard Code for Information Interchange, plain text

as fit as a fiddle fit, healthful, healthy, hearty, in good health, sound, vigorous

ash can dustbin, garbage can, garbage pail, litter basket, trash barrel, trash bin, trash can, wastebasket, waste bin, wastepaper basket

A-side featured song

asking price charge, cost, price, selling price

aspect ratio academy ratio, anamorphic, aspect format, screen proportion; tire aspect ratio, tire profile

asphalt jungle city, concrete jungle, downtown, inner city, mean streets, metropolis, municipality, urban area, urban complex, urban sprawl

assault and battery mugging, simple assault

assault rifle assault gun

assembly language assembly code

assembly line conveyor, production line

assertiveness training assertion training, positive thinking training

assisted suicide euthanasia, mercy killing

associate degree two-year degree

association football soccer, soccer football

as the crow flies beeline, direct route, most direct route, shortest route, straight, straight as an arrow, straight line

astral body astral, energy body, linga sharira, spiritual body

at fault blameworthy, culpable, erring, guilty, in error, in the wrong, liable, responsible, wrong

at hand accessible, close, imminent, impending, nearby, within reach

at heart at bottom, basically, deep down, fundamentally, in reality, inside, in spite of appearance

athlete's foot ringworm of the feet, tinea, tinea pedis

athletic contest athletic event, athletics, game, sports contest, sports event

athletic shoe aerobic shoe, basketball shoe, gym shoe, high-topped sneaker, running shoe, sneaker, tennis shoe

athletic supporter cup, jock, jockstrap

Atlantic time Atlantic Standard Time

atmospheric pressure air pressure, barometric pressure

atom bomb A-bomb, atomic bomb, atomic warhead, fission bomb, H-bomb, hydrogen bomb, neutron bomb, nuclear bomb, nuclear warhead, nuke, plutonium bomb, thermonuclear bomb

atomic age nuclear age

atomic bomb A-bomb, atom bomb, atomic warhead, fission bomb, H-bomb, hydrogen bomb, neutron bomb, nuclear bomb, nuclear warhead, nuke, plutonium bomb, thermonuclear bomb

atomic energy atomic power, nuclear energy, nuclear power, thermonuclear power

atomic mass atomic weight

atomic mass unit AMU, atomic volume, dalton

atomic number atomic weight

atomic pile atomic reactor, chain-reacting pile, chain reactor, fission reactor, nuclear reactor, pile, reactor, reactor pile

atomic theory Bohr theory, Dirac theory, Doctrine of definite proportions, Lewis-Langmuir or octet theory, quantum theory, Rutherford theory, Schrödinger theory, Thomson's hypothesis

atomic weight atomic mass, relative atomic weight

atom smasher accelerator, atomic accelerator, atomic cannon, atom smatter, particle accelerator

atrioventricular bundle atrioventricular trunk, bundle of His, truncus atrioventricularis

at risk at hazard, endangered, exposed, imperiled, in danger, in jeopardy, in peril, jeopardized, susceptible, threatened, vulnerable

at sea baffled, befuddled, bewildered, confounded, confused, dazed, disoriented, lost, mixed-up

attaché case attaché, briefcase

attention deficit disorder ADD, ADHD, attention deficit hyperactivity disorder, hyperactivity, learning disorder, short attention span

at times every so often, from time to time, now and again, now and then, occasionally, once in a while, on occasion

attitude problem bad attitude, chip on one's shoulder

attorney general AG, Attorney General of the United States, chief law officer, chief legal advisor, chief of the Department of Justice

au contraire contrarily, in opposition, on the contrary, on the other hand, to the contrary

au courant abreast of, aware, cognizant, current, enlightened, hip, informed, knowledgeable, up on, up to date, up to speed

audio book book on cassette, book on tape, taped book

audio frequency AF, audio, radio frequency

audiovisual aids AV aids

au fait expert, skillful, up to snuff, well instructed, wise to

au naturel bare, disrobed, exposed, in the buff, in the raw, naked, natural, nude, stark naked, stripped, unclad, unclothed, undressed

au pair baby-sitter, day care provider, domestic servant, live-in, nanny

au poivre with pepper

au revoir adieu, adios, arrivederci, bye, bye-bye, cheerio, good-bye, good day, sayonara, so long

aurora australis southern lights

aurora borealis aurora polaris, northern lights

Australian crawl crawl, front crawl

Authorized Version AV, King James Bible, King James Version, KJ

automated teller machine ATM, ATM machine, automated bank teller, automated teller, automatic teller, automatic teller machine, cash dispenser, cash machine

automatic focus autofocus, point and shoot

automatic pilot autopilot, Gyropilot™, robot pilot

automatic timer automatic shutoff, auto timer, self-timer

automatic transmission automatic drive

automobile racing auto racing,

car racing, drag racing, Formula 1 car racing, Indy car racing, motor sport, stock car racing

autumnal equinox fall equinox, September equinox

average deviation mean deviation, mean deviation from the mean

aversion therapy aversive conditioning

avoirdupois weight avoirdupois

Azoic era Archaeozoic, Archaeozoic era, Archeozoic, Archeozoic era

Aztec two-step diarrhea, diarrhoea, dysentery, flux, looseness of the bowels, loose stool, Montezuma's revenge, runs, tourista, trots, turistas

Bb

babe in the woods dupable person, dupe, easy mark, greenhorn, gull, innocent, simple soul, stooge, sucker, victim

baby blues depression, downheartedness, dumps, heaviness of heart, lowness, low spirits, melancholy, postpartum depression; blinkers, eyes, peepers

baby boomer boomer

baby carriage baby buggy, carriage, perambulator, pram, pushchair, stroller

baby grand baby grand piano, grand piano, parlor grand, piano

baby oil mineral oil

baby powder bath powder, talcum powder

baby's room child's room, nursery

baby tooth deciduous tooth, milk tooth, primary tooth

bachelor girl single girl, single woman, unattached female, unmarried woman

bachelor party smoker, stag party

bachelor's degree B.A., baccalaureate, bachelor of arts, bachelor of science, B.S., undergraduate degree

back and forth alternating, backwards and forwards, from pillar to post, from side to side, in and out, seesaw, to and fro, up and down, vacillating

back away back out, crawfish, retreat, withdraw

back burner abeyance, cold storage, limbo, suspension

back door back entrance, back stairs, back way, escape hatch, postern, postern door, secret exit, side door, trapdoor, wormhole

back down acquiesce, back off, bow out, cave in, chicken out, concede, give ground, give in, have no fight left, pull back, pull out, retreat, submit, surrender, wimp out, yield

back matter addendum, afterword, appendix, end matter, epilogue, index, supplement

back road backstreet, country road, side street

back rub kneading, manipulation, massage, rolfing, rubdown, shiatsu

backseat driver busybody, kibitzer, Nosey Parker

back talk back answer, backchat, comeback, guff, insolence, insult, lip, mouth, rejoinder, retort, return, riposte, rude answer, sass, sauce, short answer, uptake

backup light reverse light

backwards and forwards assiduously, completely, comprehensively, from A to Z, from top to bottom, fully, in and out, inside out, thoroughly, through and through

bad blood animosity, animus, antagonism, antipathy, bad chemistry, bad vibes, bad will, bitterness, disaccord, enmity, hard feelings, hatred, hostility, ill will, ill-disposedness, malevolence, oppugnancy, oppugnation, personality conflict, rancor, resentment

bad breath foul breath, halitosis, offensive breath

bad debt uncollectable bill, uncollectable debt, uncollectable loan, write-off

bad egg black sheep, corrupt person, evildoer, miscreant, reprobate, sorry lot, untrustworthy person, worthless person, wrong number, wrongdoer

bad experience annoyance, bad trip, bummer, disappointment, disaster, downer, drag, irritation, misfortune

bad luck bad break, devil's own luck, hard cheese, hard luck, hardship, ill luck, misfortune, raw deal, rotten break, rotten luck, setback, tough break, tough luck, tragedy

bad manners crudeness, discourtesy, ill-breeding, impoliteness, inconsideration, rudeness

bad off bankrupt, busted, destitute, down and out, impoverished, indigent, in need of, needy, poor

bad shot wrong guess

bag and baggage completely, entirely, outright, totally

bag lady bag person, bum, hobo, homeless woman, shopping bag lady, shopping cart lady, street person

bag of tricks know-how, savvy, tools of the trade, tricks of the trade, wisdom

bag of waters amnion, amniotic sac, arachnoid membrane, water bag
Baker's™ Chocolate baking chocolate, unsweetened chocolate
baker's dozen a dozen plus one, long dozen, thirteen, XIII
baking cup bake cup, cupcake liner, cupcake paper
baking mix Bisquick™
baking pan baking dish
baking sheet cookie sheet, flat pan
baking soda bicarbonate of soda, saleratus, sodium bicarbonate
balance beam balance bar
balance of payments balance of international payments, balance of trade, BOP, trade balance, trade deficit, trade gap
balance of power international equilibrium
balance of trade balance of payments, trade balance, trade deficit, trade gap, visible balance
balance wheel balance, flywheel
ball and chain girlfriend, little woman, old lady, old woman, wife
ball-and-socket joint articulatio spheroidea, cotyloid joint, enarthrodial joint, enarthrosis, spherical socket, spheroid joint
ball carrier halfback, running back
ball club baseball club, crew, nine, personnel, roster, squad, team
ball game baseball game, game, play, strategy; big picture, full particulars, how things stand, ins and outs, lay of the land, the score, whole picture
ballistic missile cruise missile, Exocet missile, guided missile, ICBM, intercontinental ballistic missile, intermediate range ballistic missile, IRBM, rocket bomb, surface-to-air missile, surface-to-surface missile, Tomahawk missile
ball of wax full monty, nine yards, shebang, show, state of affairs, whole works, works
ballpark figure approximation, educated guess, estimate, estimation, guess, guesstimate, judgment, projection, rough figure, rough guess, rough measure
ballroom dance ballroom dancing
Bamboo Curtain Iron Curtain
Band-Aid™ adhesive bandage, adhesive compress, bandage, bandage compress

bangers and mash sausage and mashed potatoes

bank account checking account, deposit, funds, savings account

bank card affinity card, ATM card, automatic teller machine card, bank credit card, charge card, charge plate, check card, credit card, debit card

bank check bank draft, cashier's check, certified check, check, treasurer's check

bank holiday government holiday, legal holiday, national holiday

bank loan car loan, home loan, mortgage, second mortgage, small business loan

baptismal name Christian name, forename, given name

baptism of fire hazing, initiation, martyrdom, ordeal, rite of passage, rude introduction, test of courage, trial by fire, trying experience

barbecue grill charcoal grill, electric grill, gas grill, outdoor grill

barbed wire barbwire, fence, fencing

barbershop quartet barbershop harmony, barbershopping

barber's itch sycosis, sycosis barbae, tinea barbae

bar chart bar graph, diagram, histogram

bar code Universal Product Code, UPC

bare bones basic, basic elements, basic facts, core, essential elements, frame, no-frills, skeleton, undercarriage

bargaining chip advantage, clout, edge, influence, leverage, power, pull, weight

bargaining table arbitration, debate, mediation, negotiation

bar graph bar chart, diagram, histogram

bar mitzvah bar mizvah, bas mitzvah, bat mitzvah

barn dance contra dance, country dance, folk dance, hoedown, square dance

barn raising barn bee

barrel roll aileron roll, outside roll, roll, snap roll, spiral

barrel vault barrel root, cradle vault, tunnel vault, wagon vault

barrier reef coral reef

bar sinister bastardy, baton sinister, bend sinister, illegitimacy, out of wedlock

basal metabolism acid-base metabolism, energy metabolism

base coat first coat, skim coat

base hit bingle, hit, safe hit, safety, single

base of operation base, base station, center of authority, central administration, central office, central station, headquarters, main office, seat

base on balls BB, free base, free ride, free ticket, pass, walk

base pay base salary, minimum wage, salary

base runner baseburner, pinch-runner, runner

basic training briefing, familiarization, initial training period, military training

basket case a bundle of nerves, nervous wreck, spastic, spaz

basket star basket fish, brittle star, sea spider

bathing beauty attractive woman, beautiful woman, beauty contest winner, beauty queen, cover girl, glamour girl, Miss America, Miss Universe, model

bathing cap swimming cap

bathing suit bathing costume, bikini, Jams™, maillot, one-piece, one-piece bathing suit, one-piece suit, string bikini, swimming suit, swimming trunks, swimsuit, swimwear, tank suit, thong, trunks, two-piece, two-piece bathing suit, two-piece suit

bath mat bath rug

bathroom tissue toilet paper, toilet tissue

bathtub gin bootleg, firewater, home brew, homemade gin, hooch, moonshine, mountain dew, white lightning

bat mitzvah bar mitzvah, bar mizvah, bas mitzvah

batten down the hatches button up, tie up, zip up

battery cell galvanic cell

batting average batting percentage, slugging average, slugging percentage

battle cry call to arms, rallying cry, rebel yell, war cry, war whoop; catchphrase, catchword, motto, slogan, watchword

battle fatigue combat disorder, combat fatigue, combat neurosis, complete exhaustion, post-traumatic stress disorder, shell shock

battle of the bulge obesity

battle royal brawl, fierce contest, fight, melee, pitched battle, riot, rumble

baud rate bandwidth, modem speed

bawl out berate, castigate, chew out, jump down one's throat, punish, rake over the coals, reprimand, rip into, scold, take to task, upbraid, yell at

bay window bow window

BB gun air gun, air rifle, pellet gun

beach buggy dune buggy

beach bum surf bum

be-all and end-all all-important element, quintessential element, summit, ultimate object, zenith

bean counter accountant, actuary, bookkeeper, certified public accountant, CPA, number cruncher, statistician

bean curd meat substitute, tofu

bear arms carry arms, defend, protect

bear false witness forswear oneself, perjure, perjure oneself, swear falsely

bear hug embrace, embracement, enfoldment, hug, squeeze

bearing wall load-bearing wall, support wall

bear in mind call to mind, consider, keep in mind, remember

bear market bearish market, bearishness, declining market, down market

beast of burden draft animal, jument, pack animal, packhorse, pack mule, sumpter, work animal

beat a dead horse belabor, dwell on, dwell upon, flog a dead horse, harp on

beat it go away, leave hastily

beat the bushes forage, nose around, poke around, search, search through

beat the drum for make a pitch for, thump the tub for

beat the rap acquit, clear of charges, escape punishment, escape without penalty, find not guilty, get off, go free, go scot free, receive not-guilty verdict, walk

Beau Brummell coxcomb, dandy, dude, fashion plate, fine gentleman, fop, ladies' man, lady-killer, lounge lizard, person of fashion, popinjay, swell

Beaufort scale Beaufort wind scale, half-Beaufort scale, wind scale

beau geste fine gesture, gracious gesture, noble gesture

beau ideal epitome, exemplar, good example, ideal, model, nonpareil, paragon, perfection, person to look up to, role model, shining example

beau monde bon ton, fashionable society, good society, haut monde, high life, high society, smart set, society

beautiful people aristocracy, beau monde, café society, cream of society, crème de la crème, cultured class, elite, famous people, glamorous people, glitterati, haut monde, high life, high society, in-crowd, jet set, privileged class, smart set, society, society people, the privileged, the upper class, the well-to-do, upper crust, wealthy people

beauty contest beauty pageant

beauty mark beauty spot, birthmark, mole, nevus

beauty parlor beauty salon, beauty shop, beauty spa, hairdresser, hairdressing establishment, hairdressing salon, hair salon, salon de beaute, spa

beauty queen bathing beauty, beauty contestant winner, cover girl, glamour girl, Miss America, Miss Universe, model

beauty sleep forty winks, full night's sleep, nap, rest, siesta, snooze

beauty spot beauty mark, birthmark, mole, nevus

bed and breakfast B and B, B&B, country inn, guest house, hotel, inn, lodging house

bed linen bed sheet, bedding, dust ruffle, duvet cover, pillow slip, pillowcase, sham, sheeting, sheets

bed of nails uncomfortable situation

bed of roses clover, comfort, comfortable situation, lap of luxury, life of ease, luxury, paradise, the good life, velvet

bed rail side rail

bedroom community residential community, satellite, suburb

bedroom eyes amorous stare, come-hither look, flirtatious look, glad eyes, ogle

bed table night table, nightstand

beer parlor bar, barroom, beer garden, neighborhood bar, neighborhood pub, pub, rathskeller, saloon, taproom, tavern

before-dinner drink aperitif

begin again breathe new life into, make a fresh start, refresh, regenerate, rejuvenate, renew, revitalize

behavioral science behavioral psychology, behavioristic psychology, Skinnerian psychology, social anthropology, social psychology, sociology, Watsonian psychology

behavior modification aversion therapy, behavioral therapy, behavior therapy, conditioning, counseling, reinforcement, retraining, reward system, therapy

behind bars confined, imprisoned, in jail, in prison, incarcerated, jailed, serving time, under lock and key

behind closed doors à huis clos, in camera, in chambers, in closed meeting, in executive session, in private conference, in secret meeting, januis clausis

behind the eight ball in Dutch, on the hot seat, on the spot, up the creek

behind the scenes backstage, behind the curtain, in a corner, in the background, in the dark, sub rosa

behind the times back number, has-been, of the old school, old hat, old-fashioned, out of date, unfashionable

bell curve bell-shaped curve, normal curve

bell jar bell glass

bells and whistles features, frills, frills and furbelows, gimcrackery, gimmickry, glitz, superaddition

bell tower belfry, campanile, spire

belly flop belly buster, belly flopper, belly whop, belly whopper, nosedive, plunge

belly laugh good one, guffaw, hoot, howler, rib tickler, riot, roar, scream, sidesplitter, thigh-slapper, wow

below average below normal, below par, inferior, low-grade, poor, second-rate, subpar, substandard

below the belt cheating, dirty, dirty pool, foul, unethically, unfair, unfairly, unsportingly

belt bag bum bag, fanny pack, waist pack

bench warrant arrest warrant

bend over backwards fall over backwards, lean over backwards

beneath contempt abominable, cheap, contemptible, despicable, detestable, ignominious, low, miserable, scummy, utterly degraded, wretched

Benedict Arnold backstabber, betrayer, Brutus, defector, deserter, double agent, double-crosser, fink, informer, Judas, quisling, snake in the grass, snitch, spy, traitor, treasonist, turncoat

bent on bound, dead set on, decided upon, determined, determined upon, fixed, fixed upon, intent, set on

Bermuda shorts Bermudas, Jamaica shorts, Jams™, surfer shorts, trunks

beside oneself agitated, anxious, bothered, distraught, distressed, frantic, hysterical, in a panic, out of one's mind, overwrought, rattled, raving, shook up, upset, worked up

beside the point immaterial, inapplicable, insignificant, irrelevant, nihil ad rem, not pertaining to, not to the purpose, off the subject, pointless, unrelated, wide of the mark, wide of the point

best bib and tucker best bib and band, best clothes, caparison, finery, full feather, full fig, investiture, regalia, Sunday best

best boy assistant chief lighting technician, best boy electric, best boy grip

best man bridesman, groomsman, paranymph

beta blocker beta-adrenergic blocking agent

beta particle cathode particle, negatron

beta test final product test, real-world test, second-phase testing

beta wave beta rhythm

bête noire adversary, anathema, antagonist, bad news, bane, bitter enemy, bugbear, competitor, curse, devil, enemy, foe, opponent, plague, rival, trouble

bet one's bottom dollar gamble on, lay money on, make book on

better half consort, espoused, feme covert, helpmate, helpmeet, husband, mate, partner, rib, significant other, soul mate, spouse, wife

better off happier, more fortunate

between the devil and the deep blue sea between a rock and a hard place, between Scylla and Charybdis, between the hammer and the anvil, between two fires, catch-22, cornered, Hobson's choice, in a dilemma, in a pickle, in a predicament, in the middle, in a tight spot, no choice, sitting on a powder keg

between you and me behind closed doors, between ourselves, confidentially, don't breathe a word, in confidence, off the record, privately

beyond a shadow of a doubt absolutely; beyond any doubt; categorically; certainly; clearly; definitely; indubitably; no ifs, ands, or buts about it; obviously; undeniably; unquestionably

bib and tucker apparel, clothes, clothing, costume, garments, habit, outfit, regalia, Sunday best

bicarbonate of soda acid neutralizer, alkalizer, antacid, baking soda, saleratus, sodium bicarbonate

Big Apple New York, New York City, NYC

big band jazz band, swing band

Big C C, cancer, carcinoma, malignancy, malignant tumor

big cheese big enchilada, big gun, big kahuna, big wheel, boss, chief, head honcho, leader, person in charge, top dog, VIP

Big Easy New Orleans

big house big cage, big school, brig, calaboose, can, city hotel, cooler, coop, correctional institution, detention facility, house of correction, house of detention, icebox, jail, joint, penal institution, penitentiary, prison, slammer, tank, up the river

big league big time, bigs, major league, majors

big name captain of industry, celebrity, headliner, heavyweight, idol, megastar, mogul, nabob, panjandrum, person to be reckoned with, star, superstar, topliner, very important person

big picture approach, attack, essence, idea, master plan, picture, plan of attack

big-screen TV projection TV

big shot big cheese, big gun, big wheel, bigwig, dignitary, fat cat, head honcho, heavy-hitter, high-muck-a-muck, important person, influential person, mogul, nabob, notable, somebody, VIP

big talk boasting, bragging, exaggeration, fancy talk, fine talk, fish story, gas, hogwash, hot air, tall story

big time big league, bigs, major league, majors

big toe great toe

big top circus, round top, three-ring, white-top

big wheel big cheese, big gun, big shot, bigwig, dignitary, fat cat, head honcho, heavy-hitter, high-muck-a-muck, important person, influential person, mogul, nabob, notable, somebody, VIP

bill of exchange bank note, draft, Federal Reserve note, order of payment

bill of fare card, carte, carte du jour, menu

bill of goods snow job, the business

bill of health clean bill of health, full pratique, pratique

bill of indictment arraignment, impeachment, indictment, true bill

bill of lading docket, invoice, manifest, waybill

bill of particulars information, information against

Bill of Rights Constitution, constitutional guarantees

bill of sale proof of purchase, receipt, sales slip, stub

billy club baton, cudgel, nightstick, police baton

billy goat billy, he-goat, male goat

binary digit bit, infobit, 0 or 1

binary star binary star system, binary system, double star

binding energy activation energy, bond energy, mass energy, separation energy

Binet test Binet-Simon test, intelligence test, IQ test, Stanford-Binet test

binge-purge syndrome binge-vomit syndrome, bingeing, bulimarexia, bulimia, bulimia nervosa, eating disorder, hyperphagia, polyphagia

biological clock biological rhythm, biorhythm, body clock, circadian rhythm, cycles, internal clock

biological father birth father, natural father

biological mother birth mother, natal mother, natural mother

biological parent biological father, biological mother, birth father, birth mother, birth parent, father, mother, natural parent

biological rhythm biological clock, biorhythm, circadian rhythm, cycles

biological warfare biological operation, BW, germ warfare

bipolar disorder bipolar affective disorder, bipolar illness, manic-depression, manic-depressive disorder, manic-depressive illness, manic-depressive psychosis

bird, the the finger

bird of prey beast of prey, predator, raptor, raptorial bird, vampire

birds and the bees facts of life

bird's-eye view aerial view, bird's-eye survey, comprehensive view, fly on the wall, overview, pandect, panorama, worm's-eye view

birds of a feather couple, matching pair, matching set, pair, peas in a pod, two of a kind

birth control abortion, birth prevention, conception prevention, contraception, family planning, planned parenthood, pregnancy prevention

birth control pill abortion pill, anovulatory drug, Brompton, Brompton's cocktail, Brompton's mixture, French abortion pill, mifepristone, morning-after pill, oral contraceptive, RU 486, the Pill

birthday suit altogether, bare skin, buff, nakedness, native buff, nude, raw, state of nature

birth defect abnormality, congenital abnormality, congenital anomaly, congenital defect, disability, mutation

birth parent biological father, biological mother, biological parent, birth father, birth mother, birth parent, father, mother, natural parent

bit by bit by degrees, drop by drop, grade by grade, gradually, inch by inch, inchmeal, in stages, little by little, piecemeal, step by step

bite one's lip bite one's tongue

bite the bullet cross the Rubicon, leap into the breach, seize the opportunity, suck it up

bite the dust buy the farm, cash in one's chips, cease living, croak, die, expire, kick off, kick the bucket, meet one's maker, pass away, pass on, push up daisies, succumb

biting midge no-see-um, punkie, punky

bit part bit, minor part, minor role, small role, speaking part, walk-on

bit player extra, mute, spear-carrier, supernumerary, supporting actor, supporting actress, supporting player

bitter end completion, conclusion, death, ending, finish

bitter pill bad part, bitter cup, bummer, downer, downside

bituminous coal soft coal

black-and-blue mark bruise, contusion, ecchymosis

black art abracadabra, black hocus-pocus, black magic, necromancy, occultism, sorcery, spell-casting, voodoo, witchcraft, witchery, wizardry

black book datebook; blacklist, shitlist

black box flight data recorder, flight recorder

black cow ice cream soda, root beer float

Black Death bubonic plague

black diamond carbonado

black eye bad name, bad reputation, black mark, blemish, disgrace, dishonor, lost face, shame, smear, stain, stigma, taint; bruise, shiner

black glass Claude glass

black gold crude oil, oil, petrol, petroleum, Texas tea

black hats bad guys, criminals, opponents, villains

black hole abyss, empty space, void; dungeon, prison cell; gravitational collapse

black letter Clarendon type, German type, Gothic, Old English

black light invisible light

black lung anthracosis, black lung disease, coal miner's lung, miner's lung, pneumoconiosis

black magic black art, demon worship, demonianism, diabolism, magic, mysticism, necromancy, Satanism, sorcery, voodoo, witchcraft, witchery, wizardry

Black Maria paddy wagon, patrol wagon, police van, police wagon

black mark black eye, blemish, censure, disgrace, dishonor, lost face, shame, smear, stain, stigma, taint

black market bootleg market, gray market, illegal commerce, illegitimate business, illicit business, run, shady dealings, underground, underground market, underworld market

black out faint, go out like a light, keel over, lose consciousness, pass out, swoon, zonk out; cover up, extinguish, hush up, put the lid on, quash, sit on, smother, squelch, stifle, suppress

black sheep bad egg, scapegrace

black tie dinner jacket, tux, tuxedo

blank verse unrhymed poetry

blaze a trail lead the way, pilot, spearhead

bleaching powder chloride of lime, chlorinated lime

bleeding heart bleeding-heart liberal, liberal, sentimental fool, softy, sympathizer

blessed event birth, birthing, childbirth, delivery, happy event, natality, parturition, visit from the stork

Blessed Virgin Blessed Virgin Mary, Madonna, Mary, mother of Jesus, Mother of our Lord, the Virgin, Virgin Mary

blind alley blank wall, cul-de-sac, dead end, dead-end street, impasse, tangent

blind date arranged date, setup

blind drunk besotted, buzzed, crocked, dead-drunk, groggy, inebriated, intoxicated, loaded, pissed, plastered, sloshed, smashed, soused, stiff, tipsy, under the table, wasted

blind side blind spot, unguarded side, weak side

blister pack bubble pack, bubble wrap, plastic bubbles

block and tackle block and fall

block letter block capital, hand-printing, lettering

block party neighborhood party

block print engraving, linoleum-block print, rubber-block print, stencil, woodblock, woodcut, woodprint, xylograph

blood alcohol level BAC, BAL, blood alcohol content

blood bank blood donor center, bloodmobile

blood brother bro, brother-german, close friend, uterine brother

blood cell blood corpuscle, corpuscle, erythrocyte, hemocyte, leukocyte, red blood cell, red corpuscle, white blood cell, white corpuscle

blood clot coagulum, crassamentum, embolus, grume, thrombus

blood count blood profile, blood work, CBC, complete blood count, full blood count

blood feud bad blood, conflict, falling out, family feud, feud, fight, grudge, vendetta

blood money wergild

blood poisoning pyemia, sepsis, septicemia, septic infection, septicopyemia, septic poisoning, toxaemia, toxemia

blood pressure BP

blood pudding black pudding, blood sausage, sausage

blood relation biological relationship, blood, blood brother, blood relationship, blood relative, blood sister, consanguinean, family, flesh, flesh and blood, genetic relationship, kindred, ties of blood, uterine kin

blood serum blood plasma, serum

blood sister close friend, sister-german, uterine sister

blood sugar blood glucose, glucose

blood type blood group, blood grouping

blood vessel arteriole, artery, capillary, metarteriole, vein, venule

bloody shirt banner, battle cry, bluidy sark, colors, gonfalon, rallying cry

blotting paper blotter

blow hot and cold chop and change, flip-flop, fluctuate, vacillate

blow job fellatio, head, oral sex

blow of mercy coup de grâce, deathblow, decisive stroke, finishing blow, mortal blow

blow one's own horn boast, brag, crow, gloat, grandstand, pat oneself on the back, toot one's own horn

blow one's stack blow one's top, blow up, get mad, lose one's temper

blow the whistle finger, inform on, rat, sell down the river, sell out, snitch, spill the beans, squawk, squeal, weasel

blue blood aristocrat, Brahmin, noble, patrician, silk stocking, thoroughbred, titled person, upper-cruster

blue chip bellwether, blue-chip stock, Nifty Fifty

blue-collar factory-working, lower-class, middle-class, proletarian, proletariat, wage-earning, working class

blue-collar worker common laborer, employee, factory worker, hand, industrial worker, laborer, lunch-bucket worker, member of the working class, nonoffice worker, proletarian, workingman, working stiff, workingwoman

blue devils blahs, blues, depression, despair, despondency, dumps, funk, gloom, low spirits, melancholy, mopes, unhappiness; blue Johnnies, delirium tremens, d.t.'s, pink elephants

blue flu sick-in, sick-out, slowdown

blue funk depression, despondency, funk, gloom

blue jeans denims, designer jeans, dungarees, jeans, Levi's™

blue moon ages, coon's age, long time, years

blue murder bloody murder

blue plate special house specialty, specialty

blue ribbon award, championship, cordon bleu, crown, cup, decoration, first place, first prize, laurels, palms, trophy, victory

blue-ribbon jury blue-ribbon panel, special jury, struck jury

boarding pass boarding card

boat person refugee

boat shoe Docksiders™

bobby pin hairpin

bodice ripper romance novel

body and soul completely, entirely, heart and soul

body check block

body clock biological clock, biorhythm, circadian rhythm, internal clock

body corporate corporation

body count death toll

body double alter ego, stand-in

body English ass English, English

body language body movement, gestures, kinesics, mannerisms, motion, nonverbal communication

body odor BO, perspiration odor, sudoresis

body piercing ear piercing

body politic commonwealth, constituency, country, electorate, land, nation, polity, res publica, state, the people

body shop automotive garage

body snatcher ghoul, grave robber

body wave perm, permanent, permanent wave

boggle the mind amaze, astonish, astound, awe, bedazzle, bewilder, blow one away, blow one's mind, confound, dazzle, dumbfound, flabbergast, knock one's socks off, perplex, stagger, stun, stupefy

boiling point boil, BP

bolo tie bolo, long string tie, string tie

bomb shelter A-bomb shelter, air-raid shelter, bombproof shelter, fallout shelter, retreat, safety island, safety isle, safety zone

bomber jacket pilot jacket

bona fide authentic, authoritative, card-carrying, credible, for real, genuine, good-faith, legitimate, natural, official, original, pure, real, rightful, straight, true to life, unquestionable, veritable

bon appetit chow down, eat hearty, eat up, enjoy your meal, good appetite

bond paper bond

bond servant chattel, drudge, peon, serf, slave, thrall, vassal

bone china porcelain, white china

bone of contention altercation, apple of discord, argument, beef, conflict, controversy, debate, difference of opinion, disagreement, dispute, grounds for war, issue, matter at hand, point in question, problem, sore point, tender spot

bone up brush up, brush up on, cram, drum, get up, grind away, polish up, read up, refresh the memory, review, study

bon vivant aficionado, connoisseur, connoisseur of food, connoisseur of wine, enthusiast, epicure, epicurean, gastronome, gastronomist, gourmand, gourmet

bon voyage adieu, adios, bye-bye, cheerio, farewell, gluckliche Reise, Godspeed, goodbye, happy landing, have a nice trip, pleasant journey, send-off, tsetchem leshalom

boob tube idiot box, small screen, television, television set, telly, the box, the tube, TV, TV set

booby hatch bedlam, bughouse, funny farm, insane asylum, laughing academy, loony bin, lunatic asylum, madhouse, mental health institution, mental home, mental hospital, mental institution, nuthouse, padded cell, psychiatric hospital, psychiatric ward, rubber room, sanatorium, sanitarium, snake pit

booby prize consolation prize

booby trap ambush, baited trap, concealed trap, deadfall, decoy, hidden danger, land mine, mine, mousetrap, pitfall, setup, snare, trap, trip wire

Boogie™ board surfboard

booking office box office, ticket office

book match matchbook, safety match

book value Blue Book value, estimated value

boom box ghetto blaster, ghetto box, portable audio system, portable radio, portable stereo, radio

boon companion boon fellow, consort

booster cable battery cable, jumper, jumper cables, jumper lead

booster shot booster, booster dose, immunization, recall dose, vaccine

boot camp basic training camp, military training, recruit training facility

bootleg recording illegal recording, pirated recording

boot up boot, initialize, load, log in, start computer

born yesterday childlike, green, gullible, inexperienced, innocent, naïve, unworldly, wet behind the ears

borscht circuit barnstorming, borscht belt, vaudeville circuit

bosom friend best friend, bosom buddy, close friend, companion, confidant, dear friend, intimate friend, pal, soul mate

botanical garden arboretum, botanic garden

bottled gas butane, compressed petroleum gas, liquefied hydrocarbon gas, liquefied petroleum gas, propane

bottle opener bottle screw, church key, corkscrew

bottle up cork, enclose, entrap, seal; contain, curb, hold back, hold in, repress, restrain, suppress

bottom feeder hungry puppy, slop sucker; base person, bottom fish, lowest common denominator, lowlife, riffraff, scum

bottomless pit abysm, abyss, chasm, crevasse, Gehenna, Hades, hell, netherworld, underground, underworld

bottom line basis, conclusion, core, crux, essence, fiber, final decision, fundamentals, last word, main idea, name of the game, nitty-gritty, point, reality, whole story; income, net, profit

bottoms up cheers, down the hatch, drink up

Boulder Dam Hoover Dam

bounce back echo, reflect, reverberate; get well, mend, overcome, pull around, rebound, recover, recuperate

bounced check bad check, kite, rubber check

bouncing Bet bouncing Bess, hedge pink, *Saponaria officinalis*, soapwort

bound and determined determined, driven, hell-bent, intent, obsessed, persistent, relentless, resolute, resolved, serious, set on, single-minded, steadfast, strong-minded, stubborn, tenacious, unrelenting, unwavering

bounty hunter criminal hunter, fugitive hunter

bovine growth hormone bovine somatotropin

bovine spongiform encephalopathy mad cow disease

bow and scrape bob a curtsy, bow, curtsy, grovel, kowtow, stoop

bowel movement BM, crap, defecation, discharge, dung, excrement, excretion, fecal matter, feces, feculence, flux, go to the bathroom, manure, number two, shit, stool, waste

bowie knife Arkansas toothpick, hunting knife, Missouri toothpick

bowled over amazed, astonished, dumbfounded, dumbstruck, flabbergasted, floored, knocked for a loop, shocked, staggered, thunderstruck

bowling alley bowling green, bowling lane, skittle alley

bow out back out, bail out, drop out, exit, leave, pull out, quit, retire, withdraw

bow tie necktie

bow window bay window

box camera box Kodak

boxer shorts boxers, drawers, shorts, underpants, undershorts, underwear

box lunch bag lunch, brown-bag lunch

box nut cap nut, dome nut

box office gate, gate receipts, receipts, take; ticket booth, ticket office

box score game summary

box seat baignoire, box, grandstand box, loge

box spring bedspring

boy wonder child prodigy, polymath, whiz kid, wunderkind

bracket creep tax-bracket creep

brain death cerebral death, irreversible coma, local death, somatic death

brain fever cerebrospinal fever, cerebrospinal meningitis, encephalitis, epidemic meningitis, meningitis

brain trust advisers, advisory board, authorities, body of advisers, cabinet, council, experts, inner circle

brain wave brainchild, brainstorm, inspiration, quantum leap

branch water plain water

branding iron brand, brand iron, hot iron

brand name brand, trademark name, trade name

brass knuckles brass knucks, knuckle-dusters, knuckles, knucks

brass ring opportunity, plum, prize, reward, trophy

brass tacks basic facts, basics, cases, essential facts, essentials, facts, nitty-gritty, realities, the dope, the scoop, truth of the matter

brazen it out brazen it through

breach of contract bad faith, breach of faith, breach of privilege, breach of promise, breach of trust

breach of peace breach of the peace, disorderly behavior, disorderly conduct, disturbance of the peace

bread and butter bread, daily bread, keep, livelihood, living, meat, staff of life, support, sustenance

bread box bread bin

bread line dole, welfare

bread machine bread maker

break bread break one's fast, eat, mange, partake, subsist, take nourishment

break camp clear out, decamp, depart, go away, leave, move, pull out, pull up stakes, ride off, set out, split, take off, vacate

break cover come out, come out in the open

break dancing break-dance

break faith betray, break one's word, forswear oneself, go back on one's word, perjure oneself, renege

breaking and entering break and entry, break-in, burglarizing, burglary, housebreaking, robbery, second-story work, unlawful entry

breaking point extreme tension, overextension, overstrain, snapping point, tension

break of day brightening, cockcrow, crack of dawn, dawn, dawning, daybreak, first blush, first brightening, first flush of the morning, first light, peep of day, prime, prime of the morning, sunrise, sunup

break service break back

break the ice break ground, cut the first turf, get one's feet wet, lay the first stone, start, take the plunge

break wind cut one, cut the cheese, fart, let her rip, pass gas, rip one

breast implant boob job, breast augmentation, breast enlargement, silicone implant

breathe freely breathe easily, breathe easy

breathing space breath, breather, breathing room, breathing spell, breathing time

breeder reactor fast breeder reactor, nuclear reactor, power breeder reactor

breeding ground birthplace, birth site, breeding place, hatchery, rookery

bride-to-be engaged woman, fiancée, future mate, future wife, prospective wife, wife-to-be

bridge loan bridge financing, swing loan

bridle path bridle road, bridle trail, bridle way

Bright's disease nephritis

Brillo™ pad scouring pad, SOS™ pad

bring home the bacon bear the palm, earn a living, take the cake

bring into play call into play, call upon, draw on, draw upon, impress, muster, recruit, set in motion

bring to bear apply, bring forward, come forward, make available, offer, proffer, put forward

bring to book call on the carpet, call to account, read the riot act, take to task, tongue-lash

bring to justice bring before the bar, bring to trial, haul into court, put on trial, take before the judge, take to court

bring to life breathe life into, bring into existence, give a new lease on life, give birth to, put new life into

bring to light blow the lid off, bring into the open, crack wide open, disclose, expose, hold up to view, lay bare, reveal, take the lid off

bring to pass bring about, bring off, deliver, do the trick, produce, put across, put through

bring to terms bring low, bring to one's knees, humble, humiliate, take down a notch, take down a peg

Brith Milah berith, bris

British Empire Britain, British Commonwealth of Nations, Commonwealth of Nations, England, perfidious Albion, the Commonwealth, United Kingdom

broad jump long jump, running broad jump, standing broad jump

Bronx cheer boo, catcall, heckle, hiss, hoot, jeer, raspberry, razz, razzing

Bronze Star Bronze Star Medal

brown goods appliances, household appliances

brownie points credibility,

credit, kudos, mark of merit, notability, pat on the back, plaudits, points, praise, strokes

brown lung brown lung disease, byssinosis

brown study absorption, abstraction, deep thought, dreamy abstraction, engrossment, preoccupation, quiet ecstasy, reverie, study

brush aside brush off, discount, dismiss, disregard, ignore, push aside

brush up on bone up, brush up, cram, polish up, read up, refresh the memory, review, study

B-side flip side, reverse side

bubble chamber cloud chamber, spark chamber

bubonic plague Black Death

bucket shop boiler room, chop shop

buckle down apply oneself, get serious, plunge into, put one's hand to the plow, put one's nose to the grindstone, swing into action, take the bull by the horns

buffer state buffer country

buffer zone area of separation, BZ, demilitarized zone, line of demarcation, neutral zone

bug off beat it, cut out, depart, go away, hit the road, leave, move out, scram, shove off, split

bug spray insectifuge, insect repellent

build castles in the air build castles in Spain, live in a dream world

building block component, constituent, elementary unit, ingredient, monad, part, piece, segment, unit of being

building code building ordinance, building regulations, construction standards

building contractor builder, contractor

building sickness SBS, sick building syndrome

bulletin board corkboard, notice board, pegboard

bulletin board system bboard, BBS, bulletin board service, electronic bulletin board

bullet train aerotrain, high-speed train, train de haute vitesse

bull market advancing market, bullish market, bullishness, rising market, up market

bull session chinfest, chin-wag, confab, gabfest, informal discussion, rap session, talkfest

bull's-eye butt, center, dead center, direct hit, omphalos, quintain, target

bumper car dodgem

bumper crop bonanza, cash crop, fat of the land, foison, gold mine, rich harvest, windfall

bumper sticker decal, decalcomania, sticker

bump off blot out, blow away, chill, deep-six, dispatch, dispose of, do away with, do in, dust, grease, hit, ice, kill, knock off, murder, off, rub out, snuff, snuff out, stretch out, waste, wax, whack, zap

bumpy ride rough time, tough time

bum rap bad break, bad charge, bad deal, false accusation, frame-up, raw deal, rotten deal, the shaft

bum's rush bounce, chuck, culling, disdain, eviction, heave-ho, push, riddance, scorn, shakeout

bum steer bad advice, bad information, bad tip, poor guidance, poor information, poor tip

Bundt™ pan fluted cake pan

Bunsen burner burner, element, etna, gas jet, heating element, jet, pilot burner, pilot light

burden of proof onus, onus probandi, responsibility

burglar alarm alarm system, security system, warning device

burial garment cerement, pall, shroud, winding-clothes, winding-sheet

burial ground bone orchard, boneyard, burial place, burial yard, burying ground, burying place, catacomb, cemetery, city of the dead, family plot, graveyard, necropolis, plot

burning question difficult question, knotty question, sixty-four-thousand-dollar question, vexed question

burn one's bridges burn one's boats, go for broke, kick down the ladder, nail one's colors to the mast

burn out become drained, exhaust, fatigue, get tired, grow weary, run down, run out of steam, stress out, tire, wear down, wear out

burn rubber dig, peel out, peel rubber, skin out

burn the candle at both ends bite off more than one can chew, do too much, keep one's nose to the grindstone, overdo, slave, spread oneself too thin, stay on the treadmill

burn the midnight oil cram, do double duty, elucubrate, grind, lucubrate, overwork, study, work day and night, work late, work overtime

burp gun machine pistol, submachine gun

bury the hatchet accept apology, bear no malice, forget, forgive, kiss and make up, let bygones be bygones, make peace, smoke the peace pipe, wipe slate clean

bush jacket bush shirt, safari jacket

bush league amateur, minor league, minors, nothing to brag about, second-rate, small potatoes, the bushes, triple-A

business administration business management

business card call card, calling card, card, carte de visite, visiting card

business cycle business fluctuations, economic cycle, trade cycle

business expense nonremunerated business expenses, out-of-pocket expenses, overhead, trade expense

business school B school, management school

business travel road warrioring

butcher block butcher board, chopping block, chopping board, cutting board

butler's pantry food pantry

butterflies in the stomach collywobbles, dithers, heart skipping a beat, nervous stomach

butter up adulate, bootlick, brownnose, build up, cajole, flatter, inveigle, lay it on thick, massage, play up to, soften, spread it on, stroke, suck up to, sweet-talk, work on

button-down collar tab collar

button man button, doberman, goodfella, gun, gunsel, hammer, high soldier, hit man, soldier, torpedo, trigger man, wiseguy

button one's lip be silent, button up, keep silent

buyer's market soft market

buying power purchasing power

buy off bribe, do business, get to, grease palm, influence, lubricate, make a deal, pay off, sweeten the pot, tamper

buy the farm bite the dust, buy it, buy the ranch, cash in one's chips, cease living, croak, die, expire, farm, kick the bucket, meet one's maker, pass away, pass on, succumb

buy time make time stand still, work against time

buzz bomb doodlebug, flying bomb, robot bomb, V-1 rocket

buzz saw circular saw

by chance accidentally, by mistake, fortuitously, unexpectedly, unintentionally, unwittingly

by degrees bit by bit, continuously, gradually, inch by inch, in small doses, little by little, piece by piece, steadily, step by step

by fits and starts impulsively, intermittently, irregularly, with many interruptions

by the numbers according to Hoyle, according to rule, according to the highest authority, by the book, by the numbers, gospel, indisputable

by the way apart from, aside, by the by, incidentally, in passing, parenthetically, speaking of, while on the subject

by turns alternately, in succession, one after another

Byzantine Church Eastern Church, Eastern Orthodox Church, Greek Church, Greek Orthodox Church, Orthodox Eastern Church

Cc

cabin class coach, second class

cabin cruiser cruiser, outboard cruiser, pleasure boat, pleasure craft, power cruiser, sedan cruiser

cabinet minister cabinet member, minister of state, undersecretary

cabin fever claustrophobia, climbing the walls, restlessness, SAD, seasonal affective disorder, temporary insanity, winter blues

cable car grip car, streetcar, tram, tramcar, trolley, trolley bus, trolley car

cable television cable, cable system, cable TV, cablevision, community antenna television, pay television, subscription television

caesarean section abdominal delivery, caesarean, caesarian, cesarean, cesarean section, C-section, surgical birth, surgical delivery

café society beau monde, beautiful people, cream of society, elite, fashionable society, glitterati, haut monde, high society, in-crowd, jet set, right people, smart set, société

cafeteria plan flexible benefit plan

cake rack cooling rack, wire rack

cakes and ale all the comforts of home, amenities, conveniences, egg in one's beer, good things of life, material pleasures, worldly pleasures

cake server cake knife, pie server

calcium blocker calcium channel blocker

calendar year annual accounting period, civil year, CY, fiscal year, twelve-month period

call box coin telephone, pay phone, pay station, phone booth, public telephone, telephone booth, telephone box, telephone kiosk

caller ID caller identification

call girl B-girl, harlot, hooker, hustler, lady of the evening, prostitute, scarlet woman, streetwalker, whore, working girl

calling card phone card; business card, call card, card, visiting card

call into question bring into question, cast doubt on, dispute, raise a question, raise doubt

call letters call sign

call number call mark, pressmark

call one's bluff accept a challenge, take a dare, take one up on

call sign call letters

call the shots be in charge, be in the driver's seat, be in the saddle, call the tune, lay down the law, make the rules

call to account blame, hold accountable, hold answerable, hold responsible

call to arms bid to combat, gauntlet, glove, invitation to combat, mobilize, open hostilities, rally, take up arms

call to mind bear in mind, conjure up, dig into the past, have memories, look back, recall, recollect, refresh memory, remember, summon up

calorie counting dieting, fasting, food abstinence, regimen, watching one's calories, watching one's weight, weight-watching

camera obscura camera lucida

campaign promise campaign pledge

camp bed charpoy, cot

camp follower acolyte, groupie, hanger-on, satellite; call girl, hooker, prostitute, whore

Canada Day Dominion Day

cancer stick butt, cigarette, coffin nail, fag, smokes

C and W country and western, country music, country western, hillbilly music, old-time country rock, western swing

candy bar chocolate bar

candy store confectionery, sweetshop, tuckshop

canicular days canicule, dog days, heat wave, hot spell, hot wave

canker sore canker, cold sore, fever blister, herpes labialis, herpes simplex, lesion, mouth ulcer, oral herpes

canned laughter laugh soundtrack, laugh track, recorded laughter

cannon fodder food for powder, fresh fish, militiaman, trooper

can of worms complexity, complication, difficult situation, difficulty, dog's breakfast, Gordian knot, hard nut to crack, headache, hornet's nest, hot water, mare's nest, mess, Pandora's box, predicament, problem, quagmire, quandary, snafu, snake pit, snarl, trouble, unpredictable situation

canonical hour divine office

canon law church law, ecclesiastical law

can opener tin opener

cap and gown academic costume, academic gown, graduation gown

capital expenditure capital expense, capital investment, capital spending

capital goods assets, available funds, available means, available resources, black-ink items, capital, capitalization, cash flow, financial resources, liquid assets, pluses, producer goods, stock in trade

capital investment capital expenditure, capital expense, capital spending

capital letter big letter, uppercase letter

capital punishment death penalty, death sentence, death warrant, execution, extreme penalty, judicial murder

capital sin carnal sin, deadly sin, grave sin, mortal sin, unpardonable sin, unutterable sin

capital spending capital expenditures, capital expense, capital investment, equipment expenditures, equipment expenses

capital stock authorized capital stock, authorized shares, authorized stock, issued capital stock

Capitol Hill the Hill, U.S. Congress

capsule radio radio pill

caramel apple candied apple, candy apple, taffy apple

carbon copy carbon, clone, copy, double, duplicate, facsimile, imitation, replica, reproduction, spit and image, spitting image, twin

carbon dating carbon-14 dating, dating, radioactive carbon dating, radiocarbon dating

carbon dioxide carbonic acid, carbonic acid gas, CO_2

Carboniferous period Carboniferous, Mississippian period, Pennsylvanian period

carbon monoxide carbon monoxide gas, CO, exhaust fumes

carbon paper carbon

card catalog bibliography, card catalogue, finding list, hand list, reference list

cardiac arrest asystole, cardiac

infarction, cardiopulmonary arrest, congestive heart failure, coronary infarction, coronary thrombosis, heart attack, heart failure, myocardial infarction, tachycardia

cardinal number cardinal

cardinal point great point, key point, salient point

cardinal points compass rose, degrees, half points, points of the compass, quarter points

cardinal virtues basic virtues, natural virtues, preeminent virtues; fortitude, justice, prudence, temperance

cardiopulmonary resuscitation cardiac resuscitation, CPR

card page ad card

card table folding table

career woman businesswoman, career girl

car for hire cab, hack, limo, limousine, rental car, taxi, taxicab

carnal knowledge coition, coitus, copulation, fornication, intercourse, intimacy, love making, procreation, relations, sex, sex act, sexual intercourse, sexual relation

carotid artery arteria carotis

carpal tunnel syndrome CTS, overuse strain injury, repetitive motion disorder, repetitive motion injury, repetitive strain disorder, repetitive strain injury, repetitive stress injury, RSI

carpe diem live for the day, live for today, seize the day, seize the present day, take no thought of the morrow

carpet bombing intense bombing, saturation bombing

carpet sweeper electric broom, vacuum, vacuum cleaner, vacuum sweeper

car pool ride share, van pool

carriage return enter, enter key, return key

carrying capacity ecological capacity

carrying charge carrying cost, cost of carry

carry-on luggage overhead luggage

carry the ball assume the leading role, bear the burden, carry on, carry one's weight, carry through, do one's part, make go, perform

carry weight be influential, count, cut ice, have a lot to do with, have influence, have weight, tell, weigh, weigh heavy

car seat booster seat, child seat, convertible seat, infant seat, safety seat

carte blanche blank check, franchise, free hand, free rein, freedom, full authority, full power, grant, latitude, leeway, no holds barred, permission, unconditional authority, warrant

carte du jour bill of fare, card, carte, menu

cartoon animation animated cartoon, animated movie, animation, cartoon, cell animation, Claymation™, comic, comic strip, drawing

cartridge belt ammunition belt, bandolier

carved in stone adamant, dyed-in-the-wool, firm, inflexible, unalterable, unbending, unchangeable, uncompromising

case goods case furniture, furniture

case history anamnesis, case study, dossier, medical history, medical record, psychiatric history

case in point case, instance, object lesson, precedent, relevant instance, typical case, typical example

case knife sheath knife; table knife

case law common law, non-statutory law, precedent

case study anamnesis, case history, dossier, medical history, medical record, psychiatric history

cash cow golden goose, grubstaker, meal ticket, money-maker, money-spinner

cash crop crop sold for money, root crop

cash flow available funds, available means, available resources, capital, means, pecuniary resources, stock in trade

cashier's check bank check, bank draft, certified check, check, treasurer's check

cash machine ATM, automated teller, automated teller machine, automatic teller machine, cash dispenser

cash on delivery COD

cash register cashbox, coin box, register

cast a spell bewitch, charm, conjure, enchant

cast aspersions asperse, cast reflections on, damage one's good name, give one a black eye, injure one's reputation

casting director casting manager

castle in the air air castle, castle in Spain, castle in the sky, daydream, dreamscape, fantasy, flight of fancy, fond illusion, fool's paradise, pipe dream, unrealistic goal, wishful thinking

cast lots cut lots, draw lots, draw straws, lot

casual acquaintance associate, colleague, friend

catalogue raisonné classified catalog, dictionary catalog

catbird seat commanding position, complete control, controlling position, enviable position, high perch, high place, lofty perch, position of influence, position of power, power position, seat of power, throne

cat box kitty box, litter box

cat burglar cat man, cracksman, housebreaker, second-story man, second-story thief, yegg

catch one's breath breathe, ease off, mellow out, recuperate, relax, rest, sit down, slow down, stop for a breath, take a break, take ten, wind down

catch phrase buzzword, catchword, motto, shibboleth, slogan

catch-22 between a rock and a hard place, bind, contradiction, dilemma, Gordian knot, in a pickle, lose-lose situation, no-win situation, paradox, predicament, problematic situation, quagmire, spot

categorical imperative golden rule, utilitarianism

cathode ray tube computer display, CRT, display, monitor, screen

CAT scan body scan, brain scan, computer-assisted tomography scan, computerized axial tomography scan, computerized tomography scan, CT scan, x-ray, x-ray image, x-ray scan

cat's cradle cratch cradle, scratch cradle

cat's meow cat's pajamas

cattle call audition, mass audition

cauliflower ear bat ear, jug ear

cause célèbre affair, celebrated case, controversial issue, controversy, debate, fuss, grist for the gossip mill, hot potato, matter of the moment, political football, rumor, scandal, talk of the town, topic of the day, uproar, war of words

cautionary tale admonition, advisory, a few words of wisdom, caution light, caveat, deterrent example, enough said, forewarning, hint, lesson, message, moral, omen, piece of advice, portent, red flag, sign of things to come, wake-up call, warning, word to the wise

caveat emptor buy at your own risk, buyer beware, let the buyer beware
cave dweller aboriginal, caveman, troglodyte
cayenne pepper chili pepper, hot pepper, jalapeño, long pepper, red pepper
CB radio amateur band, CB, citizens band, citizens band radio, ham radio
CD player compact disc player, compact disk player
CD-ROM compact disc read-only memory, laser disk
ceasefire agreement armistice, cooling-off period, olive branch, peace, stand-down, suspension of hostilities, truce
CE key backspace key, clear entry key
celestial body celestial object, celestial sphere, heavenly body
celestial equator equator, equinoctial, equinoctial circle, equinoctial line
celestial horizon rational horizon
celestial mechanics gravitational astronomy
celestial navigation astro-inertial guidance, astronavigation, celestial guidance, celonavigation
celestial object celestial body, celestial sphere, heavenly body
celestial pole pole
cell body perikaryon, soma
cell division amitosis, cellular division, meiosis, mitosis
cell fusion fusion of cells
cell membrane cell surface, cell wall, cytomembrane, plasma membrane, plasmalemma
cellular telephone car telephone, cell phone, cell telephone, cellular phone, cellular telephone, digital telephone, field telephone, mobile telephone
Cenozoic era Age of Mammals, Cenozoic, Quaternary period, Tertiary period
census-taking demography, head counting, population study
center of gravity center of mass, mass center, point of balance
center punch hand punch
center stage attention, celebrity, fame, limelight, notoriety, public eye, spotlight
central air-conditioning A/C, AC, air-conditioning, air cooling, C/A, central air, climate control, climatization
central nervous system CNS

central processing unit central processor, CPU, mainframe, processor

centrifugal force centrifugal action

centripetal force centripetal action

cerebral palsy athetosis, mobile spasm, palsy, spastic paralysis

cerebrovascular accident apoplexy, CVA, stroke

certificate of deposit CD, certificate, credit memorandum, credit slip, deposit slip

certified check bank check, bank draft, cashier's check, check, treasurer's check

certified mail registered mail

certified public accountant accountant, chartered accountant, CPA, state-licensed accountant

cesarean section abdominal delivery, caesarean, caesarean section, caesarian, cesarean, C-section, surgical birth, surgical delivery

c'est la vie it's in the cards, oh well, que sera sera, such is life, that's how the cookie crumbles, that's life, that's reality, what will be will be

chafing dish chafing pan

chain gang hard labor, labor camp, rock pile

chain letter circular letter

chain-link fence Cyclone™ fence, steel wire fence, wire mesh fence

chain mail chain armor, coat of mail, mail, ring armor, ring mail

chain reaction causal nexus, cause and effect, chain of circumstances, chemical reaction, concatenation of events, domino effect, powder train, ripples in a pond, vicious circle

chain store retail chain

chair car drawing-room car, palace car, parlor car

chamber music concert music, longhair music, symphonic music

chamber of commerce C of C, junior chamber of commerce

chamber pot chamber, jerry, jordan, pisspot, potty, thunder mug

champ at the bit burst with energy, chafe at the bit, feel one's oats, thrive

championship game bowl game, championship match, conference championship, division championship, national championship, playoff game, post-season game

change hands change ownership, sell, transfer

change of heart about-face, apostasy, backpedaling, change of mind, defection, flip-flop, 180, reversal, turnaround, volte-face

change of life climacteric, grand climacteric, menopause, midlife crisis

change one's tune dance to another tune, do an about-face, reverse, sing a different tune

change ringing bell ringing, campanology, peal ringing, ringing the changes

chaos theory chaology, chaos dynamics

chapter and verse documentation, goods, gospel, gospel truth, lowdown, quotation, real McCoy, skinny, substantiation

Chapter 11 bankruptcy, Chapter Eleven, Chapter XI, declaring bankruptcy, default, failure, insolvency, receivership

character assassination ad hominem, blackening, dirty politics, dirty pool, dirty tricks, muckraking, mudslinging, name-calling, personal attack, slanderous attack, smear, smear campaign

character reference certificate of character, good character, letter of introduction, letter of recommendation, letter of reference, recommendation, reference, testimonial, voucher

charge account credit account, open account

charge card affinity card, bank card, charge plate, credit card, debit card, gold card, plastic, plastic money, platinum card

chargé d'affaires chargé, chargé d'affaires ad interim

charity drive appeal for funds, charity event, fundraiser, philanthropic enterprise, pledge campaign, pledge drive, radiothon, telethon

Charles's law Gay-Lussac's law, law of volumes

charmed circle closed circle, elite, fairy ring, in-crowd, in-group, inner circle, magic circle, popular crowd

charmed life all the luck, nine lives

charnel house bone house, charnel, lichhouse, morgue, ossuarium, ossuary

chartered accountant CA, certified public accountant

charter member club member, founding member, original member

chat room channel

chat show talk show

cheap wine plonk

checking account bank account

check valve clack valve, cock, cork, faucet, nonreturn valve, plug, spigot

cheek by jowl arm in arm, cheek to cheek, close, close together, crowded, hand in glove, hand in hand, in close proximity, shoulder to shoulder, side by side, very intimate, yardarm to yardarm

chemical engineering technology of chemistry

chemical formula formula, molecular formula

chemical warfare chemical operations, CW

cherry pitter cherry stoner

cherry tomato plum tomato

Cheshire cat chessy cat, Chessy cat

chest of drawers bureau, chest, chifforobe, dresser, highboy, tallboy, Yorkshire dresser

chewing gum bubble gum, gum

chewing tobacco eating tobacco, oral tobacco, snuff

chew the cud chew the fat, converse, digest, meditate, muse, ponder over, ruminate, think about

Chicago-style pizza thick-crust pizza

chicken feed chump change, Mickey Mouse, nickels and dimes, paltry sum, peanuts, pittance, pocket money, small amount, small change, small potatoes, spending money

chicken out avoid, back down, back out, beg off, cop out, funk out, get cold feet, give way, have no stomach for, make concessions, shy from, weasel out, wimp out, worm out, yield

chief executive president, president of the United States

chief executive officer boss, CEO, chief executive, chief operating officer, president

chief priest archpriest, hierarch, high priest, prelate, primate

child care baby-minding, babysitting, day care, family service, governance, infant care

child prodigy boy wonder, genius, gifted child, gifted student, girl wonder, phenom, polymath, prodigy, sensation, talented child, whiz kid, wonder, wunderkind

child's play breeze, cinch, drop in the bucket, duck soup, easy thing, picnic, piece of cake, pushover, simple matter, small potatoes

chill out calm down, chill, cool it, cool off, loosen up, mellow, relax, settle down, simmer down, take a chill pill

chimney sweep chimney sweeper, flue cleaner, sweep, sweeper

china cabinet breakfront, china closet, china cupboard, hutch

China Syndrome nuclear accident, nuclear meltdown accident, nuclear winter

Chinese lantern Japanese lantern

Chinese puzzle brainteaser, conundrum, difficult problem, labyrinth, maze, puzzlement

Chinese restaurant syndrome Kwok's disease

Chinese Wall Great Wall of China

chink in one's armor Achilles' heel, failing, foible, frailty, shortcoming, soft spot, underbelly, vulnerable place, weak link, weakness, weak point, weak side

chip off the old block alter ego, counterpart, second self, spitting image

chip on one's shoulder fight, gauntlet, truculence

chip shot chip, short shot

chock-full brimming, bulging, bursting, chockablock, cramfull, crammed, filled to capacity, jam-packed, overcrowded, overflowing, packed, packed like sardines, stuffed

choke collar choke chain

chopping block butcher block, butcher board, chopping board, cutting board

chorus girl chorine, chorus line, coryphée, showgirl

Christian Science Church of Christ, Scientist

Christmas box Christmas gift

chronic fatigue syndrome fatigue disease, fatigue syndrome, post-viral fatigue syndrome, yuppie flu

chuck wagon cookhouse, cookshack, lunch wagon

chump change chicken feed, Mickey Mouse, nickels and dimes, paltry sum, peanuts, pittance, pocket money, small amount, small change, small potatoes, spending money

church key bottle opener, bottle screw, can opener

Church of England Anglican Church, Anglican Communion, English church

Church of the Brethren Dippers, Dunkers

Church of the New Jerusalem Swedenborgians

cinder block concrete block, concrete building block

circuit board board, card, circuit card, motherboard, printed circuit board

circuit box electrical box, junction box, service panel

circuit breaker breaker, fuse

circuit rider itinerant preacher

circular file garbage can, wastebasket, wastepaper basket

circular function inverse trigonometrical function, trigonometric function

circulating decimal recurring decimal, repeating decimal

circulating medium currency, legal tender, medium of exchange

circulatory system cardiovascular system

circumstantial evidence inconclusive evidence, indirect evidence, inferred evidence

citizens band amateur band, CB, CB radio, citizens band radio, ham radio

city council board of aldermen, board of selectmen, city board, city government, common council, selectboard

city editor news editor, newspaper editor

city father councillor, councilor, elder

city hall city center, municipal building, municipal center, town hall; city government, municipal government, town government, town hall

city manager burgomaster, first selectman, lord mayor, maire, mayor, supervisor

City of God Celestial City, City Celestial, Civitas Dei, Heavenly City, Holy City, Jerusalem; heaven, New Jerusalem, Zion

city slicker big-city person, city boy, city dweller, city person, metropolitan, townie, urbanite

civil action civil suit

civil disobedience noncooperation, nonviolent resistance, passive resistance, protest, resistance movement

civil law Justinian Code, Roman law; noncriminal law

civil liberty civil rights, constitutional freedom, constitutional rights, Four Freedoms, freedom, freedom from fear, freedom from want, freedom of expression, freedom of religion, freedom of speech, freedom of worship, God-given right, political liberty, rights

civil rights civil liberties, constitutional rights, freedom, human rights, legal rights, natural rights, rights, rights of citizenship, unalienable rights

civil servant government employee, public employee, public official, public servant

civil service government workers

Civil War War Between the States, War of Secession

class consciousness class difference, class distinction, class hatred, class identity, class politics, class prejudice, class struggle, class war, discrimination, snobbery

classical conditioning Pavlovian conditioning

classical education classicism

classical music chamber music, classic, concert music, longhair music, operatic music, semiclassical music, serious music, symphonic music

classic car antique automobile, antique car, classic automobile, vintage automobile, vintage car

classic revival neoclassicism

classified ad classified advertisement, classifieds, want ad

classified advertisement classified ad, classifieds, want ad

classified information secret information, top secret information

clay pigeon bird, clay disk, skeet

clean bill of health bill of health, full pratique, good health, pink, pratique

clean-cut button-down, clean-shaven, groomed, neat, tidy, trim

cleaning woman charwoman, cleaning lady, cleaning service, daily, daily woman, housecleaner, household help, housekeeper, housemaid, maid, maidservant

clean room white room

clean slate clean hands, clean sweep, clear conscience, fresh start, new beginning, new start, square one, tabula rasa

clearance sale closing-out sale, inventory-clearance sale

clear the air clarify, clear up, decipher, define, elucidate, explain, interpret, make clear, make plain, shed light on, show, simplify, solve, spell out

clear the decks clear away, clear out, flush out, groom, make a clean sweep, spruce up

clerical collar dog collar, priest's collar, Roman collar

clever remark bon mot, clever comment, quip, witticism, witty remark

client state dependency, dependent state, puppet government, satellite, satellite state

climbing iron climber, crampon, crampoon

climbing perch *Anabas, Labyrinthici*

clip art click art

clip joint brace house, bust-out joint, deadfall, flat joint, flat store, gambling house, juice joint, low den, nick joint, snap house, sneak joint, steer joint, wire joint, wolf trap

clipper ship clipper

cloak-and-dagger clandestine, covert, hugger-mugger, hush-hush, intriguing, mysterious, quiet, secret, sly, sneaky, stealthy, surreptitious, undercover

clog dance clog, clog dancing

close call close shave, close squeeze, hairbreadth escape, heart-stopper, narrow escape, narrow squeak, near go, near miss, near squeak, near thing, squeaker, tight squeeze

closed-circuit television closed-circuit TV

closed shop preferential shop, union shop

close-minded blind, deaf, intolerant, narrow-minded, resistant, shortsighted, unpersuadable

close out close the books, close the door on, liquidate, sell out, terminate the account

close quarters close range, confined space, grips, place of confinement

close ranks go into a huddle, huddle, join fortunes with, stand together

closet auger snake, toilet auger

clothes chute laundry chute

clothes closet armoire, cloakroom, closet, clothespress, linen closet, wardrobe

clothes hamper clothes basket, hamper, laundry basket, laundry hamper

cloud chamber Wilson cloud chamber

cloud nine bliss, blissfulness, heaven, over the moon, paradise, seventh heaven, top of the world, walking on air

cloud seeding artificial nucleation, nucleation, rainmaking, seeding

club car bar car, lounge car

club soda carbonated water, seltzer, soda water, sparkling water

club steak Delmonico steak

cluster headache histamine headache

clutch bag clutch purse

coach class economy class, third class, tourist class

coal gas blackdamp, chokedamp, firedamp

coalition government caretaker government, interregnum, provisional government

coal oil crude, crude oil, fossil oil, kerosene, paraffin, petroleum, rock oil, shale oil

coat hanger clothes hanger, dress hanger

coat of arms armorial bearings, armory, arms, bearings, blazon, blazonry

coat of mail armored coat, chain armor, chain mail, hauberk, mail, ring armor, ring mail

coaxial cable coax, coax cable, coaxial line, concentric cable, fiber cable, fiber-optic cable, transmission line

cock-and-bull story fanciful tale, farfetched story, fish story, flight of fancy, song and dance, tall story, tall tale, unbelievable tale

cocktail lounge bar, barroom, bistro, night club, piano bar

cocktail table coffee table

code of conduct code of behavior, custom, decorum, diplomatic code, etiquette, formalities, guideline, manners, protocol, rules of conduct, social code, social procedures, standard procedure

code word code book, code name, euphemism, password, secret language, secret message, secret word, secret writing, watchword

coffee break break, pause, recess, tea break

coffee filter coffee cone

coffee grinder coffee mill

coffee klatch kaffeeklatsch

coffee maker coffeepot, drip coffee maker

coffee measure coffee scoop

coffee shop café, coffee bar, coffee room, coffeehouse, java shop, tearoom, tea shop

coffee table cocktail table

coffin nail butt, cancer stick, cigarette, fag, smokes

cognitive dissonance babel, confoundment, confusion, sensory overload

coign of vantage high ground, perspective, point of vantage, point of view, standpoint, vantage point, viewpoint, where one stands

coin collecting numismatics, numismatology

cold call hard sell, sales call, spam, unsolicited call

cold cash cash, hard cash, money, sterling

cold cream face cream, hand cream, hand lotion, lanolin, vanishing cream

cold cuts cold meats, lunch meat

cold duck sparkling wine

cold feet anxiety, apprehension, chicken heart, doubt, faint heart, fear, reservations, second thoughts, weak knees, white feather, yellow streak

cold frame gardening frame

cold front cold sector, cold snap, cold spell, cold wave, polar front, snap

cold pack cold sheet, ice bag, ice pack

cold shoulder aloofness, brush-off, coldness, coolness, cut, cut direct, disregard, distance, go-by, slight, snub, spurn, spurning, standoffishness

cold snap cold spell, cold wave, cold weather

cold sore canker, canker sore, fever blister, herpes labialis, herpes simplex, lesion, mouth ulcer, oral herpes

cold steel naked steel, steel

cold storage cold store, freezer, freezer locker, frigidarium, frozen-food locker, locker

cold turkey abrupt withdrawal, crash, detox, detoxification, sudden withdrawal, taking the cure

cold war antagonism, hostilities, one-upsmanship, rivalry, tension

cold-water flat walk-up

cole slaw cabbage salad

collapsed lung pneumatothorax, pneumothorax

collateral damage civilian casualties

collect call reverse-charge call

collective bargaining package bargaining, pattern bargaining

collective farm co-op, co-op farm, communal farm, cooperative, cooperative farm, kibbutz, kolkhoz

collective mark service mark, trademark

collective noun group noun

collective unconscious race memory, racial unconscious, spiritus mundi

collect on delivery COD, cash on delivery

collector's item catch, collectible, pièce de résistance, showpiece, trouvaille

college try all-out effort, best effort, good effort, old college try, valiant effort

collision course clash, encounter

color bar color line, Jim Crow

color blindness achromatic vision, daltonism, dichromatic vision

color guard honor guard

color line color bar, Jim Crow

color scheme color arrangement, coloration, color compatibility, color coordination, color design, color pattern, decorator colors

combat boot army boot, buskin, chukka boot, jackboot, military boot, top boot

combat drone drone aircraft

combat fatigue battle fatigue, combat disorder, combat neurosis, complete exhaustion, posttraumatic stress disorder, shell shock

combat zone battle zone, battlefront, combat area, communications zone, firing line, theater, theater of operations, war zone

come a cropper be felled, fail miserably, run aground, suffer a misfortune

come clean admit, confess, implicate oneself, incriminate oneself, own up, reveal, spill, tell the truth

come to a head cap, climax, conclude, culminate, end, finish, wind up

come to blows assault, attack, battle, bear arms, box, brawl, challenge, clash, cross swords, dispute, do battle, duel, exchange blows, feud, fight, joust, mix it up, ply weapons, quarrel, scrap, scuffle, skirmish, wage war

come to grips with bear, bite the bullet, brace, brave, confront, contend, cope with, deal with, endure, face, grapple with, make a stand, stomach, suffer, sustain, take, withstand

come unglued break down, come apart at the seams, come unwrapped, fall apart, fall to bits, fall to pieces, go to pieces

comfort station bathroom, comfort room, ladies' room, lavatory, men's room, public convenience, public lavatory, public rest room, public toilet, rest room, washroom

comic book caricatures, cartoons, comics, comic section, funnies, funny book, funny paper

comic opera bouffe, opéra bouffe, opéra comique

comic strip cartoon, cartoon strip, funnies

command economy socialism

commander in chief captain general, generalissimo, president, U.S. president

commanding officer CO, commandant, commander, general, hetman, old man, sirdar

command post base, company headquarters, CP, field headquarters, general headquarters, GHQ

commercial bank full-service bank

commercial paper bill, bills of exchange, negotiable instrument, negotiable paper, paper

commercial traveler bagman, drummer, knight of the road, roadman, road warrior, traveler, traveling agent, traveling man, traveling salesman, traveling sales representative, traveling saleswoman

commissioned officer military leader, military officer, officer

commodity exchange commodities exchange, corn pit, pit, wheat pit

common brick red brick

common carrier carrier, conveyer, driver, shipper, transporter, truck driver, trucker

common cold catarrh, cold, coryza

common denominator common divisor, common factor, common measure, denominator

Common Era AD, anno Domini, CE, Christian Era

common ground communion, community, commutuality, mutuality, mutual understanding

common labor manual labor, manual work, physical work, unskilled labor, unskilled work

common law case law, non-statutory law, precedent

common-law marriage cohabitation, living as man and wife

common market customs union, economic community, EEC, European Economic Community, free trade area

common measure common meter, hymnal stanza; common time, four-four time

common people folk, hillbilly, hoi polloi, lower class, masses, proletariat, working class

commonplace book adversaria, diary, journal, memo book, memorandum book

common room community room, faculty lounge, sitting room

common salt halite, rock salt, sodium chloride

common school public elementary school, public school

common sense experience, good sense, horse sense, levelheadedness, logic, mother wit, practicality, prudence, rationality, reason, reasonableness, sensibleness, sound judgment, soundness, sound sense, sweet reason, wits

common stock common shares, junior equity, ordinary shares

common year regular year, 365 days

communications satellite active communications satellite, communications relay satellite, comsat, relay satellite

communion table altar, chancel table, holy table, Lord's table, table of the Lord

community center civic center, rec center, recreation center

community theater amateur theater, community playhouse, little theater, neighborhood playhouse, neighborhood theater, summer playhouse

commutation ticket season ticket

compact disc CD, compact disk, DVD, laser disk, multimedia CD

company man conformist, lackey, organization man, yes-man

compass rose cardinal points, degrees, direction symbol, map symbol, points of the compass

complementary angle complement

complementary distribution complementary relation, complementation

complex carbohydrate polysaccharide

complex fraction compound fraction, continued fraction

complex number complex quantity, imaginary number

complex plane Argand diagram, Gauss plane

complimentary close complimentary closing

composing room pressroom, proofroom

composing stick galley chase, job stick

compost heap compost, compost pile, kitchen midden, refuse heap

compound fraction complex fraction, continued fraction

compound fracture open fracture

compound number denominate number

compressed-air sickness aeroembolism, bends, caisson disease, decompression sickness

computer-aided design CAD

computer-aided manufacture CAM

computer-assisted tomography CAT, computer-aided tomography

computer graphics animation, computer-aided design

computer hacker computer crackerjack, computer enthusiast, computer geek, computer nerd, computer programmer, computer wiz, cracker, cyberpunk, hacker

computer hardware central processing unit, computer, computer unit, CPU, data processor, disk drive, floppy disk, hard drive, hardware, magnetic disk, microcomputer, microelectronics device, modem, output device, personal computer, supercomputer, tape drive

computerized axial tomography CAT, computed axial tomography, computed tomography, computer-assisted tomography, computerized tomography

computer literacy computeracy

computer science artificial intelligence, computer-aided learning, computer-aided testing, cybernetics, data processing, information retrieval, information technology, natural language processing, neural networks, operating systems, programming, programming languages, robotics, simulation, systems analysis

computer virus bug, computer bug, Trojan horse, virus

comrade in arms comrade, fellow soldier

con artist bilker, bunco, cheater, clip artist, confidence man, con man, crook, deceiver, fleecer, flimflammer, fraud, hoser, hustler, mountebank, scammer, shark, sharpie, smoothie, swindler

concentration camp death

camp, detention camp, forced-labor camp, gas chamber, gulag, internment camp, killing fields, Konzentrationslager, labor camp, prison camp, prisoner-of-war camp

concert grand concert piano, grand piano

concert pitch best, international pitch, philharmonic pitch

concrete jungle asphalt jungle, city, downtown, inner city, mean streets, metropolis, municipality, urban area, urban complex, urban sprawl

concrete music musique concrète

condensation trail contrail, vapor trail

condensed milk evaporated milk

conditioned reflex acquired reflex, conditional reaction, conditional reflex, conditional response, conditioned reaction, conditioned response, conditioned stimulus

confectioners' sugar powdered sugar

conference call phone meeting, teleconference, video teleconference

conference room boardroom, meeting room

confidence game bait and switch, boiler room, bunco game, bunko, con, confidence trick, con game, con job, flimflam, hustle, Ponzi, racket, rip-off, shell game, skin game, sting, swindle

confidence man bilker, bunco, cheater, clip artist, con artist, con man, fleecer, flimflammer, hoser, hustler, scammer, shark, sharpie, smoothie

con game bait and switch, boiler room, bunco game, bunko, con, confidence game, confidence trick, con job, flimflam, hustle, Ponzi, racket, rip-off, shell game, skin game, sting, swindle

congenital defect birth defect, congenital abnormality, congenital anomaly, congenital disorder

congenital disease gene disease, genetic abnormality, genetic disease, genetic disorder, gene-transmitted disease, hereditary disease, inherited disease, inherited disorder

conic projection conical projection

conjugal love married love, uxoriousness

con man bilker, bunco, cheater,

clip artist, con artist, confidence man, crook, deceiver, fleecer, flimflammer, fraud, hoser, hustler, mountebank, scammer, shark, sharpie, smoothie, swindler

connective tissue cellular tissue, connective tissue, connectivum

conning tower bridge, crow's nest

conscience money amends, redress, reparations, restitution

conscientious objector CO, conchie, draft dodger, passive resister, peacemonger

consent decree consent judgment

consent judgment consent decree

conservation law conservation

conservation of energy conservation of force, law of conservation of energy

conservation of mass conservation of matter, law of conservation of mass, law of conservation of matter

consolation prize booby prize, runner-up prize, second prize, silver medal

conspicuous consumption conspicuous waste, opulence, waste

constitutional monarchy absolute monarchy, kingship, monarchical government, queenship

construction wood dimension lumber

consumer credit installment credit, retail credit

consumer electronics home electronics

consumer goods consumer items, goods for sale, retail goods

consumer price index cost-of-living index, CPI, price index, retail price index

contact lenses contacts, disposable lenses, extended-wear lenses, hard lenses, soft lenses

contact print projection print

continental breakfast English breakfast, petit déjeuner

continental divide continental drift, divide, Great Divide

continental margin continent's edge

continental shelf continental platform, continental slope, land bridge, offshore rights, submarine canyon, territorial waters, three-mile limit, twelve-mile limit

continuing education adult education, continuation school, postgraduate work

continuous budget month-by-month budget, rolling budget
contour feather body feather, down feather, penna, plume feather, plumule
contour line hachure, isoheight, isohypse, isoline, layer tint
contour map relief map, topographic map
contrast medium barium, iodine
control experiment controlled experiment
controlled substance abused substance, addictive drug, dangerous drug, designer drug, dope, drug, hard drug, illegal drug, narcotic drug
controlling interest majority ownership
control panel console, control board, instrument panel, panel
control surface aerofoil, airfoil
control tower Air Traffic Control Center, island
convenience food canned food, dehydrated food, fast food, frozen food, precooked food
convenience store corner store, mom-and-pop store, 7-Eleven™
conventionalized art stylized art
conventional weapon nonnuclear weapon
conventional wisdom commonplace, lieu commun, locus communis, platitude, truism
convergent evolution biological evolution, convergence, parallel evolution, speciation
conversation piece curio
conveyor belt transporter
cookie sheet baking sheet
coon's age ages, donkey's years, long time
coonskin hat coonskin, coonskin cap, Davy Crockett hat, raccoon hat
cooperative apartment condo, condominium, co-op, cooperative apartment house
coordinate bond coordinate covalent bond, coordinate valence, dative bond
Coordinated Universal Time Greenwich Mean Time, International Atomic Time, Universal Coordinated Time, Universal Time Coordinated, UTC, World Time
coordination compound complex compound, coordination complex
cop a plea get off on a technicality, plea-bargain, plead guilty
copy machine copier, copying machine, duplicator, photocopier, photocopy machine, Xerox™

cordial glass liqueur glass
cordon bleu blue ribbon, high quality
core curriculum required course, requirement
Coriolis effect Coriolis deflection
cork cambium phellogen
corneal transplant corneal graft, keratoplasty
coronary artery arteria coronaria
coronary bypass open-heart surgery
coronary infarction cardiac arrest, congestive heart failure, heart attack, heart failure, myocardial infarction, tachycardia
coronary occlusion coronary thrombosis
coronary thrombosis coronary occlusion
corporal punishment beating, flagellation, flogging, paddling, spanking, whipping
correction fluid Liquid Paper™, Wite-Out™
correlation coefficient coefficient of correlation
correspondence course adult education, matchbook course
correspondence school adult education, matchbook school
Cosa Nostra Black Hand, gangdom, gangland, Mafia, mob, organized crime, organized crime family, rackets, the mob, the Syndicate, the underworld
cosmetic surgery anaplasty, esthetic surgery, face-lift, plastic surgery, reconstructive surgery, rhinoplasty
cosmic dust meteor dust, space dust
cosmic noise galactic noise
cosmic ray aurora particles, cosmic particles, intergalactic matter, radiation
cost accounting cost-accounting system, costing, cost system, managerial accounting
cost-effective cost-efficient, economical, frugal, labor-saving, penny-wise, practical, profitable, prudent, thrifty, time-saving, worthwhile
cost-of-living index consumer price index, CPI, price index, retail price index
cost-push inflation cost inflation, cost-push, hot economy, inflationary pressure, inflationary spiral, inflationary trend
costume film period piece
costume jewelry glass, junk jewelry, paste

cottage cheese Dutch cheese, farmer cheese, pot cheese, smearcase

cottage fries home fries

cotton candy candy floss, spun sugar

cotton swab cotton bud, Q-tip™

couch potato drone, goof-off, lazybones, sofa spud, spud, televiewer, television viewer, TV-viewer, video-gazer

cough drop horehound, lozenge, medicated lozenge, pastil, pastille, throat lozenge, troche

cough syrup cough medicine, expectorant

could care less apathetic, neutral, unbothered, unconcerned, uninterested

counterfeit money counterfeit currency, fake money, funny money

counting number natural number, positive integer

country bumpkin clodhopper, hayseed, hick, hillbilly, yokel

country club club, lodge, tennis club, yacht club

country gentleman cottager, provincial, ruralist, rustic, squire

country mile long distance

country music C&W, country and western, hillbilly music, old-time country rock, western swing

country singer folk singer

county agent agricultural agent, extension agent

county seat county site, county town, shiretown

coup de grâce blow of mercy, deathblow, finishing blow, knockout punch, mortal blow, Sunday punch

coup de main surprise attack

coup d'état coup, insurrection, mutiny, overthrow, power play, putsch, rebellion, revolt, revolution, seizure of power, takeover, uprising, usurpation

course of study class, course of instruction, curriculum, program

court case case, cause, cause in court, legal case, trial

court-martial military court, military trial, military tribunal

court of appeals appeals court, appellate court, court of appeal

court of domestic relations domestic relations court, family court

court of inquiry military court

court of law court of arbitration, court of justice, judicature, law court, legal tribunal

court of record trial court

court reporter brachygrapher, stenographer

court tennis real tennis, royal tennis

Cousin Jack Cornish miner, Cornishman

covalent bond covalence, covalent bonding, electron-pair bond

cover charge admission charge

covered wagon Conestoga wagon, prairie schooner, prairie wagon, stagecoach

cover girl glamour girl, model, pinup, pinup girl, supermodel

cover glass cover slip

cover ground make good time, make headway, make strides, travel

cover letter covering letter

cover-up camouflage, concealment, disguising, hush-up, masking, placing under wraps, seal of secrecy, veil of secrecy

cowboy hat Stetson, ten-gallon hat

cowboy picture cowboy movie, horse opera, oater, shoot-'em-up, spaghetti western, western, western movie

cow college agricultural college, college of agriculture, cow tech, farming college, school of agriculture

cow horse cow pony

craft union guild, horizontal union

crash diet bare subsistence, bread and water, fad diet, starvation diet, water diet

crash pad houseroom, living space, nest, place to rest one's head, sleeping place

crazy bone elbow, funny bone

crazy person deranged person, insane person, lunatic, maniac, nut, nut case, psychopath, sociopath

cream of the crop aristocracy, beau monde, beautiful people, best of the best, cream of society, cream of the cream, crème de la crème, haut monde, high society, pick of the litter, privileged class, smart set, the best and brightest, the elite, the finest, the privileged, upper class, upper crust

cream puff cannoli, chou, cream horn, croquembouche, profiterole, puff

creation science creationism, divine creation

creature comforts all the comforts of home, amenities, bodily pleasure, comforts, conveniences, fare, good things of life, physical pleasure, sense pleasure

credibility gap discrepancy, disparity, doubtfulness, forswearing, inconsistency, perjury, question, unreliability, untrustworthiness, untruthfulness
credit card affinity card, bank card, charge card, charge plate, debit card, gold card, plastic, plastic credit, plastic money, platinum card
credit line bank line, credit limit, line of credit, personal line of credit
credit union cooperative credit union, lending institution, savings institution, thrift institution
crepe rubber sponge rubber
crew cut burr cut, buzz cut, buzzer, close-cropped, flattop, fuzz cut, military haircut, number 2 buzz
crib death cot death, SIDS, sudden infant death syndrome
crime against humanity atrocity, enormity, evil, genocide, outrage, savagery, war crime
criminally insane dangerous
critical mass climax, crisis, critical juncture, critical point, critical stage, crossroads, crucial moment, crucial point, decisive moment, defining moment, emergency, high noon, moment of truth, pivotal point, point of no return, turning point, zero hour
critical point climacteric, climax, crisis, critical juncture, critical mass, critical stage, crucial moment, crucial point, crunch, defining moment, moment of truth, nexus, pivot, pivotal point, point of no return, turning point
crocodile tears Academy Award performance, affected tears, fake tears, false show of emotion, false tears, insincere tears
Cro-Magnon man cave dweller, caveman, cavewoman, Cro-Magnon, Cro-Magnon race, *Homo sapiens*, human, Paleolithic man, Stone Age man
crop dusting pesticide spraying
cross bridging herringbone bridging
cross-examine cross-question, give the third degree, go over with a fine-tooth comb, grill, inquire, interrogate, pump, put on the hotseat, question, scrutinize
cross-eye cockeye, convergent strabismus, crossed eye, exotropia, strabismus
cross-purposes contrary

purpose, crossed wires, misunderstanding, mutual misunderstanding

cross section random sample, sample, sampling, transection

cross swords bandy words, brawl, chop logic, contend, cut and thrust, fight, lock horns, quarrel, spar

cross the Rubicon bite the bullet, choose one's fate, jump in with both feet, leap into the breach, leave a crossroads, make one's move, pass the Rubicon, prendre la balle au bond, take the bull by the horns, take the plunge

crown glass optical crown

crowning achievement bestseller, bull's-eye, chef d'oeuvre, classic, coup, crowning accomplishment, crowning stroke, feather in one's cap, grand slam, hole in one, home run, icing on the cake, masterpiece, masterwork, Meisterstuck, showpiece, smash hit, success story, work of a master, work of a past master

crow's-feet crow's-foot, laugh lines, wrinkles

crow's nest bridge, conning tower

crude oil black gold, coal oil, crude, fossil oil, oil, petrol, petroleum, rock oil, Texas tea

cruise missile ballistic missile, Exocet missile, guided missile, surface-to-air missile, surface-to-surface missile, Tomahawk missile

cruise ship floating hotel, floating palace, liner, luxury liner, ocean greyhound, ocean liner, passenger ship, passenger steamer

crumb tray toaster bottom, toaster tray

crunch time critical mass, critical moment, crucial moment, do-or-die time, high noon, moment of truth, pivotal point

crystal ball clairvoyance, divination, envisagement, forward look, prediction, prevenience

cry uncle break, cave in, give way, put one's tail between one's legs, say uncle, surrender

cry wolf cry before one is hurt, give a false alarm

CT scanner CAT scanner, computerized axial tomography scanner

cubic measure capacity measure, capacity unit, cubage, cubage unit, cubature unit, cubic measurement, displacement unit, volume unit

cubic zirconia artificial diamond
cub reporter beginning reporter, greenie
cue ball white ball
cue card flip card, idiot card, idiot sheet, teleprompter
cul-de-sac blind alley, dead end, dead-end street, impasse
culinary art cookery, cooking, cuisine, culinary science, gastronomy
cultural alienation anomie
cultural geography human geography
culture shock alienation, anxiety, confusion
curb service drive-in service, take-out service
cure-all catholicon, elixir, magic bullet, magic potion, nostrum, panacea, theriac, universal remedy
curling iron crimper, crimping iron, curler, hot iron, hot rollers, straightening iron
current affairs current events, happenings, hard news
curry favor back-scratch, bootlick, brownnose, butter up, cajole, court, dance attendance on, fall all over, fawn over, flatter, kiss up to, pay court to, suck up to, sweet-talk, toady to, win over
curtain call applause, bow, curtain, ovation
curtain-raiser countdown, curtain-lifter, curtain-warmer, inaugural, kickoff, lead-in, opener, opening gun, opening shot, preliminary, preview, run-up, warm-up
curtain wall nonbearing wall
curvature of the spine kyphosis, lordosis, scoliosis
customer service CS, help line, product service, troubleshooting
cut-and-dried familiar, old hat, ordained, ordinary, routine, trite, warmed-over; destined, fated, fixed, in the cards, plotted, prearranged, set, settled, written
cut loose go berserk, kick up one's heels, let go, let loose, let one's hair down, run amok, run riot, run wild
cut short abbreviate, break short, check, checkmate, clip, curtail, freeze, stop cold, stop dead, stop short
cut the Gordian knot clear, cut through red tape, free, get to the bottom of, resolve, solve, unravel, unsnarl, untangle, work out
cutting board butcher block, butcher board, chopping block, chopping board

cutting edge advance guard, avant-garde, forefront, front, front line, leading edge, new wave, pioneer, point, spear-head, van, vanguard

cutting horse cow-cutting horse

cyclone cellar fallout shelter, storm cave, storm cellar, storm shelter, tornado shelter

Dd

dabbling duck dabbler
Dagwood sandwich club sandwich, triple-decker
daily double late double
daily dozen calisthenics, constitutional, exercise, exercising, physical jerks, warm-up, workout
daily grind grind, nine-to-five, squirrel cage, treadmill, working day
dairy compartment butter compartment
daisy wheel daisy print wheel, print wheel
damage control compensation, correction, disaster control, recompense, troubleshooting
damper pedal forte pedal, loud pedal, sustain pedal, sustaining pedal
D and C dilatation and curettage, dilation and curettage
Danish pastry Danish, French pastry
dark adaptation night vision, scotopia, scotopic vision
Dark Ages medieval times, Middle Ages
dark horse also-ran, little chance, little opportunity, long shot, outside chance, outside shot, poor bet, poor lookout, poor possibility, poor prognosis, poor prospect, remote possibility, sleeper, slim chance, small chance, stalking horse, underdog, unexpected winner, unknown, unknown quantity, unlikelihood, unlikely winner, upsetter
dark meat leg meat, thigh meat {compare *white meat*}
data highway I-bahn, infobahn, information superhighway, Infostrada, Internet, Net, Web, World Wide Web, WWW
data processing data storage, DP, electronic data processing, information processing
data retrieval data obtainment, data procurement, information retrieval
date line International Date Line
date rape acquaintance rape, indecent assault, violation
Davy Jones's locker bottom of the ocean, bottom of the sea, ocean bottom, ocean floor, seabed, sea bottom

day care after-school care, child care, crèche, day nursery, infant school, nursery, nursery school, playschool, preschool

day in and day out all the time, everyday, regularly

day laborer common laborer, laborer, navvy, roustabout, unskilled laborer, unskilled worker

daylight savings time DST

Day of Atonement Yom Kippur

Day of Judgment day of reckoning, Doomsday, Judgment Day, Last Day, Last Judgment, the Judgment

day of reckoning crack of doom, day of doom, Day of Judgment, doom, Doomsday, Judgment Day, trumpet of doom

day of rest day off, Lord's day, rest day, Sabbath, Sabbath Day, Saturday, Sunday

dead body body, cadaver, carcass, clay, corpse, dead man, mortal remains, remains, stiff

dead end blank wall, blind alley, corner, cul-de-sac, dead-end street, impasse; box, deadlock, hole, impasse, logjam, stalemate, standstill

dead giveaway betrayal, communication leak, exposure of secret, giveaway, leak, obvious clue, telltale, telltale sign, unwitting disclosure

dead hand mortmain, past history

dead heat blanket finish, draw, even money, Garrison finish, Mexican standoff, neck-and-neck race, photo finish, standoff, tie, wash

deadly sin anger, covetousness, envy, gluttony, lust, pride, sloth; mortal sin, seven deadly sins

dead-on absolutely right, accurate, exact, on the mark, on the money, pinpoint, precise, to the point, unerring

dead on arrival DOA

dead ringer carbon copy, copy, doppelgänger, eidetic image, exact counterpart, exact duplicate, facsimile, living image, living picture, lookalike, mirror image, replica, spit and image, spitting image, very image, very picture

dead storage cold storage, cold store, dry storage

dead time downtime, insensitive time, limbo, time delay, unproductive time

Dear John letter breakup letter

death benefit life insurance payment

death camp Auschwitz, concentration camp, gas chamber, killing fields

death instinct death wish, Thanatos

death march cortege, dead march, funeral procession

death notice death announcement, mortuary tribute, necrology, obit, obituary

death penalty capital punishment, death sentence, death warrant, execution, judicial execution, judicial murder, legalized killing

death rattle death groan, rale

death row death house

death squad executioners, firing squad, hired assassins

death tax death duty, estate tax, inheritance tax

death warrant apocalypse, bane, coup de grâce, cutoff, death knell, deathblow, doom, end of the world, fate, final blow, quietus

death wish black despondency, death instinct, gloom and doom, pessimism, self-destructive urge, suicidal despair

debit card plastic money, smart card

debt of honor solemn declaration, solemn promise, solemn word, word of honor

debt of nature curtains, death, last debt, reward

decaffeinated coffee decaf, Sanka™

decimal fraction compound fraction, continued fraction

deck chair beach chair

decompression chamber altitude chamber, compression chamber, diving chamber, hyperbaric chamber, hypobaric chamber, recompression chamber

decompression sickness aeroembolism, air embolism, bends, caisson disease, diver's palsy, the bends, tunnel disease

Decoration Day Memorial Day

deep blue sea high seas, ocean, open sea, sea, the brine, the briny deep, the deep, the deep sea, the seven seas

deep-dish thick

deep freeze arctic frost, big freeze, cold, cold storage, freeze, frost, hard freeze, hard frost, sharp freeze

deep pocket baron, Daddy Warbucks, magnate, moneybags, Mr. Moneybags, richling, tycoon

deep pockets bottomless purse, bulging purse, embarras de richesses, embarrassment of riches, fat purse, full purse, heavy purse, money to burn, well-lined purse

deep-seated deep-rooted, deep-settled, embedded, implanted, ingrained, inherent, instilled

deep six burial, burial at sea, bury; dumping, jettison, throw away

deep space celestial spaces, cosmic space, cosmos, empty space, ether space, intercosmic space, intergalactic space, interplanetary space, interstellar space, metagalactic space, ocean of emptiness, outer space, pressureless space, the heavens, the universe, the void, the void above

deep structure semantic content, underlying structure

deep thought absorption, concentration, contemplation, engrossment, meditation, preoccupation, profound thought, reflection, study

de facto actual, existing, factual, from fact, in fact, in reality, real

defense attorney defense counsel, defense lawyer

defense mechanism conversion, defense, defense reaction, repression, sublimation, suppression, symbolization

deficit spending budget deficit, compensatory spending, pump priming

defining moment climax, critical moment, crucial moment, crunch, decisive moment, kairos, kairotic moment, loaded moment, moment of truth, point of no return, pregnant moment, turning point

degenerative joint disease degenerative arthritis, osteoarthritis

dehydrating agent desiccant, drying agent

déjà vu familiarity, hallucination, memory, paramnesia, past-life experience, recall, remembrance, revisiting

delirium tremens blue devils, blue Johnnies, delirium alcoholicum, delirium ebriositatis, dementia a potu, DT's, heebie-jeebies, horrors, jimjams, mania, pink elephants, pink spiders, screaming meemies, shakes, snakes in the boots

delivery date delivery day, prompt date, release date, release day, shipment date

delivery room birthing room, labor room

delivery truck delivery van, panel truck

delta wave delta rhythm

delusions of grandeur airs, pretensions, swank, vain pretensions, vaporing

demand loan call loan

dementia praecox dissociation of personality, mental dissociation, schizophrenia, schizophrenic disorder, schizophrenic psychosis

denim jacket jean jacket

dental caries cavity, tooth decay

dental floss floss, tooth floss

dental surgery oral surgery

Denver boot boot, Boston boot, wheel-locking clamp

deoxyribonucleic acid desoxyribonucleic acid, DNA

department store emporium, mart, retail store, store

depletion allowance price support, subsidization, subsidy, subvention, support, tax benefit, tax write-off

depository library library

depth charge ash can, blockbuster, depth bomb, fire bomb, incendiary bomb

depth of field depth of focus

depth psychology analysis, psychoanalysis, psychology of depths

de rigueur a must, called for, comme il faut, conventional, correct, mandatory, necessary, obligatory, proper, required, right, socially obligatory

dernier cri all the rage, avant-garde, craze, fad, hip, in vogue, latest wrinkle, look, mode, new look, the in thing, the last word, the latest cry, the latest fad, the latest fashion, the latest thing

derring-do adventurousness, audacity, bravado, courage, daring deed, overboldness, risk-taking, valor, venturousness

descending order reverse order, Z to A {compare *ascending order*}

designated hitter DH

designer drug controlled substance, illegal drug

designer pizza gourmet pizza

designer's colors opaque watercolors

desktop computer home computer, PC, personal computer, workstation {compare *laptop computer*}

desktop publishing computer

graphics design program, DTP, print formatter, text editor, word processor

destroying angel *Amanita phalloides*, death angel, death cap, death cup

detention camp concentration camp, forced-labor camp, gulag, internment camp, Konzentrationslager, labor camp, prison camp, prison farm

deus ex machina contrivance, device, divine intervention, gimmick, god in the machine, happy coincidence

developing nation developing country, Third World country, Third World nation

developmental biology embryology

devil-may-care careless, cavalier, easygoing, foolhardy, free and easy, happy-go-lucky, heedless, inattentive, lackadaisical, negligent, nonchalant, rash, reckless, unconcerned

devil's advocate apologist, defender, mediator, polemicist

devil worship demonism, diabolism, Satanism

Dewey decimal classification abridged decimal classification, Dewey decimal system, universal decimal classification

dew point dew point temperature, humidification, humidity, saturation, saturation point

dewy-eyed childlike, guileless, innocent, naïve, trusting, unguarded

dialect atlas linguistic atlas

dialect geography linguistic geography

dialectical materialism historical materialism, Marxism

diesel engine compression-ignition engine, diesel, diesel motor

difference of opinion altercation, argument, bone of contention, conflict, debate, disagreement, dispute, dissension, dissent, friction, strife

differential gear differential, differential gearing

difficult situation sticky wicket, tight spot, touchy situation

digital computer computer, electronic brain, electronic data processor, general purpose computer, information processor

digital recording digital transcription, transcription

dilation and curettage D and C, dilatation and curettage

dill pickle garlic pickle, kosher dill pickle, sour pickle

dime a dozen cheap and commonplace, superabundant
dime novel penny dreadful
dime store five-and-dime, five-and-ten, five-and-ten-cent store, ten-cent store, variety shop, variety store, Woolworth™
diminishing returns going belly up, losings, losses
dining car buffet car, diner, dining compartment
dining room breakfast nook, dinette, eating place, salle à manger
dinner jacket black tie, tux, tuxedo, tuxedo jacket
dinner theater café theater
diplomatic immunity congressional immunity, indemnity, legislative immunity, nonprosecution, privilege, special case, special privilege
direct access random access
direct action acting, activism, DA, doing, happening, willed activity
direct current DC, pulsating direct current
direct discourse direct quotation, direct speech
direction finder DF, HFDF, high-frequency direction finder, huff duff, radio direction finder, RDF
direct mail direct-mail advertising, direct-mail selling, mail advertising, mail-order selling, mail solicitation
director of photography cinematographer
direct primary open primary
direct tax direct taxation
dire straits desperate straits, difficulties, hardship, hock, straits
dirt farmer crop farmer, truck farmer
dirty old man lecher, old goat, pedophile, pervert, satyr, sleazebag
dirty pool conjuration, dirty game, dirty politics, dirty tricks, dirty work, escamotage, foul play, jugglery, legerdemain, mudslinging, prestidigitation, sleight of hand, smoke and mirrors, trickery
dirty word bad word, curse, cuss, cuss word, dirty name, expletive, foul invective, four-letter word, naughty word, oath, obscenity, profane oath, profanity, swear word, vulgarity
dirty work donkeywork, grunt work, scut work, thankless task
disaster area area of devastation,

crisis zone, desolation, disaster relief area, flood zoné, path of destruction, storm center

disc brake disk brake

disc jockey deejay, disk jockey, DJ, radio announcer

dish antenna dish aerial, satellite dish, saucer

dish drainer dish rack, drying rack

disk drive disc drive, drive, floppy disk drive, hard disk, removable drive, tape drive, Winchester drive, Zip™ drive

disk jockey deejay, disc jockey, DJ, radio announcer

disk operating system DOS, operating system, OS, system software

disorderly conduct aggro, breach of peace, disorder, disorderliness, disorderly behavior, disruption, disruptiveness, disturbance of the peace, hoodlumism, hooliganism, riotousness, rowdiness, rowdyism, ruffianism

dispatch case attaché case, briefcase, dispatch box

displaced person DP, exile, expatriate, man without a country, persona non grata, stateless person, unacceptable person, undesirable

distaff side womanhood, womankind, womenfolk, womenfolks

distilled water pure water

distinctive feature feature, keynote, lineament, mannerism, particularity, peculiarity, point of character, quirk, redeeming feature, singularity, trait

distress signal flare, Mayday, notice to mariners, signal of distress, SOS, upside-down flag

district attorney attorney general, DA, Dist. Atty., judge advocate, prosecution officer, prosecutor, public prosecutor

dive-bomber bomber, fighter-bomber, jet bomber, strategic bomber

Divine Liturgy eucharistic right, Liturgy

Divine Office Breviary, canonical hours, Cursus ecclesiasticus, Diurnal Office, Ecclesiastical Office, Nocturnal Office

divine providence dealings of providence, dispensations of providence, providence, visitations of providence

divine right of kings divine kingship

divine service devotions, duty,

exercises, liturgy, office, public worship, religious service, service

diving bell bathyscaphe, bathysphere, diving chamber

diving board springboard

diving suit diving dress

divining rod divining stick, doodlebug, dowser, dowsing rod, wand, wiggle stick, witching stick

division of labor industrialization

DNA fingerprinting DNA probe, genetic fingerprinting

doctor of medicine doctor, Dr., MD, physician

doctor's degree doctor, doctorate, Ph.D., postgraduate degree

documentary film docudrama, documentary movie, docutainment, infotainment

dog and pony show ambitious presentation, elaborate presentation

dog collar clerical collar, Roman collar; choker, neckband

dog days canicular days, canicule, hot weather, summer, very hot days

dog-eat-dog aggressive, brutal, competitive, cutthroat, merciless, ruthless, unmerciful, vicious, voracious, without mercy

doggy bag doggie bag, leftovers, tidbit bag

dog's life hard case, hard life, hard plight, miserable life, tough row to hoe, vale of tears

Dog Star Canicula, Sirius, Sothis

doing business as d/b/a

dollar diplomacy dollar imperialism

dollar sign $, dollar mark

dollars to doughnuts hundred to one, sure bet, sure thing, ten to one

domestic affairs domestic business, domestic concerns, domestic issues, domestic matters, national affairs, national issues, national matters, native affairs

domestic animal domesticated animal

domestic arts culinary science, domestic science, home arts, home economics, home management

domestic relations court court of domestic relations, family court

domestic science home economics, housekeeping

domestic violence family violence

domino effect causal sequence,

cause and effect, chain of events, contagion effect, domino theory, knock-on, knock-on effect, ripple effect, slippery slope

done for ausgespielt, beaten, cooked, dead, defeated, done in, doomed, dying, eighty-sixed, exhausted, finished, gone to Davy Jones's locker, had it, kaput, on ice, packed-up, ruined, shot, six feet under, sunk, tired, washed up

done to a turn bien cuit, cooked just right, done to perfection

Don Juan Casanova, heartbreaker, ladies' man, lady-killer, libertine, Lothario, philanderer, playboy, Prince Charming, rake, Romeo, roué, seducer, stud, wolf, woman chaser, womanizer

donkey's years aeon, all one's born days, coon's age, eternity, forever and a day, long time, month of Sundays, right smart spell, time immemorial, time out of mind, years on end

donkey work dirty work, grunt work, scut work, thankless task

do-nothing bum, couch potato, deadbeat, good-for-nothing, goof-off, idler, laggard, layabout, lazy person, lazybones, loafer, lotus eater, lounger, malingerer, moocher, shirker, slacker, sloth, sponger

dormer window dormer

dos and don'ts customs, established ways, etiquette, method, mode, practice, regulations, rules, system, traditional action

dot product inner product, scalar product

double agent counterspy, espionage agent, spy

double back back up, backpedal, backtrack, retrace steps, return, reverse, turn back

double bassoon contrabassoon, contrafagotto

double bed full bed

double bogey two strokes over par

double-cross betray, cheat, deceive, double deal, dupe, scam, sell down the river, sell out, stab in the back, trick, two-time

double dagger diesis, double obelisk

double-dealing backstabbing, betrayal, cheating, deceit, disloyalty, double-crossing, duplicity, treachery, two-facedness, two-timing

double decomposition metathesis

double Dutch babble, baloney, Choctaw, gibberish, Greek, hogwash, hokum, hooey, malarkey, nonsense

double entry double-entry bookkeeping

double feature double bill, doubleheader, twin bill

double indemnity accidental death benefit

double refraction birefringence

double star binary star

double take afterthought, arrière-pensée, delayed reaction, esprit d'escalier, second thought

double talk babble, doublespeak, drivel, gibberish, nonsense

double time double march, double-quick, forced march, haste, on the double

double vision diplopia, double sight

double whammy evil eye, hex, jinx, malocchio, whammy

doubting Thomas cynic, disbeliever, doubter, dubitante, Humist, naysayer, nonbeliever, pooh-pooher, Pyrrhonist, scoffer, skeptic, unbeliever

Dow Jones Industrial Average Big Board, DJIA, Dow, Dow Jones' Average, Dow Thirty, the Big Board, the Dow

down-and-out bankrupt, broke, broken, destitute, impoverished, insolvent, in the gutter, in the poorhouse, moneyless, on the skids, penniless, ruined

down cold down pat, mastered

down in the mouth chapfallen, dejected, depressed, discouraged, down in the dumps, in the doldrums, in the dumps, low-spirited, sad

down payment binder, deposit, earnest, earnest money, front money, security

Down syndrome Down's syndrome, mongolianism, mongolism, trisomy, trisomy 21

down the drain done for, down the tubes, finished, kaput, pffft, unrecoverable

down to earth earthy, folksy, informal, levelheaded, matter-of-fact, natural, plainspoken, practical, pragmatic, real, realistic, reasonable, rustic, sensible, simple, sober-minded, unassuming, unpretentious

draft animal beast of burden, jument, pack animal, plow animal, work animal

drafting pencil bow pen

draft pick draft choice, draftee, lot pick, lottery pick, selection

drag bunt bleeder, chopper, dying quail, nubber, roller, slow roller, squibbler, wormburner

drag queen closet queen, cross-dresser, female impersonator, fruitcake, queen, transvestite

drainage basin catchment area, catchment basin, drainage area, watershed

drain opener drain cleaner, Drano™, unclogger

dramatic arts acting, Broadway, burlesque, musical theater, stage, stage arts, stagecraft, theater, theatercraft, theatre, theatricals, thespian arts, vaudeville

dramatic irony tragic irony

drawing board drafting board; square one

drawing card attraction, draw-card, gimmick, hook, loss leader

drawing room parlor, salon

drawing table drafting table, easel

drawn butter clarified butter, melted butter

drawn work drawn threadwork

draw the line draw a line, fix a limit, set a limit, set a stopping point, set an end point

dream team all-star team

dregs of society one-percenters, rabble, riffraff, rubbish, scum of the earth, trash, undesirables, vermin

dressed to the nines dressed to advantage, dressed to kill, dressed to the teeth, dressed up, gussied up, in full dress, in full feather, soignée, spiffed up, spruced up, well dressed

dressing gown bathrobe, caftan, housecoat, lounging robe, morning dress, robe, robe de chambre, yukata

dressing room changing room, fitting room, greenroom

dressing table toilet table, vanity

dress rehearsal blocking, dry run, final dress, full rehearsal, gypsy rehearsal, rehearsal, run, run-through, technical run, tech rehearsal, tech run, walk-through

dress shirt button-down shirt, evening shirt

dress uniform court dress, dress whites, formal uniform, full-dress uniform, regalia, social full-dress uniform, special full-dress uniform, whites

drinking fountain bubbler, water cooler, water fountain

driver's seat command, control, head, helm, reins, saddle, seat of authority, throne, wheel

drive-through delivery drive-by delivery
drive time commute time, rush hour
driving range golf range
driving test driver's test, road test
drone aircraft combat drone
drop charges cease prosecution, dismiss case
drop cloth ground cloth, groundsheet, tarp, tarpaulin
drop curtain act curtain, act drop, back cloth, backdrop, cloth, drop, drop cloth, drop scene, scrim, tab, tableau curtain
drop dead buy the farm, croak, die suddenly, die unexpectedly, kick the bucket, pop off
drop-down menu pull-down menu
drop in the bucket band-aid, cosmetic measure, disappointment, drop in the ocean, lick and a promise, miniscule amount, pittance, small change, small potatoes, spit in the sea, too little too late, trifle, trivial amount
drop-kick calcitration, kicking, place kick, punt
drop leaf table gate leg table
drug addict addict, burnout, dopehead, doper, drug abuser, drug fiend, druggie, drug user, freak, hophead, junkie, narcotics addict, space cadet, user
drug dealer bagman, candy man, connection, dealer, dope peddler, dope pusher, drug peddler, drug seller, drug supplier, drug trafficker, man, pusher, source
drum table capstan table, rent table
drunk driving driving under the influence, driving while intoxicated, DUI, DWI
drunk tank detention cell, holding cell, jail cell, lockup, tank
dry cell battery
dry dock dockyard, graving dock, shipyard
dryer sheet antistatic sheet, fabric softener
dry farming dryland farming
dry goods off-the-rack clothes, ready-to-wear, soft goods, store-bought clothes, textile products, textiles
dry ice solid carbon dioxide, solidified carbon dioxide
dry ingredients powdered ingredients
dry measure British imperial dry measure, dry unit, U.S. dry measure {compare *liquid measure*}

dry run bench test, combat rehearsal, dress rehearsal, dummy run, kriegspiel, maneuver, maneuvers, practical test, practice run, rehearsal, road test, test performance, test run, trial, trial run, tryout, war game

ducking stool castigatory, cucking stool, trebuche

duck soup breeze, cakewalk, cherry pie, child's play, cinch, easy, kid stuff, no-brainer, picnic, pie, piece of cake, pushover, snap, turkey shoot, velvet, walkover, waltz

duffel bag duffel, duffle, duffle bag

du jour of the day; all the rage, chic, current, faddy, fashionable, hot, in style, in vogue, latest, now, popular, stylish, trendy

duke it out battle, do battle, fight, fight it out, fight to the finish, give no quarter

dump truck dumper

dune buggy beach buggy

dunk shot dunk, slam dunk, stuff shot

duplex apartment duplex, duplex house

durable goods consumer durables, durables, hard goods

durable press durable-press fabric, permanent press, permanent-press fabric

dust storm black blizzard, devil, dust devil, duster, harmattan, khamsin, peesash, samiel, sand column, sand spout, sandstorm, shaitan, simoom, sirocco

Dutch courage bold front, dipsomania, hard drinking, hitting the bottle, pot-valiance, pot-valiancy, pot-valor

Dutch door half door

Dutch uncle admonisher, monitor

dyed-in-the-wool absolute, complete, confirmed, congenital, deep-down, deep-dyed, deep-rooted, deep-seated, full-fledged, genuine, infixed, ingrained, instilled, out and out, thorough, thoroughgoing, through and through, to the core, true, uncompromising, utter

dying day end of life, last day of life, on one's deathbed

Ee

eager beaver aholic, beaver, busy bee, live wire, no slouch, sharpy

eagle eye hawkeye, keen eye, lidless eye, peeled eye, penetrating eye, sharp eye, sleepless eye, watchful eye, weather eye, X-ray eye

ear candy music

early bird early comer, early riser, first arrival, firstcomer, first on the scene, Johnny-on-the-spot

early release parole

earned run average ERA

ear stone otolith

earth inductor dip inductor, earth inductor compass, inclinometer, induction compass, induction inclinometer

earth science geoscience

earth tone earth color

Eastern Empire Byzantine Empire, Eastern Roman Empire

Eastern Orthodox Church Byzantine Church, Eastern Church, Orthodox Catholic Church, Orthodox Eastern Church

easy chair lounge chair, overstuffed chair

easy mark chump, cinch, doormat, easy pickings, easy touch, fall guy, jay, mark, mug, patsy, pigeon, pushover, scapegoat, sitting duck, soft touch, sucker

easy rock pop, pop music, soft rock

easy street affluence, bed of roses, clover, Elysium, Fat City, hog heaven, lap of luxury, life of luxury, prosperity, velvet, wealth

eat crow eat dirt, eat humble pie, eat one's words, eat shit, swallow one's pride, tuck one's tail

eating disorder anorexia, anorexia nervosa, bingeing, binge-purge syndrome, binging, binging and purging, bulimia, bulimia nervosa, dieting disorder, hyperphagia, polyphagia

eau de toilette cologne, perfume, toilet water

ebb tide diminishing tide, falling tide, outgoing tide, receding tide, retiring tide

economic expansion boom, economic growth, economic upswing, economic upturn, prosperity

economic rent rent

economy class cheap airfare, coach class, Y class

economy size family size, giant size, king size, large size, queen size, very large size

editor in chief editorial director, executive editor, managing editor, senior editor

efficiency expert efficiency engineer, management consultant

egg case egg capsule, egg sac, ootheca

egg on one's face abashment, chagrin, embarrassment, humiliation, look foolish, mortification, red face, self-consciousness, shame

eighteen-wheeler big rig, 18-wheeler, rig, semi, semitrailer, tractor trailer, trailer truck, truck trailer

800 number 1-800 number, toll-free number, toll-free telephone number

eighty-six cast aside, cast off, chuck, discard, 86, get rid of, reject, throw away, throw out

elastic bandage Ace™ bandage, elastic support bandage, stretchable bandage

elbow grease blood, sweat and tears; effort; exertion; hard work; labor; muscle; oomph; strain; strength; sweat; sweat of one's brow; toil; travail

elder statesman elder, mentor, starets, wise old man

electrical outlet electric receptacle, outlet, receptacle

electrical storm lightning storm, thunder and lightning, thunderstorm

electric chair death chair, hot seat, the chair

electric eye electron-ray tube, magic eye, photocell, photoelectric cell, photosensitive device

electric frying pan electric skillet

electric mixer beater, Mixmaster™

electric razor electric shaver, shaver

electric shock therapy ECT, electroconvulsive therapy, electroshock, electroshock therapy, shock therapy, shock treatment

electroconvulsive therapy convulsive therapy, ECT, electric shock therapy, electroshock, electroshock therapy, shock therapy, shock treatment

electronic banking cyberbanking, e-banking, Internet banking, Web banking
electronic bulletin board BBS, bulletin board, bulletin board system, EBB
electronic countermeasure jamming
electronic mail E-mail, e-mail, E-message, online correspondence, online mail
electronic money cybercash, digital cash, digital money, electronic cash, e-money
electronic news gathering ENG
electronic publishing Internet publishing, online demand publishing, online publishing
electronic surveillance bugging, tapping, wiretap, wiretapping
electron microscope scanning electron microscope, transmission electron microscope
electron optics electro-optics
electron tube converter, thermionic tube, thermionic vacuum tube, thermionic valve, tube, vacuum tube
electrostatic generator electrostatic machine, static machine, Van de Graaff generator, Wimshurst machine
elementary particle atomic particle, fundamental particle, subatomic particle, ultraelementary particle
elementary school folk school, graded school, grade school, grammar school, junior school, primary school, the grades
elephant man's disease multiple neurofibromas, neurofibromatosis, neuromatosis, Recklinghausen's disease, von Recklinghausen's disease
elevated railroad el, elevated railway, overhead railway
elevator music background music, Muzak™, piped music
eleventh hour high time, just in time, last minute, nick of time, the last moment, zero hour
e-mail electronic mail, e-mail, E-message, online correspondence, online mail
emergency brake hand brake, parking brake
emergency lights flashers, four-way flashers, hazard lights, idiot lights, warning lights
emergency medical technician EMT, lifesaver, paramedic
emergency room critical care facility, emergency, ER, medical crisis unit, trauma center, triage room
emery board filing board, fingernail file, manicuring stick, nail file, orange stick

emery wheel buff wheel, glazer, grinding wheel

eminent domain angary, divine right, lawful authority, legal authority, legitimacy, right of angary, rightful authority, right of eminent domain

emission control smog control

employment agency employment recruiter, employment service, executive search agency, headhunter, recruiter, temporary agency, temporary service

employment agreement covenant, employment contract

employment history bio, résumé, work history

employment opportunity employment possibility, job opportunity, open position

empty-headed airheaded, blank-minded, brainless, clueless, dizzy, dumb, empty-minded, featherbrained, ignorant, scatterbrained, silly, simple, stupid, unintelligent, vacant, witless

empty talk empty words, gossip, hot air, palaver, propaganda, rhetoric, rumor

endangered species threatened species

end of the world apocalypse, Armageddon, catastrophe, final battle, final battleground, holocaust, showdown between good and evil, total annihilation

end product finished product, handiwork, manufacture, output, product, production, result

end user final user, ultimate consumer

end zone crossbar, end line, goal, goal line, goalpost

energy efficiency ratio EER

energy level electron state, energy state

enfant terrible holy terror, juvenile delinquent, little terror, punk kid, snotnose kid, spoiled brat, spoiled child, whippersnapper

engine block block, cylinder block

engine company fire brigade, fire company, fire department

engineering feat engineering achievement

English horn cor anglais, corno inglese

English saddle English cavalry saddle

en masse all at once, all together, as a body, as a group, as one, collectively, communally, cooperatively, en bloc, ensemble, in a group, in chorus, in unison, jointly, together, unanimously, unitedly, wholly, with one voice

en route along the way, bound for, headed for, in passage, in transit, on the road, on the way

enteric fever paratyphoid fever, typhoid, typhoid fever

enterprise zone business district, factory district, industrial area, industrial park, industrial zone, manufacturing quarter, merchant area

entitlement program alms, benefit program, government assistance, public welfare, relief program, social insurance, social program, social security, welfare program

entrance ramp on-ramp {compare *exit ramp*}

environmental protection ecology, environmental control, environmental impact analysis, environmental management, environmental monitoring, environmental policy, environmental science, environmentology

epicanthic fold epicanthus

epicyclic train epicyclic gear train, gear, wheels, wheels within wheels, wheelworks

Epstein-Barr virus EBV, Epstein-Barr syndrome, glandular fever, mononucleosis

equal-area projection aphylactic projection, authalic projection, equal-area map projection, equiareal projection, equivalent projection, homalographic projection, homological projection

equal sign equality sign, equals sign

equity capital risk capital, venture capital, working capital

equivalence point end point

erotic dance burlesque dance, lap dance, strip show, striptease

erotic dancer bump-and-grinder, burlesque queen, ecdysiast, exotic dancer, lap dancer, peeler, stripper, striptease artist, striptease dancer, stripteaser, stripteuse

escape artist escapee, escaper, escapist, escapologist, evader, fugitive, Houdini, runaway

escape clause clause, escalator clause, escape hatch, escapeway, fine print, hole to creep out of, loophole, saving clause, technicality, way of escape, way out

escape mechanism avoidance

reaction, bunker atmosphere, bunker mentality, defense mechanism, defenses, ego defenses, negative taxis, negative tropism, psychological defenses

escape velocity burn, thrust

esprit de corps camaraderie, common bond, communion, community, community of interests, esprit, fellowship, group loyalty, group spirit, morale, solidarity, team morale, team spirit

essential oil volatile oil

estate tax death duty, death tax, inheritance tax

estrogen replacement therapy ERT

estrous cycle estral cycle, estrum, estrus

et al and others, et alia, et alii

ethnic cleansing final solution, genocide, holocaust, mass destruction, mass extermination, mass murder, pogrom, race extermination, race murder, Roman holiday, ruthless clearance of populace, wholesale murder

European Economic Community Common Market, EEC, European Community

evaporated milk condensed milk

evaporator coil cooling coil

evening dress dress clothes, evening clothes, evening gown, evening wear, formal, formal dress, formalwear, soup and fish, white tie and tails

evening star Hesper, Hesperus, Venus, Vesper

even-tempered calm, cool, dispassionate, easygoing, equable, good-tempered, inexcitable, level-headed, patient, placid, relaxed, serene, steady, unflappable, unirritable

event horizon singularity

ever and again ever and anon, evermore, now and then, occasionally

every now and then ever so often, every once in a while, every so often, from time to time, now and again, now and then, occasionally, once and again, once in a while, sometimes

every which way all over the place, at every turn, everyway, everywhere, everywhither, in all directions, in all manner of ways, in every direction, in every quarter; arbitrarily, haphazardly, indiscriminately, irregularly, randomly

evil eye double whammy, hex, ill wishes, jinx, malocchio, silent curse, whammy

exchange rate currency exchange rate, foreign exchange rate, rate of exchange

exclamation point exclamation mark

exclusion principle Pauli exclusion principle

executive branch Executive Department

Executive Mansion 1600 Pennsylvania Avenue, White House

executive officer chief, chief executive, executive director, executive secretary, lieutenant

executive order regulation

executive session closed meeting, closed session, private conference, secret meeting

exhaust pipe tailpipe

existential quantifier existential operator

exit poll canvass, canvassing, counting hands, counting heads, counting noses, division, polling

exit ramp off ramp, turnoff {compare *entrance ramp*}

exotic dancer bump-and-grinder, burlesque queen, ecdysiast, erotic dancer, lap dancer, peeler, stripper, striptease artist, striptease dancer, stripteaser, stripteuse

expanding universe big bang model, inflationary universe, open universe, oscillating universe, pulsating universe

expansion card add-ins, add-ons, expansion board

expense account expenses, travel and entertainment account

experimental philosophy natural philosophy, natural science, physical science, physics

experimental psychology psychonomics

exploded view cross-section, cutaway, diagram

exponential growth logarithmic growth

exponential notation scientific notation

ex post facto after the fact, attendant, posterior, post factum, postmortem, retroactive, retrospective, sequent, subsequent, succeeding

exposure meter ASA scale, light meter, photometer, Scheiner scale

express mail airmail, next-day air, priority mail, special delivery

extended family binuclear family, kinship group, ménage, relations

extenuating circumstances mitigating circumstances

exterior angle external angle

extra-base hit double, home run, triple

extracurricular activity after-school activity, extraclassroom activity, noncollegiate activity, nonscholastic activity

extradition treaty deportation treaty

extramarital affair affaire, amour, fling, goings-on, hanky-panky, illicit love affair, liaison, playing around, romance, thing, two-timing

extrasensory perception clairvoyance, ESP, intuitionism, intuitivism, precognition, presentiment, psychic power, second sight, telepathy

extravehicular mobility unit EVMU, space suit

extremely high frequency EHF

extreme unction anointing of the sick, last rites, sacrament of the sick, viaticum

eye-catching alluring, appetizing, attention-getting, attracting, bold, captivating, charismatic, engaging, interesting, intriguing, irresistible, noticeable, riveting, seductive, sexy, spellbinding, tantalizing, titillating, winning

eye contact visual contact

eye doctor oculist, ophthalmologist, optometrist

eye for an eye avenging, getting even, payback, reprisal, retaliation, retribution, revenge, vengeance, vindication

eye of the storm eye of the hurricane, storm center, war of the elements

eye socket orbit, orbital cavity

Ff

fabric making weaving
face card coat card, court card, picture card
face the music bite the bullet, come to grips with, face the facts, face up to it, grin and bear it, look square in the eye, make one's bed and lie on it, pay the piper, swallow the pill, take one's lumps, take one's medicine, take the consequences
face value face, maturity value, nominal value, par value
facial nerve cranial nerve seven, cranial nerve VII, nervus facialis, seventh cranial nerve
facial tissue Kleenex™
fact finder finder of fact, researcher, researchist, research worker
facts of life birds and the bees
fair and square aboveboard, honest, honest and aboveboard, impartial, just, straightforward
fair game clear stage, even break, fair field, fair play, fair shake, level playing field; prey, quarry, target
fair market price market prices
fair sex female sex, gentle sex, second sex, softer sex, weaker sex, women, womenfolk
fair shake even break, even chance, even odds, fair chance, fair treatment, fifty-fifty, square deal, square odds
fair to middling adequate, fair, fairish, indifferent, mediocre, middling, moderate, modest, ok, passable, so-so
fair trade balance of trade, fair-trading, free trade, managed prices, multilateral trade, reciprocal trade
fair-trade agreement managed-price agreement
fair-weather friend false friend
fairy tale fable, fairy story, ghost story, marchen, myth, tale, yarn
fait accompli accomplished fact, a truth, certainty, cold hard facts, done deal, done deed, fact of life, grim reality, irreversible act, irreversible truth, matter of fact, self-evident fact, undeniable fact

faith healer alternative practitioner, healer, nonmedical therapist, priest-doctor, shaman, spiritual healer, witch doctor

faith healing alternative medicine, faith cure, unorthodox medicine

fallen angel âme damnée, backslider, lost sheep, lost soul, recidivist

fall from grace backslide, backsliding, fall, fall from favor, lapse, original sin, recidivation, recidivism, slip, trip

fall guy boob, can-carrier, chump, dupe, easy mark, fool, goat, lamb to the slaughter, mark, patsy, pigeon, sap, scapegoat, schlemiel, stooge, sucker, victim, whipping boy

falling-out argument, bicker, brawl, contention, disagreement, dispute, feud, fight, fracas, fuss, misunderstanding, quarrel, row, run-in, sharp words, snarl, spat, squabble, strife, tiff

falling star meteor, shooting star

false alarm cry of wolf, dud, nonstarter

false arrest unjustifiable arrest, unlawful arrest

false face disguise, facade, mask, masquerade

false front disguise, display, facade, front, guise, image, mask, mere facade, public image, sham, veneer, window dressing

false fruit accessory fruit, pome, pseudocarp

false imprisonment illegal detention, unjustifiable imprisonment, unlawful imprisonment

false-memory syndrome false memory, misremembrance, paramnesia, retrospective falsification

false pregnancy pseudocyesis, pseudopregnancy

false pretense false colors, false pretension, feign, hollow pretense, pretension, pretext

false start premature start

false step fall, flop, misstep, slip, stumble, trip, tumble

false teeth artificial teeth, choppers, dental implants, dentures, fake teeth, implants

false witness false charge, frame, frame-up, planted evidence, put-up job, trumped-up charge

family court court of domestic relations, domestic-relations court

family doctor family physician, family practitioner, general practitioner, GP

family feud bad blood, blood feud, fight, vendetta

family jewels ballocks, balls, cullions, gonads, male genitalia, male genitals, nuts, rocks, testes, testicles

family man husband, man of the family, married man, patriarch

family name byname, cognomen, last name, surname

family planning birth control, birth prevention, contraception, planned parenthood

family practice family medicine, private practice

family room den, game room, playroom, recreation room, rec room, rumpus room

family tree ancestral tree, ancestry, bloodline, descent, genealogical chart, genealogical tree, genealogy, line, lineage, pedigree, stemma, tree

family way carrying a child, expecting, gravid, pregnant, with child

fancy-free carefree, footloose, independent, unattached, without commitments, without ties

fancy woman call girl, fancy lady, harlot, hooker, lady in red, lady of pleasure, lady of the evening, mistress, prostitute, streetwalker, tart, whore, working girl

fanjet engine turbofan, turbofan engine, turbojet, turbojet engine

fan mail fan letter

fanny pack belt bag, bum bag, fanny bag, waist pack

far and away by a great deal, by far, far and wide, to the highest degree, without doubt

far and wide broadly, everywhere, far and near, great lengths, near and far, wide, widely

far cry great distance, long way

far-flung extensive, far-extending, far-going, far-reaching, far-spread, far-stretched, long, wide-extending, wide-ranging, widespread; wide-stretching; distant, far away, remote

farm out farm, hire out, job, rent out, subcontract, sublet

far out avant-garde, Bohemian, contemporary, cool, deep, groovy, hippie, mod, modern, modernistic, out of this world, rad, radical, ultramodern, unconventional, way out, weird, wild

far-reaching big, broad, crucial,

extensive, far-flung, huge, important, influential, long, pervasive, significant, sweeping, wide-ranging, widespread, wide-stretching

fashion business apparel industry, fashion industry, garment industry, rag trade

fashion plate best-dressed, clotheshorse, dandy, dude, fop, fribble, sharpy, snappy dresser, swell

fashion victim clothes buyer, obsessive shopper

fast and loose irresponsible, reckless, uncontrolled, undisciplined, unrestrained

fast break run-and-shoot offense

fast food convenience food, junk food

fast-forward double-time, full speed, maximum speed

fast friend best friend, constant friend, devoted friend, faithful friend, fidus Achates, good friend, great friend, staunch friend, trusted friend, trusty friend

fast lane burning the candle at both ends, fast pace, fast track, free living, high living, killing pace

fatal flaw hamartia, tragic flaw

fat cat baron, big shot, deep pocket, magnate, moneybags, moneyed person, person of means, person of substance, richling, rich person, tycoon, wealthy person

fat chance chance in a million, ghost of a chance, no chance, poor outlook, poor possibility, poor prospect, slim chance, small chance

Fat City bed of roses, clover, easy street, good life, hog heaven, lap of luxury, life of Riley, velvet

fat farm health resort, health salon, health spa, weight loss clinic

Father Christmas Kriss Kringle, Saint Nicholas, Saint Nick, Santa, Santa Claus

father confessor confessor, holy father, priest, spiritual director, spiritual father, spiritual leader

father figure father image, father substitute, father surrogate, substitute, surrogate

fatigue clothes combat fatigues, fatigues, military clothes, military uniform

fault line break, fault, fault trace, fault trend, geological fault, rift, split

faux pas blooper, blunder, botch, bungle, colossal blunder, error, gaffe, gaucherie, hash, indiscretion, mess, misstep, mistake, offense, slip, social blunder, social error, solecism, transgression

favonian wind wester, westerly, west wind

fax machine facsimile, facsimile machine, telephotograph machine, Telephoto™ machine, Wirephoto™ machine

fear campaign bullying, hostage-taking, intimidation tactics, terrorism

feature film feature, feature-length film, main attraction

feature story headliner

federal case big deal

federal district court district court

feel in one's bones expect, feel deeply, have a feeling, have a funny feeling, have a gut feeling, have a hunch, have a sensation, just know, perceive, predict, sense

feel sorry for bleed for, comfort, commiserate, condole with, console, empathize with, express sympathy, feel compassion for, feel for, grieve with, have mercy on, lament for, open one's heart, pity, sympathize

feet of clay character flaw, fault, flaw, vice, weakness

fellow feeling agape, brotherly love, Christian love, concern, empathy, good feeling, identification, loving concern, rapport, relating, responsiveness, sympathetic response, sympathy, vibes, warmth

fellow traveler companion, comrade, sidekick, supporter, sympathetic person, sympathizer, travel companion

feminine napkin feminine pad, Kotex™, sanitary napkin, sanitary pad

femme fatale coquette, courtesan, deadly lady, deadly woman, enchantress, flirt, seductress, siren, temptress, vamp

fender bender minor automobile accident, minor car accident

ferret out chase down, dig out, dig up, discover, hunt down, probe, root out, scout out, search out, smoke out, sniff out, track down, uncover, unearth, worm out

fetal alcohol syndrome FAS

fever blister blister, bulla, cold sore, herpes labialis, herpes simplex lesion, oral herpes, vesicle

fever pitch all haste, fast-forward, great haste, mad rush, rush

fiber optics catoptrics, dioptrics, fibre optics; glass fiber, optical fiber

field artillery heavy artillery, heavy field artillery, light mobile artillery

field event broad jump, discus throw, hammer throw, high jump, javelin throw, long jump, pole vault, shot put, triple jump

field glasses binoculars

field goal basket, bucket

field guide guidebook, nature book

field hockey bandy, banty, hurley, hurling, shinny, shinty, street hockey

field hospital MASH, MASH unit

field house armory; sports arena

field lens field glass

field marshal five-star general, general of the army, marshal

field officer field grade officer

field of honor battlefield, battleground, field of battle

field of vision field of view, horizon, ken, line of sight, line of vision, peripheral field, peripheral vision, purview, range, scope, sight line, sweep, visual field

field theory supersymmetry theory, unified field theory

field trip day trip, excursion, expedition, jaunt, junket, outing, school outing, school trip, sight-seeing tour

fifth column collaborators, collaborators of enemy, infiltrators, saboteurs, subversives, Trojan horse, underground

fifth wheel spare, spare tire; boot lagniappe, superfluity, triviality

fighting chance bare possibility, gambling chance, outside chance, remote possibility, slim chance

fighting words taunt, threat, threatening words

figment of the imagination creation of the brain, creature of the imagination, fabrication, fantasy, fiction, fiction of the mind, figment, imagination, invention, phantom of the mind, whimsy, wildest dream

figure eight figure of eight

figure of speech allusion, analogy, device, expression, flourish, flower, hyperbole, imagery, malapropism, manner of speaking, metaphor, ornament, oxymoron, sarcasm, simile, trope, turn of expression, way of speaking

file clerk filer, filing clerk

file server client-server, client/ server

filling station gasoline station, gas station, petrol station, service station

film holder black back

filter bed bacteria bed

final rest death, decease, dying, eternal rest, final sleep, gravepassing

financial backing backing, financial support, financing, funding, patronization, sponsorship, support, venture capital

fine arts arts and crafts, arts of design, beaux arts, graphic arts, visual arts

fine print fine print at the bottom, minutiae, particulars, small print, specifications

finger food finger sandwiches

finger in the pie hand in, kibitz, nose in

finish line destination, finishing line, goal, journey's end, last stop, resting place, stopping place, tape, wire

fire alarm emergency alarm, heat sensor, smoke alarm, smoke detector, sprinkler system

fire and brimstone everlasting fire, everlasting torment, hellfire, lake of fire and brimstone

fire and water black and white, day and night, light and darkness

fire escape emergency exit, escape hatch, escapeway, fire egress, fire exit

fire extinguisher carbon dioxide extinguisher, extinguisher

fire hydrant fireplug, hydrant

fire truck fire engine, hook and ladder

fire wall asbestos curtain

fireworks display fireworks, fireworks exhibition, pyrotechnics, pyrotechny

firing line battlefront, battle line, enemy line, front, front line, line, line of battle

firing squad firing party, fusillade, shooters, shooting

first aid emergency assistance, emergency care, emergency treatment

first blush break of day, brightening, crack of dawn, early morning, first brightening, first flush of morning, first glance, first impression, first light, first sight, morning, outset, peep of day, prime

first-class best, elite, excellent, exceptional, first-rate, highest-quality, marvelous, outstanding, premium, superb, top of the line, top-drawer, top-notch

first estate clergy, Lords Spiritual

first fruits bang for the buck, crop, fruits, harvest, output, payoff, produce, yield

first law of thermodynamics law of conservation of energy

first light aurora, break of day, cocklight, dawn, dawning, dawnlight, daybreak, daylight, day-peep, glow, half-light, morning, sunrise, sunup

first mate first officer, mate

first name baptismal name, Christian name, forename, given name

first night opening night

first off firstly, first of all, first thing, foremost, immediately, in the first place, primo, up front

first officer first mate, mate

first-order consumer herbivore, plant eater

first principle(s) first reader, first step, groundwork, outline, primer, principia, principles, rudiment

first-rate A number 1, A1, bang-up, best, excellent, exceptional, first-class, great, highest-quality, marvelous, outstanding, premium, super, superb, superior, superlative, supreme, top-drawer, top-notch, top of the line, unmatched, world-class

first refusal first option, option, preemption, prior right of purchase, refusal, right of preemption

first sergeant command sergeant major, sergeant first class, sergeant major, top sergeant

first strike descent on, descent upon, preemptive nuclear attack, preventive strike, preventive war, surgical strike

first string first team, starters, varsity

first water best quality, highest grade, highest quality, highest rank

fiscal year accounting year, annual accounting period, calendar year, financial year, twelve-month period

fish hatchery fishery, piscary

fishing expedition inquisition, witch hunt

fishing pole bait-casting rod, boat rod, casting rod, fiberglass rod, fishing rod, fly rod, jigging rod, muskie rod, popping rod, rod, spinning rod, surf rod

fishing rod bait-casting rod, boat rod, casting rod, fiberglass rod, fishing pole, fly rod, jigging rod, muskie rod, popping rod, rod, spinning rod, surf rod

fish out of water misfit, out of place, square peg in a round hole, ugly duckling

fish story bunk, cock-and-bull story, embellishment, exaggeration, far-fetched story, incredible story, lie, overstatement, tall story, tall tale, trumped-up story, yarn

fitted sheet bedsheet, contour sheet

fit to be tied angry, annoyed, bent out of shape, boiling, good and mad, hot and bothered, outraged, steamed

five o'clock shadow bristles, bristly stubble, peach fuzz, stubble, whiskers

five senses hearing, sensorium, sight, smell, taste, touch

five wits common wit, estimation, fantasy, imagination, memory

fixed assets current assets, frozen assets, net assets, nonliquid assets

fixed star real star, starry host

flake tool flake

flare-up bang, blast, blaze, blowup, boom, burst, detonation, disruption, epidemic, eruption, explosion, gush, outbreak, outburst, spurt, upheaval, uprising

flash flood deluge, freshet, sudden rainfall, torrent, wall of water, waterflood

flash in the pan brief success, bugbear, dud, fad, failure, misfire, momentary success, nine days' wonder, wet squib

flash point critical mass, flashing point, incandescence; moment of truth, zero hour

flat on one's back horizontal, laying down, lying flat, parallel, recumbent, supine

flat out all out, peak performance, top speed; bluffly, bluntly, directly, openly

flea market farmers' market, flea fair, marche aux puces, street market, swap meet, tag sale, trading post, yard sale

fleet admiral admiral, Admiral of the Fleet, five-star admiral, navarch

flesh and blood children, clay, consanguinean, family, fellow creature, kids, kin, offspring, ordinary clay, organic complex, organism, relatives, uterine kin

flight attendant airline hostess, airline steward, airline stewardess, cabin attendant, cabin crew, hostess, purser, skycap, stew, steward, stewardess

flight deck landing deck

flight engineer third officer

flight of fancy creation of the brain, exaggeration, facon de parler, fish story, fumes of fancy, imagination, mind's eye, stretch of fancy, stretch of the imagination

flight of stairs escalier, flight of steps, pair of stairs, staircase, stairs, stairway

flight path air lane

flight pay combat pay, danger pay

flight recorder black box, flight data recorder

flip-flop about-face, change, change of heart, change of mind, changeover, reversal, second thoughts, switch, switchover, turnabout, turnaround, U-turn

flip one's wig blow a gasket, blow one's cool, blow one's top, blow up, flip, flip one's lid, flip out, go off the deep end, hit the ceiling, lose one's cool, pop one's cork, wig out

flip side back, B-side, B side, converse, inverse, obverse, opposite side, other side, other side of the coin, reverse side, the other side of the picture

flood lamp flood, floodlight, photoflood

flood plain alluvial plain, coastal plain, delta, delta plain, tidal plain

flood tide flood, high tide, high water, mean high water, spring tide, storm surge

floor exercise balance beam, horizontal bar, pommel horse, side horse, stationary rings, trampolining, tumbling, uneven parallel bars, vaulting

floor lamp standing lamp, tall lamp

floor manager director, floor man, floorwalker

floor plan horizontal section, longitudinal section, scale drawing

floor sample demonstration model, display merchandise

floor show cabaret, nightclub acts

floppy disk disk, diskette, floppy, magnetic disk, microfloppy, minifloppy {compare *hard disk*}

Florida room sunroom

flotsam and jetsam floating debris, floating population, floating wreckage, lagan

flow chart flow diagram, flow sheet, schema, scheme, step-by-step diagram, structural outline

flower child beatnik, Bohemian, free spirit, freethinker, hippie, hipster, liberal, New Age traveler

fluid mechanics hydraulics

flutter kick scissors kick, swimming kick, whip kick

fly ball fly, high fly

fly-by-night disreputable, irresponsible, not to be trusted, undependable, unprofessional, unreliable, untrustworthy; ephemeral, evanescent, fleeting, momentary, passing, short-lived, temporary

flying boat amphibian, clipper, hydroplane, seaplane

flying bomb buzz bomb, cruising missile, doodlebug, robomb, robot bomb, rocket bomb, torpedo, V-1

flying bridge catwalk, fly bridge, flying walkway, skybridge, skywalk, temporary bridge, walkway

flying buttress arc-boutant, arch buttress

flying colors flags unfurled, flourish of trumpet, triumph

flying field airfield, field, landing field

flying machine aeroplane, aircraft, airplane, avion

flying saucer extraterrestrial spacecraft, extraterrestrial vessel, spacecraft, spaceship, UFO, unidentified flying object

flying start running start

flying wedge wedge-shaped formation

fly on the wall bird's-eye view, bystander, listener-in, little pitcher with big ears, snoop, worm's-eye view

fly sheet advertising sheet, flier, handbill

fly swatter fly swat

foam at the mouth froth at the mouth, go berserk, run amok, run mad

foam rubber spongy rubber

focal point center of attention, centerpiece, focus, focus of attention, point of convergence, prime focus

focus group marketing study, market survey

foldaway bed cot, foldable bed, folding bed, Murphy bed, rollaway, truckle bed, trundle bed

folding chair camp chair, collapsible chair

folding door accordion door, hinged door

folding money bills, folding green, green stuff, greenbacks, lettuce, long green, paper currency, paper money, skins

folding table card table, tray table, TV table

folk medicine healing, herbal remedies, shamanism, traditional medicine

folk music balladry, country music, ethnic music, ethnomusicology, folk, folk ballads, folk songs, regional music

folk rock country rock, rockabilly

folk tale folk history, folk story, legend, myth, oral tradition

follow suit follow in the footsteps of, follow the example of, jump on the bandwagon

food additive artificial additive, artificial coloring, artificial flavoring, preservative, preservative medium

food chain food cycle, food web

food for thought something to chew on, subject for thought

food poisoning botulism, gastrointestinal disorder, ptomaine, ptomaine poisoning, salmonella poisoning, salmonellosis

food processor blender, Cuisinart™, food mill, mixer

food pyramid food chain hierarchy, RDA, recommended daily vitamins and minerals

food stamp food coupon, government-issued stamps, meal ticket, welfare aid

fool's gold iron pyrites, pyrite

fool's paradise castle in the air, chimera, delusive contentment, dreamscape, false hope, fond illusion, pipe dream, quixotic ideal, utopia

foot in the door access, first step, initial opportunity, means of access, opening wedge, point of entry

foot soldier infantryman, infantry trooper

foot the bill bear the cost, finance, pay the bill, pick up the check, pick up the tab, pop for, redeem, spring for

forbidden fruit forbidden indulgence, illegal indulgence, illegal pleasure, immoral indulgence, prohibited article

force majeure act of God, brute force, inevitable accident, main force, main strength, predetermination, unavoidable casualty, vis major

force of habit creature of habit, habit pattern, knee-jerk reaction, pattern

force one's hand browbeat, hold a gun to one's head, impel

foregone conclusion cinch, par for the course, preconceived notion, preconceived opinion, sure-fire proposition, sure success, sure thing

foreign affairs diplomacy, foreign policy, foreign relations, world politics

foreign aid economic assistance, military assistance

foreign correspondent correspondent, special correspondent, stringer, war correspondent

foreign exchange convertibility, negotiable bills

foreign minister cabinet minister, government minister, secretary of state

foreign mission legation, mission, missionary post, missionary station, permanent diplomatic mission

foreign office consular service, corps diplomatique, diplomatic corps, diplomatic mission, diplomatic service, diplomatic staff, embassy, foreign service, legation

foreign policy diplomacy, diplomatic policy, diplomatics, foreign affairs, international relations, world politics

foreign service consular service, consular staff, diplomatic service, diplomatic staff, FS

forest ranger forester, forest manager, forest protector, ranger

formal logic material logic, mathematical logic, symbolic logic

form letter mailing list letter, standard letter

forte pedal damper pedal, sustain pedal

fortune hunter gold digger, moneygrubber, self-server, tufthunter

forty winks blanket drill, catnap, crash, nap, power nap, rack time, sack time, short sleep, siesta, snooze, some Zs, spot of sleep, wink, wink of sleep, zizz

forward pass aerial, bomb, pass, pass pattern

fossil fuel hydrocarbon deposit, nonrenewable energy, nonrenewable fuel source

foster home halfway house, safe harbor, safe house

foul play abomination, atrocity, crime, mischief, murder

foul shot charity shot, free throw

foundation garment bandeau, bra, brassiere, corset, girdle

found object objet trouvé

fountain of youth eternal youth, mythical fountain

fountain pen ink pen, reservoir pen

four elements air, earth, fire, water

four-letter word bad word, curse, cuss, cuss word, dirty word, expletive, naughty word, oath, obscenity, profane oath, profanity, swear, swearword, vulgarity

fourth dimension continuum, four-dimensional space, space-time, space-time continuum, time, time-space

fourth estate broadcast journalism, electronic journalism, journalism, journalists, press, press corps, print journalism, public press, public print, the press

Fourth of July Independence Day, July 4, July 4th, July Fourth, U.S. Independence Day

four-ways emergency lights, flashers

four-wheel drive all-wheel drive, 4WD, sport utility vehicle

frame of mind disposition, feelings, humor, mindset, mood, shape, spirits, standing, state, state of mind, temper, temporary psychological state, tone, vein

frame of reference coordinate system, framework, reference frame, reference system, universe of discourse

Franklin stove woodstove

fraternal twin carbon copy, dead ringer, exact mate, identical twin, look-alike, mirror image, spitting image

freak of nature freak, lusus naturae

freak out blow one's stack, blow one's top, flip one's lid, flip out, fly off the handle, go ballistic, go bananas, go crazy, go nuts, go off the deep end, hit the ceiling, lose one's mind, lose one's temper, wig out, work oneself up

free agent freelance, independent, individualist, rugged individualist

free and easy boon, casual, convivial, easygoing, footloose, footloose and fancy-free, free as a bird, free as the wind, informal, loose, nonformal, unstudied

free association association by similarity, idea association, idea suggestion, word association

freedom of speech civil liberty, freedom of expression, free speech, lack of censorship, poetic license

freedom of the press constitutional freedom, lack of censorship

free enterprise capitalism, free competition, free economy, free market, free trade, free-enterprise economy, free-enterprise system, liberalism, open market, private enterprise, self-regulating market

free fall decline, dive, nosedive, plummet, plummeting, plunge, sag, slump

free-for-all brawl, commotion, donnybrook, fight, fracas, fray, melee, pandemonium, racket, rhubarb, riot, ruckus, rumble, rumpus, shindy, tussle, uproar

free form free morpheme, minimum free form, semanteme, word

free hand carte blanche, free choice, free course, freedom, free play, free scope, free will, full scope, independence, latitude, leeway, liberty, one's choice, one's discretion, one's initiative

free kick direct free kick, indirect free kick, onside kick, penalty kick, squib kick

free love extracurricular relations, extracurricular sex, extramarital sex, free-lovism, new morality, premarital sex, sexual freedom, sexual liberation, sexual revolution

free port harbor, home port, port of call, treaty port

free radical diradical, radical

free rein play, unlimited freedom, unrestraint

free ride complimentariness, freebie, free ticket, gimme, no charge

free speech first amendment, freedom of speech

free spirit beatnik, Bohemian, eccentric, flower child, freethinker, gonzo, hippie, maverick, New Ager, nonconformist, original

free thought freethinking, latitudinarianism, liberalism

free throw charity shot, foul shot

free throw line charity line, foul lane, foul line, free throw lane, keyhole, the key, the line

free trade capitalism, common market, economic community, fair trade, multilateral trade, noninvolvement, open market, reciprocal trade

free verse unrhymed verse, vers libre

free weight barbell, dumbbell

free will choice, conation, free choice, one's discretion, one's own will, volition

free world anticommunist countries, capitalistic countries, democratic countries

freeze-frame motionless image, motionless scene, still picture, stop motion

freezer paper freezer wrap

freezing rain sleet

freight train goods train, nonpassenger train, rattler

French braid fishbone braid

French cuff cuff-link cuff

French fries French-fried potatoes, fries

French kiss deep kiss, soul kiss, tongue

French leave abrupt departure, absenteeism, absent without leave, AWOL, cut, hooky, secret departure, truancy, unannounced departure

French window casement window, French casement

frequency distribution frequency curve, frequency polygon, probability curve, probability function

Freudian slip lapsus linguae, misstep, slip of the tongue, sus linguae

friction match Congreve, Congreve match, fusee, locofoco, safety match, vesta, vesuvian

friction tape insulating tape, water-resistant tape

friend of the court amicus curiae

frig around diddle around, fool around, muck about, waste time

fringe area static

fringe benefit allowances, benefits, bonus, compensation package, employee benefit, gravy, lagniappe, perk, perks, perquisite, perquisites, reward, solatium

frog kick scissors kick, swimming kick, whip kick

from time to time ever so often, every now and then, every once in a while, infrequently, not often, now and again, now and then, occasionally, once and again, once in a while, periodically, sometimes, sporadically

frontage road access road

front burner important position

front matter explanatory matter, introduction, preface, preliminary

front money advance payment, early payment, startup money

front office anteriority, executive hierarchy, executive office, top brass, upstairs

front room best room, drawing room, foreroom, living room, morning room, parlor, salon, sitting room, withdrawing room

frozen dinner fast food, frozen entrée, frozen meal, TV dinner

fruit leather fruit rollup

frying pan fryer, fry pan, griddle, skillet

fuddy-duddy dotard, fogy, fussbudget, fusspot, granny, old fart, old fogy, old maid, square

fudge factor ad hoc correction, correction

fuel indicator fuel gauge, gas gauge

full blast all-out, flat-out, full force, full speed, full steam, full tilt, full volume

full boil rolling boil

full-blooded blue-blooded, of good breed, pure-blooded, purebred, red-blooded, thoroughbred, unmixed, well-bred

full-bodied flavorful, full-flavored, rich, strong, thick

full circle circuit, cycle, go-round, orbit, pass, revolution, round trip

full court press press, trapping

full dress dress clothes, evening dress, evening wear, formal dress, formals, full feather

full-fledged developed, experienced, full-grown, grown, in full bloom, mature, qualified, schooled, seasoned, skilled, trained, well-developed

full-grown adult, complete, developed, full-fledged, full-sized, fully developed, grown, mature, ripe, well-developed

full house capacity, fill, full hand, full measure, max, sellout

full marks due praise, full credit

full monty complete, the works, whole ball of wax, whole deal, whole nine yards, whole shebang, whole thing, whole works

full moon harvest moon, hunter's moon

full of beans full of ginger, full of pep, full of piss and vinegar, full of vitality, peppy, vivacious, zingy

full orchestra symphony

full speed flat-out, full sail, full steam, full swing, full tilt, heavy right foot, maximum speed, open throttle

full stop dead stop, decimal point, dot, period, point, screeching halt

full throttle full stroke, top speed

functional illiteracy grammarlessness, illiteracy, illiterateness, semiliteracy

function key Alt, Ctrl, F key

fundamental units International System of Units, Système Internationale

funeral director embalmer, mortician, undertaker

funeral home funeral chapel, funeral church, funeral parlor, funeral residence, undertaker's establishment

funeral procession cortege, dead march, death march, exequy, funeral march

fun fair amusement park, carnival, Tivoli

funnel cloud tornado

funny bone crazy bone, elbow, sense of humor

funny book comic, comic book

funny farm bedlam, booby hatch, bughouse, insane asylum, laughing academy, loony bin, lunatic asylum, madhouse, mental health institution, mental home, mental hospital, mental institution, nuthouse, padded cell, psychiatric hospital, psychiatric ward, rubber room, sanatorium, sanitarium, snake pit

funny feeling bad vibes, gut feeling, hunch, suspicion, wariness

funny money counterfeit currency, counterfeit money, fake money

funny paper comics, comic section, funnies

fusion bomb hydrogen bomb

future life afterlife, future state, life after death, next life, postexistence

fuzzy logic Boolean logic

Gg

gable roof double sloping roof

gag order gag rule, taboo

gain ground advance, make up for lost time, pick up speed, progress

gal Friday alter ego, assistant, confidant, fidus Achates, girl Friday, hired hand, man Friday, right-hand girl, second self

galley proof blue, blueprint, foundry proof, galley, page proof, plate proof, press proof, slip

gallows humor black humor, grim humor, sick humor

game bird curlew, grouse, partridge, pheasant, plover, quail, sandpiper, snipe, wild turkey, wildfowl, woodcock

game of chance bingo, bridge, canasta, craps, crazy eights, gambling game, gin, gin rummy, lottery, lotto, penny ante, pinochle, poker, roulette, twenty-one, wheel of fortune

game plan approach, blueprint, design, scenario, scheme, strategic plan, strategy, tactical plan, tactics, working plan

game show giveaway show, quiz show

game theory mathematical probability, theory of games

gamma ray high-energy photon, invisible radiation, S-ray

garage band amateur band, neighborhood band

garage sale bazaar, flea market, rummage sale, tag sale, white elephant sale, yard sale

garbage can ash can, circular file, Dumpster™, dustbin, garbage pail, trash basket, trash can, wastebasket, waste bin, wastepaper basket

garbage disposal compactor, compost, compost heap, Disposall™, garbage disposer, garbage grinder, waste disposal unit

garden clippers hedge clippers, hedge trimmers, trimmers

garter belt girdle, suspender belt

gas chamber death camp, death chamber

gas gauge fuel gauge, fuel indicator

gas station filling station, petrol station, service station

gateleg table drop-leaf table
gateway drug soft drug
Gay-Lussac's law Charles's law
Geiger counter Geiger-Müller tube
gelatin dessert gelatin, gelatine, Jell-O™
gem cutting lapidary
gender bender cross-dresser, gender-crossing clothing, unisex
gender gap culture gap
gene map gene mapping, gene splice, genetic map, recombination DNA technology
gene pool gene complex, gene flow, genetic drift
general admission unreserved seating
general delivery domestic mail, post, snail mail
general election by-election, election, presidential election
general manager highest-ranking manager
general partnership business partnership
general post office GPO, postal service, postal system, U.S. Post Office
general practitioner family doctor, family physician, GP
general relativity general relativity theory, general theory of relativity
general store convenience store, corner store, country store, mom-and-pop store, trading post, variety store
general strike strike
generation gap culture gap, generational difference
Generation X GenX, Gen-X, Gen X, new generation, young blood
genetic code DNA, replication, RNA
genetic counseling genetic screening, hereditary counseling
genetic drift gene complex, gene flow
genetic engineering biogenetics, DNA fingerprinting, genetic fingerprinting, recombinant DNA technology
genetic marker marker, marker gene
gene transfer gene transplantation, germline insertion
gentleman's gentleman chauffeur, coachman, driver, gentleman, manservant, valet, valet de chambre
gentlemen's agreement bond, contract, deal, gentleman's bet, handshake, nonformal agreement, pact, pactum, pledge,

tacit agreement, understanding, unspoken agreement, unwritten agreement, verbal agreement

gentle sex fair sex, female sex, softer sex, weaker sex, womankind, women

geographical mile Admiralty mile, nautical mile

geologic time geological time

geometric mean nth root

geometric ratio arithmetical proportion, geometric proportion, harmonic proportion

geometric series geometric progression

geothermal energy geothermal gradient, geothermal heat

German measles rubella

German shepherd Alsatian

German submarine U-boat

germ warfare bacteriological warfare, biological warfare

gestational carrier gestational mother, surrogate mother

get rid of assassinate, do away with, exterminate, kill, murder, slaughter; cast aside, chuck, cut, deep-six, discard, dispose of, ditch, do away with, dump, eighty-six, eliminate, exclude, expel, omit, part with, reject, remove, throw away, throw out

get the ball rolling keep the ball rolling, start the ball rolling

getting old aging, fading, getting up in years, growing, maturing, not as young as one used to be, seasoning, senescent, wearing out, wilting

get together party, social event

get-together congregation, function, gathering, meeting, party, social affair, social event

get under one's skin annoy, bother, drive up the wall, exasperate, get in one's hair, infuriate, irk, irritate, madden, needle, pester, provoke, push one's buttons, rattle one's cage, rile, ruffle, upset, vex

get used to acclimate, accustom, acquaint, adapt, adjust, familiarize, habituate

ghetto blaster beat box, boom box, box, ghetto box, ministereo, personal stereo, portable radio, portable stereo

ghost town abandoned town, deserted town

ghost word ghost name

ghost writer ghost, surrogate

gift of gab blarney, cacoethes loquendi, diarrhea of the mouth, flowing tongue, furor loquendi, gift of the gab, logomania, logorrhea, verbal diarrhea, volubility, way with words

gift of tongues charismatic gift, glossolalia, speaking in tongues

gift wrap decorative wrap, wrap, wrapping, wrapping paper

GI Joe dough, doughboy, GI, grunt, John Dogface, Yank

gilded age golden age, Reconstruction Era

gimlet eye eagle eye, hawk eye, keen eye, sharp eye, X-ray eye

girl Friday assistant, gal Friday, hired hand, man Friday, right-hand girl

give-and-take banter, collaboration, compromise, concession, cooperation, deal-making, exchange, mutual concession, offset, reciprocity, settlement, swap, trade, trade-off, wheeling and dealing

given name baptismal name, Christian name, first name, forename

give the cold shoulder ignore, neglect, overlook, pass over, rebuff, shun, slight, snub

giving up crying uncle, giving in, surrendering, throwing in the towel

glad hand accueil, cordial welcome, open arms, pleasant reception, warm welcome, welcome

glad rags best bib and tucker, best clothes, dressy clothes, ostrich feathers, party dress, Sunday best, Sunday-go-to-meeting clothes

glass block glass brick

glass ceiling class prejudice, social prejudice

glass eye artificial eye

glass jaw glass house, vulnerability

glee club a cappella choir, choir, chorale, chorus, Liederkranz, Liedertafel, singing club, singing society

global village entire world

global warming greenhouse effect

glove compartment glove box

go back on betray, renege on

go-between agent, arbitrator, broker, connection, contact, intermediary, intermediate, liaison, mediator, middleman, middleperson, middlewoman, negotiator

God-fearing devoted, devout, faithful, good, holy, observant, pious, pure, religious, reverent

God-given talent aptitude, capability, gift, innate ability, natural ability

God's acre churchyard, final resting place

God's will destiny, fate, God's plan, karma, kismet, predestination, predetermination, what is in the books, what is written

go insane crack up, flip, flip out, go bananas, go crazy, go nuts, lose one's mind

gold card custom credit card, platinum card

gold digger bloodsucker, exploiter, leech, opportunist, parasite, sponge, user; forty-niner, goldminer, gold panner, mineworker

golden age gilded age, golden days, golden era, golden time

golden-ager old person, senior, senior citizen

golden boy admired person

golden calf almighty dollar, effigy, graven image, idol, mammon

golden handshake emeritus status, golden handcuffs, golden parachute, pensioning off, putting out to pasture, retirement gift, superannuation

golden mean happy medium, juste milieu, mean, moderation, via media

golden oldie classic, fossil, oldie

golden rule dictum

gold mine bonanza, cash cow, El Dorado, Golconda, goose that laid the golden egg, mother lode, rich lode, rich source, vein

golf bag caddie bag

Good Book American Standard Version, Bible, Book of Books, Christian Bible, Holy Bible, Holy Writ, King James Bible

good deed accommodation, act of kindness, aid, assistance, benevolence, courtesy, favor, good turn, help, kind deed, kindly act, kindness, special favor

good egg good guy, good person, Mr. Nice Guy, nice guy, sweetheart, sweetie

good faith bona fides, bonne foi, pledge, promise, troth, word

good fellow capital fellow, good lot, good sort, right sort

good humor good mood, happiness

good life bed of roses, clover, easy street, Fat City, hog heaven, lap of luxury, life of ease, life of Riley, velvet

good-looking attractive, beautiful, becoming, bonny, cute, gorgeous, handsome, hunky, lovely, nice-looking, pleasing to the eye, pretty, ravishing, stunning, well-built, well-proportioned

good luck fluke, lucky break, lucky strike, Midas touch, streak of luck, stroke of luck
good-luck charm amulet, rabbit's foot, talisman
good manners courtesy, etiquette, formality, graciousness, mannerliness, politeness, respect, social graces
good-natured agreeable, amiable, cheerful, cordial, easygoing, easy to get along with, even-tempered, genial, good-humored, good-tempered, kindly, mild-mannered, nice, pleasant, sweet, well-natured
good offices coattails, good deed, instrumentality, ministration, mitzvah, offices, support, troubleshooting
good old boy good ol' boy, good ole boy
good old days days of old, good old times, horse and buggy days, olden days, olden times, past, times of old, times of yore, yesterday, yesteryear
Good Samaritan Boy Scout, do-gooder, good neighbor, helping hand, humanitarian, Johnny-on-the-spot, Samaritan
goody two-shoes goody-goody, prig, prissy, prude, prudish, Puritan, straightlaced, straitlaced, upright, Victorian
gooney bird black-footed albatross, Diomedea nigripes, goon, gooney, goonie, goony
goose bumps cold creeps, cold shivers, creeps, gooseflesh, goose pimples, heebie-jeebies, horripilation, jimjams, willies
goose egg nix, zero, zilch, zip, zippo
gospel music spirituals
gospel truth absolute truth, Bible truth, chapter and verse, gospel, hard truth, lowdown, naked truth, plain truth, real McCoy, skinny, straight truth, unalloyed truth
gossip column choice bit of dirt, juicy morsel, scandalmongering, scandal sheet
gossip columnist gossipmonger, reporter, taleteller
go to pieces break down, go mad
government agency administrative unit, agency, authority, bureau, office
government employee civil servant, government worker, public official, public servant
Graafian follicle ovarian follicle
grab bag grab barrel, grab box, mixed bag, ragbag, tontine
grace note appoggiatura
grace period forgiveness period, moratorium

grade crossing crossover, level crossing
grade point average GPA, grades, QPA, quality point average
grade school elementary school, folk school, graded school, grammar school, preparatory school, primary school
graduation gown academic gown, cap and gown
grammar school elementary school, grade school, primary school
grande dame belle, fine lady, précieuse, toast
grandfather clause grandfathering, special case, special privilege
grandfather clock longcase clock
grand jury grand inquest
Grand Lama Dalai Lama
grand larceny grand theft
grand master champion, master, master hand, past master, specialist, virtuoso, wizard
Grand Old Party GOP, Republican Party
grand piano grand
grand slam four-run home run, slam, total victory
grand touring car GT
grand unification theory grand unified theory, GUT
granny glasses harlequin glasses, mini specs, Windsor glasses
granny knot granny
graphical user interface GUI
graphic arts engraving, graphics, lithography, photography, printing, printmaking, typesetting, typography
grappling iron grappling hook
grass roots common people, hoi polloi, laboring class, Middle America, middle class, ordinary people, proletariat, rank and file, the masses, wage earners, working class, working people
grass skirt hula skirt
grass widow grass widower
graven image effigy, golden calf, idol, sacred cow
graveyard shift anchor watch, dogwatch, graveyard watch, lobster shift, night shift, sunrise watch, swing shift, third shift
gravy train lap of luxury, life of ease, life of Riley
gray eminence behind-the-scenes operator, eminence grise, friend at court, hidden

hand, kingmaker, power behind the throne, powerbroker, wire-puller

gray matter bean, brains, cerebrum, noggin, noodle, pate, smarts, upper story

greased lightning blue streak, flash, lightning, streak

grease monkey auto mechanic, automobile mechanic, mechanic, mechanician

grease someone's palm bribe, grease someone's hand

greasy spoon beanery, diner, dog wagon, eatery, hashery, hash house

great beyond afterlife, hereafter, life after death, next world, the beyond, the great unknown, the unknown, world beyond

great circle circle of the sphere

Great Depression economic crisis

Great Divide continental divide, watershed

great guns extremely well, very successfully

Great Wall of China Chinese Wall

green apple crab apple

green around the gills blue around the gills, nauseous, pale around the gills, pallid, sick

green card clearance

green-eyed monster envy, green in the eye, jaundiced eye, jealousy

greenhouse effect global warming

green lumber undried lumber

green room dressing room, waiting room

green thumb gardener, grower, horticulturist, propagator

green with envy begrudging, envious, envying, green, green-eyed, jaundiced, jealous, resentful, yellow

greeting card birthday card, Christmas card, e-card, Valentine card

griddle cake batter cake, buckwheat cake, flannel cake, flap cake, flapjack, hotcake, pancake

grief-stricken anguished, bereaved, bereft, brokenhearted, depressed, despairing, despondent, devastated, forlorn, grieving, heartbroken, heartsick, heavyhearted, inconsolable, melancholy, miserable, mourning, sad, sorrowing

Grim Reaper angel of death, Death, death, Pale Death, Reaper

grinding wheel emery wheel

grit one's teeth brace oneself, set one's teeth, steel oneself

grocery store food mart, food store, market, mom-and-pop store, supermarket

grog blossom alcoholism, bottle nose

groom-to-be fiancé, future mate, husband-to-be

gross domestic product GDP

gross income gross earnings, taxable income

gross national product GNP

gross out turn the stomach

ground ball bleeder, bunt, chopper, comebacker, drag bunt, dying quail, grounder, nubber, roller, slow roller, squibbler, wormburner

ground beef burger, chopped steak, ground round, ground sirloin, hamburger, hamburger patty, hamburger sandwich, hamburger steak

ground cloth drop cloth, groundsheet

ground cover covert, earth, ground covering, leaf litter, leaf mold, terra firma, tree litter, turf

ground crew chase crew, landing crew, maintenance crew, plane handlers

ground-effect machine air-cushion vehicle, cushioncraft, GEM, hovercraft

ground floor beginnings, first crack, first stage, head start, preliminaries, very beginning

ground fog dense fog, fog drip, radiation fog

ground substance matrix

ground zero nuclear destruction

group practice family practice, group medicine

growing pains adolescent pain, awkward age

grown-up adult, developed, full-fledged, full-grown, fully developed, grown, mature, of age

growth factor growth regulator, nutrilite

growth fund dual-purpose fund, income fund

growth hormone somatotropin

G spot Gräfenberg spot, horniness, hots, lustfulness

guard dog attack dog, bandog, watchdog

guard duty guard, guardedness, peeled eye, sharp eye, weather eye

guardian angel advocate, angel, champion, fairy godmother, good angel, guardian spirit, lifesaver, ministering angel, personal angel, protector

guard of honor formal escort, honor guard

guerrilla theater street theater

guerrilla war guerrilla warfare, trench war

guest book visitors' book

guest of honor honored guest, honoree, important invitee

guided missile automaton, ballistic missile, missile, rocket, steerable missile

guide dog Seeing Eye™ dog

guide word catchword, headword

guilt trip exaggerated guilty feeling, guilty conscience

guinea pig Cavia porcellus, cavy, rodent; examinee, experimental animal, experimental subject, lab animal, laboratory animal, lab rat, subject, test animal, testee, test subject, victim

gum arabic acacia, gum acacia

gum disease periodontal disease, periodontitis, pyorrhea

gum elastic rubber

gum inflammation bleeding gums, gingivitis, gum disease, inflammation of the gums, oulitis, ulitis

gun control firearm restriction

gung ho aggressive, ardent, banzai, can-do, eager, energetic, enthused, enthusiastic, fanatical, fired up, full of enthusiasm, intense, proactive, take-charge

gut course cram course, easy class, easy course

gut reaction knee jerk, Pavlovian response, reflex, spontaneous reaction, unthinking response

gypsum board drywall, gyp board, plasterboard

gypsy cab hack, restricted-license cab, taxi, taxicab

gyro horizon artificial horizon

Hh

Hail Mary Ave, Ave Maria; Hail Mary pass, Hail Mary play, last-ditch effort, last-minute pass

hair of the dog hair of the dog that bit one, hangover remedy, pick-me-up, refresher, tonic

hair-raising alarming, bloodcurdling, breathtaking, chilling, electrifying, fearsome, frightening, frightful, hellish, horrifying, nightmarish, scary, shocking, spine-tingling, startling, terrifying, unnerving

hair roller curler, hair curler, roller

hair shirt self-flagellation, self-hatred, self-punishment

hair stylist barber, beautician, coiffeur, coiffeuse, coiffurist, hairdresser

hair transplant hair implant, hair weave

half blood crossbreed, cur, half-bred, half-breed, half-caste, hybrid, mestizo, mixblood, mongrel

half boot short boot

half-dollar \$.50, .50, 50 cents, fifty cents

half note minim

half step halftone, minor second, semitone

halfway house rehabilitation center, safe house, stopping place

half-wit born fool, clod, dimwit, dolt, dope, dullard, dunce, idiot, imbecile, moron, nitwit, pea brain, simpleton, stupid person

halls of ivy college, university

ham it up be theatrical, burlesque, caricature, chew up the scenery, emote, ham, overact, theatricalize, travesty

hammer and sickle Communist emblem

hammer and tongs bec et ongles, heart and soul, hog-wild, tooth and nail

ham radio amateur radio, citizens band

hand brake emergency brake

hand grenade fire bomb, grenade, incendiary, incendiary bomb, pineapple

handheld vacuum Dustbuster™

hand in glove arm in arm, hand and glove, hand in hand, thick, thick as thieves

hand-me-down not new, passed down, previously owned, reach-me-down, secondhand, used, worn

hand over fist amain, apace, ASAP, at once, immediately, increasingly, instantly, speedily

hand-rolled cigarette roll-your-own, twist

hands down easily, effortlessly, going away, in a walk, with both eyes closed, with one hand tied behind one's back

hand truck handcart

handwriting on the wall forewarning, inevitability, portents and evils imminent, warning

handyman's special fixer-upper

hang around frequent, hang about, hang out, haunt, linger, loiter

hang back hang fire, hang off, hold off, hover, pause, procrastinate, stick, straggle

hang glider unpowered aircraft

hanging folder Pendaflex™

hang in the balance be touch and go, hang, hang in suspense

hang in there endure, persevere

hang-up complex, compulsion, fascination, fear, fixation, inhibition, irrestible impulse, obsession, phobia, preoccupation, quirk; barrier, block, blockage, delay, difficulty, drawback, hazard, hurdle, obstacle, obstruction, problem, stumbling block, tie-up

hanky-panky affair, amour, dalliance, fling, flirtation, fooling around, liaison, love affair, romance, sexual activity; dirty pool, funny business, hokey-pokey, mischief, monkey business, trickery

happy event birth

happy hour bread and circuses, cocktail hour

happy hunting ground better place, heaven, home, kingdom come, last home

happy-go-lucky carefree, content, easygoing, free and easy, lighthearted, living the life of Riley, nonchalant, unconcerned, untroubled, without care

happy medium gray area, middle ground, neutral ground

hara-kiri disembowelment, ritual suicide, seppuku, suttee

hard-and-fast absolute, binding, carved in stone, compulsory, conclusive, decisive, dictated, exacting, final, inflexible, irrevocable, mandatory, set, set in concrete, strict, unalterable, unbending, written

hard cash cash, cash on the barrelhead, cash payment, cold cash, legal tender

hard coal anthracite

hard copy computer printout, paper copy, printout

hard-core ardent, committed, dedicated, devoted, die-hard, enthusiastic, exuberant, fanatic, fervent, fiery, firm, hard-line, inflexible, intense, irreconcilable, passionate, resistant, rigid, spirited, staunch, steadfast, stubborn, totally committed, unbending, uncompromising, ungiving, unwavering, unyielding, zealous

hard disk hard disk drive, hard drive, tape drive, Winchester drive {compare *floppy disk*}

hard feelings bitterness, resentment

hard goods durable goods, durables

hard hat crash helmet, helmet

hard-hearted as hard as nails, callous, case-hardened, cold, cold-blooded, coldhearted, cruel, hardened, heartless, inhuman, insensitive, merciless, pitiless, stony, uncaring, unfeeling, unmerciful, unsympathetic

hard knocks adverse circumstances, adversity, difficulties, hardship, rough going, stress, troubles

hard labor chain gang, labor camp, rock pile

hard line literalism

hard news current affairs, happenings

hard-nosed bullheaded, hard-boiled, hardheaded, inflexible, mulish, obdurate, obstinate, pigheaded, stubborn, stubborn as a mule, tough, uncompromising

hard of hearing deaf, hearing-impaired, stone-deaf

hard put at a loss, embarrassed

hard rock acid rock, hard-core rock, heavy metal, punk rock

hard rubber vulcanized rubber

hard sauce brandy butter

hard science astronomy, chemistry, geology, physical science, physics

hard sell cold call, high-pressure salesmanship {compare *soft sell*}

hard-to-please choosy, critical, detailed, finicky, fussy, meticulous, nitpicking, particular, picky, scrutinizing

hard work backbreaking work,

donkey work, drudgery, hard way, labor, long haul, tough grind, uphill battle

hare and hounds game of chase

harmonic motion simple harmonic motion

harmonic progression arithmetic progression, geometric progression

harm's way razor's edge, thin ice

harum-scarum careless, disorganized, reckless

harvest home harvest festival, Oktoberfest

harvest moon full moon, hunter's moon

hash browns American fries, cottage fries, hash brown potatoes, hashed browns, home fries

hash mark Hershey bar, overseas bar, pip, service stripe; inbounds marker

hatchet job dismantlement, poison-pen letter, unmaking

hatchet man gun, professional murderer, rodman, torpedo, trigger man

hat trick three goals, three successes, three wins

haute couture designer fashion, fashion design, garment industry, high fashion, rag trade, Seventh Avenue

haute cuisine gastronomy, nouvelle cuisine

haut monde bon ton, Four Hundred, gentry, high society, Social Register

Hawaiian shirt aloha shirt, floral-print shirt

hay fever allergic rhinitis, pollinosis, rose cold

hazard lights emergency lights, flashers, 4-way flashers, four-way flashers, idiot lights, warning lights

hazardous waste atomic waste, contaminated materials, dumping, environmental pollutant, industrial waste, nuclear waste, poison, pollution, toxic waste

head cold common cold

head count bean-counting, body count, census, inventory, muster, nose count, poll, reckoning, repertory, roll call, roster

head over heels à corps perdu, completely, far gone, heels over head, intensely

head shot identification photo, identification photograph, mug shot, passport photo

head start first crack, running start

head-to-head direct encounter

head trip ego trip, introspection

health care health maintenance, health management, health protection, medical management, preventive medicine, wellness program

health club gym, health farm, health spa, spa

health food fiber, lite food, low-calorie food, low-fat food, natural food, nonfat food, organic food, roughage

health insurance comprehensive medical insurance, group medical insurance, health plan, major medical, managed care, Medicaid, medical insurance, Medicare, private insurance

health maintenance organization HMO

health spa fitness center, gym, gymnasium, health club, health resort, spa, therapeutic facility

hearing aid ear trumpet, electronic hearing aid, hard-of-hearing aid, listening device, transistor hearing aid, vacuum-tube hearing aid

hearing-impaired deaf, hard of hearing, stone-deaf

heart attack cardiac arrest, chest pains, congestive heart failure, coronary, coronary infarction, heart failure, myocardial infarction, tachycardia

heart disease angina, cardiac infarction, congenital heart disease, congestive heart failure, coronary thrombosis, ischemic heart disease, myocardial infarction

heart-to-heart talk face-to-face chat, intimate discussion, tête-à-tête

heat exchanger heat pump, heat-transfer device

heat exhaustion heat prostration

heating pad hot pad, hot-water bottle

heat lightning dark lightning, sheet lightning, summer lightning

heat rash prickly heat

heat shield heat barrier, thermal barrier

heat wave canicular days, dog days, high summer, hot spell, hot wave, warm front

heavenly body celestial body, celestial sphere, orb, sphere

heavy cream whipping cream

heavy hand big stick, firm hand, iron boot, iron hand, strong hand, tight rein, tight ship

heavy heart aching heart, agony of mind, bathos, bleeding heart, broken heart, heartache, heaviness of heart, pathos, sad heart

heavy hitter powerful batter, powerful person

heavy hydrogen deuterium, isotope of hydrogen, tritium

heavy metal hard rock music

heavy petting cuddling, fondling, foreplay, lovemaking

heavy with child carrying, family way, gravid, heavy with young, pregnant, the family way, with child

Hebrew Scriptures Hebrew Bible

hedge trimmers garden clippers, hedge clippers, shears

Heimlich maneuver Heimlich

heir apparent apparent heir, crown prince, heir expectant

heir presumptive legal heir, presumptive heir, statutory next of kin

hell-bent bound and determined, determined, driven, intent, obsessed, persistent, relentless, resolute, resolved, serious, set on, single-minded, steadfast, strong-minded, stubborn, tenacious, unrelenting, unwavering

hell week hazing week

helping hand aid, assist, assistance, boost, leg up, lift

helter-skelter arbitrary, carelessly, chaotic, confused, disorderly, haphazard, hastily, hit or miss, hurried, hurry-scurry, in disorder, random, recklessly, slapdash

hem and haw back and fill, beat around the bush, beg the question, dance around, equivocate, euphemize, fudge and mudge, hum and haw, mince words, shilly-shally, tap-dance

Henle's loop loop of Henle

hen party girls' night out, hen night, women's celebration

hen track chicken scratch, doodle, hen scratch, pothooks, scrawl, scribble

herb doctor herbalist

here and now actuality, hic et nunc, immediately, present moment, present time, real world, reality

herniated disk slipped disk

heroic verse heroic poem

hero sandwich grinder, hero, hoagie, poor boy, sub, submarine, submarine sandwich

hero worship adoration, apotheosis, breathless adoration, deification, exaggerated respect, idolization, worship

herpes zoster shingles

het up burning, hot and bothered, hot under the collar, indignant, irate, upset; enthusiastic

hex sign whammy sign

hidden agenda ax to grind, parti pris, prejudice, ulterior motive

hidden tax indirect tax

high and dry aground, deserted, foundered, marooned, shipwrecked, stranded, stuck

high and low everywhere, everywhere possible, in every nook and cranny, inside and out, upstairs and downstairs

high and mighty aristocratic, arrogant, conceited, egotistical, eminent, exalted, imperious, lordly, magisterial, mighty, pompous, presumptuous, smug, snobbish, snotty, supereminent

high bar horizontal bar

high beams bright lights

high blood pressure hypertension

high comedy witty comedy

high court court of record, superior court, Supreme Court, trial court

high-definition television HDTV

high-density lipoprotein HDL

high-energy physics particle physics

higher education college, graduate school, institute, tertiary school, university

high explosive dynamite, explosive, TNT

high fashion haute couture

high fidelity hi-fi

high frequency HF

high gear double-quick, high

high hat top hat

high heels pumps, stilettos

High Holiday High Holy Day

high horse condescension, hoity-toitiness, patronization

high jinks antic, caper, escapade, frolic, monkeyshines, practical joke, prank, shenanigans, stunt, tomfoolery

high jump running high jump, standing high jump

Highland fling jig, morris, Scottish dance

high life fast lane, high society

high-muck-a-muck big man, bigwig, high-muckety-muck, kingpin, muck-a-muck, VIP

high noon eight bells, meridian, meridiem, midday, noon; 1200 hours, 12 o'clock, noonday, nooning, noontide, noontime, peak

high-occupancy vehicle HOV

high place eminence, rank, stature, status

high priest archbishop, bishop, cardinal, chief priest, Cohen, dean, ecclesiarch, Kohen, monsignor, provost

high profile conspicuousness, exposure, high relief, pronounced, public exposure

high relief alto-relievo, alto-rilievo, bold

high-rise high-rise apartment building

high road direct route, main road, no-brainer

high roller bettor, high-stakes gambler, money player, plunger

high school eleventh grade, grades nine through twelve, gymnasium, ninth grade, secondary school, senior high, senior high school, tenth grade, twelfth grade

high seas high sea, international waters, open ocean, open sea, seven seas

high sign alert, signal, the nod, the wink, warning signal

high society aristocracy, beau monde, beautiful people, best people, café society, cream of society, crème de la crème, cultured class, elite, fashionable society, Four Hundred, good society, haut monde, high life, jet set, privileged class, right people, smart set, société, society, the better sorts, the Four Hundred, the privileged, upper class, upper crust

high tea afternoon tea, cream tea, five-o'clock tea, light supper

high technology high tech, hi tech, technicology, technics

high tide full tide, high water

high time ball, big time, due season, good time, great fun, high old time, picnic

high treason misprision of treason

high-water mark apogee, ceiling, flood mark, tidemark, upper limit, watermark

highway robbery armed robbery, banditry, gouge, holdup, rip-off

high wire tightrope

hillbilly music C&W, country-and-western, country music

hip boot wader, wading boot

Hippocratic oath doctor's oath, doctor's promise

hip to attuned, aware of, knowledgable

hired gun assassin, butcher, contract killer, executioner, gunman, hatchet man, hired killer, hit man, killer, murderer, professional killer, sniper, trigger man

historical linguistics comparative linguistics

historical materialism historicism

hitching post Samson post, snubbing post

hither and thither here and there

hit it off cotton to, fall in with, get along

hit list drop-dead list, laundry list, shit list, want list

hit man assassin, butcher, contract killer, executioner, gunman, hatchet man, hired gun, hired killer, killer, murderer, professional killer, sniper, trigger man

hit-or-miss careless, casual, erratic, haphazard, planless, random, sporadic, unarranged, undirected, unorganized

hit or miss at random, by chance, haphazardly

hit parade music best-sellers

hit squad hired killers, team of assassins

hit the books apply oneself, con, crack a book, study

hit the bottle drink heavily, hit the sauce

hit the bricks go on strike, strike, walk out

hit the ceiling blow a gasket, flip out, fly off the handle, hit the roof, lose one's cool, lose one's temper, wig out

hit the deck fall to the ground, pile out, roll out, show a leg

hit the hay crash, go to bed, go to sleep, hit the sack, kip down, sack out, turn in

hit the jackpot break the bank, clean up, hit the mark, make a killing, score, strike it rich

hit the road count ties, get going, hit the trail, leave, pound the pavement, walk the tracks

hit the spot be just the ticket, go over big, make a hit, satisfy

Hobson's choice lack of choice, no alternative, no choice, only choice, zero option

hocus-pocus abracadabra, conjuring, deception, hocus, incantation, legerdemain, magic, magic words, monkey business, mumbo jumbo, mystification, nonsense, occultism, sleight of hand, smoke and mirrors, trick, trickery

hog heaven bed of roses, easy street, fat city, lap of luxury

hog wild ape, around the bend, bananas

hoi polloi commonality, commoners, great unwashed, huddled masses, infrastructure, masses, Middle America, multitude, plebians, proletariat, rabble, rank and file, riffraff, the common people, the herd, the many, the masses, the working class, vulgus

hold back balk, check, hesitate, restrain

holding company investment trust

holding pattern limbo, stack-up, waiting path

hold one's ground hold fast, not budge, persevere, persist, stand one's ground, stay put

hold the line block, check, hinder, hold the fort, keep at bay, obstruct, stop

hold your horses be patient, hold everything, hold your water, keep your shirt on

hole in one ace, hole

hole up burrow, go underground, hide, sit tight, take refuge

holier-than-thou goody-goody, hypocritical, judgmental, pious, sanctimonious, self-righteous, self-satisfied, smug, snobbish

Holy Bible American Standard Version, Bible, Book of Books, Christian Bible, Douay Bible, Good Book, Holy Scripture, Holy Writ, King James Bible, Revised Standard Version, Scriptures, Septuagint, Testament, Vulgate, Word of God

Holy Communion Communion, Eucharist, Holy Sacrament, Last Supper, Lord's Supper, the Sacrament

holy day fast day, hallowday, holiday, holytide, saint's day

Holy Father confessor, father confessor, pope, spiritual father, spiritual leader

Holy Ghost Comforter, Dove, Holy Spirit, Intercessor, Paraclete, Spirit, Spirit of God, Spirit of Truth

Holy Grail Grail, Sangreal

Holy Land Canaan, Palestine

Holy Mother Madonna, Mother of God, Mother Superior, Our Lady, Virgin Mary

Holy Office College of Cardinals, committee of Cardinals

Holy Orders minister's rank, orders, priest's rank, rite of ordination, sacraments

Holy See See of Rome, Vatican

Holy Spirit Comforter, Dove, Holy Ghost, Intercessor, Paraclete, Spirit, Spirit of God, Spirit of Truth

holy terror enfant terrible, little terror, terror, troublemaker, whippersnapper

Holy Thursday Ascension Day; Maundy Thursday

holy war crusade, holy crusade, jihad

holy water blessed water

Holy Writ Bible, sacred writings, Scripture

home base home, home plate

home computer briefcase computer, desktop computer, handheld computer, laptop computer, notebook computer, PC, PDA, personal computer, personal digital assistant, personal organizer, pocket computer

home economics domestic economy, domestic science, home ec, home management, life management

home fries American fries, cottage fries, hash browns

home office center of operations, corporate headquarters, executive office, headquarters, HQ, main office

home page Web page, Web site

home plate dish, home, home base, platter, the plate

home rule autarchy, autonomy, independence, self-determination, self-direction, self-government, self-rule

home screen television, TV

home truth a priori truth, basic truth, general truth, honest truth, indisputable truth, intrinsic truth, naked truth, obvious truth, plain truth, self-evident truth, simple truth, straight truth, truism, unadorned truth, universal truth, unvarnished truth

honest broker arbitrator

honorable mention citation, kudos, mention, praise

honor guard guard of honor

honor roll dean's list

honor system system of trust

hook-and-loop fastener Velcro™

hook, line and sinker completely; entirely; lock, stock and barrel

hope chest bottom drawer

hornet's nest controversial issue, controversial situation, dangerous ground, trouble

horn in butt in, interrupt, intrude, muscle in

horn of plenty bottomless well, cornucopia, endless supply, horn of Amalthea

hors d'oeuvre antepast, antipasto, aperitif, appetizer, canapé, crostato, crudités, finger food, finger sandwich, foretaste, nibbles, sample, snack, starter, tidbit, whet

horse around carry on, cut up, fool around, roughhouse

horseless carriage auto, automobile, car, motor car

horse opera cowboy picture, oater, shoot-'em-up, spaghetti western, western, western movie

horse race Belmont Stakes, derby, Grand National, Kentucky Derby, Preakness Stakes, race, sport of kings

horse sense common sense, good sense, gumption, levelheadedness, plain sense, savvy, understanding

horse trade barter, hard bargaining

horse trader barterer, confidence man, horse coper, swindler, wheeler-dealer, Yankee horse trader

host computer main computer, server

hot air big talk, blah-blah-blah, bunk, gas, idle talk, wind

hot-air balloon gasbag, gas balloon, lighter-than-air craft

hot and heavy intense, passionate, vehement

hot corner hot box, third, third base

hot dish casserole, covered dish, potluck, stew

hot dog boaster, crowd-pleaser, flaunter, grandstander, hotshot, showboat, show-off; dog, footlong, frank, frankfurter, Georgia hot, red hot, sausage, weenie, wiener

hot flash hot flush

hot money temporary funds

hot pad cozy, pot holder

hot pants lederhosen, short shorts, tight shorts

hot rod drag racer, Formula car, Indy car, sports car, stock car, turbocharger

hot rollers heated curlers

hot sauce Tabasco™

hot seat hot spot, powder keg, spot, sticky wicket

hot spring mineral spring, warm spring

hot tub Jacuzzi™, plunge bath, sauna, sauna bath, steam bath, whirlpool, whirlpool bath

hot under the collar angry, boiling, burning with excitement, excited, het up, mad, pissed off, steaming, upset

hot water hot spot, jam, scrape, soup, trouble

house arrest close arrest, preventive custody, protective custody, purdah

house brand house specialty

house detective hotel detective, house dick, store detective

house doctor house physician

household effects furnishings, furnishments, furniture, home furnishings, house furnishings, household goods

household troops ceremonial troops, corps d'elite, guards, guardsmen

household word byword, common speech, plain English, vernacular

housemaid's knee rheumatism

house of cards cardhouse, glass house

house of correction Borstal, detention center, detention home, house of detention, reformatory, reform school

house of God bethel, church, church house, house of prayer, house of worship, meetinghouse, mosque, place of worship, shul, synagogue, tabernacle, temple

house of ill repute bawdy house, bordello, brothel, cathouse, den of vice, house of ill fame, house of prostitution, joy house, massage parlor, whorehouse

house of worship cathedral, church, holy place, mosque, place of worship, shrine, shul, synagogue, tabernacle, temple

house organ house magazine, house publication, newsletter, organ

house party at-home, housewarming, weekend party

house rule routine, rules and regulations, standing order

house sitter caretaker, house minder

house trailer Airstream™, camper, mobile home

housing development subdivision, tract

housing project tenement house, tenement housing, welfare housing

hue and cry alarm, brouhaha, clamor, cry, hubbub, hullabaloo, noise and shouting, outcry, outrage, protest, uproar

hula skirt grass skirt

human being earthling, higher animal, human, living person, living soul, mortal, person, soul

human ecology ecology, sociology branch

human engineering ergonomics, ergonomy, human factors engineering

human geography anthropogeography, anthropography, cultural geography

human immunodeficiency virus AIDS virus, HIV, virus that causes AIDS

human nature frail humanity, human equation, human fallibility, human frailty, humanity, human weakness, way you are, weakness of the flesh

human resources forces, personnel, staff

human rights civil liberties, civil rights, constitutional rights, natural rights, rights of citizenship, rights of man, unalienable rights

humble pie crow, dirt, pride

hunger strike fasting, religious fasting, voluntary fast

hunker down crouch, get down, hunch, hunch down, hunker, scrunch, squat, squat down

hunting expedition hunt, safari

hurricane lamp kerosene lamp, oil lamp

husband-to-be fiancé, future mate, groom-to-be

hush money blackmail, bribe, payoff, payola

hush puppy corn dab, corn dodger, dodger

hydrogen bomb fusion bomb, H-bomb, nuclear bomb, thermonuclear bomb

hypodermic injection bing, hypodermal injection, hypodermic, hypospray, injection, intracutaneous injection, intramuscular injection, intravenous injection, jet injection, shot, subcutaneous injection

hypodermic syringe needleless syringe, piston syringe

Ii

iambic pentameter blank verse, dactylic hexameter, iamb, iambus

ICBM guided missile, intercontinental ballistic missile, missile weapon, nuclear missile

ice age glacial epoch, glacial period

ice chest chiller, cooler, fridge, icebox, ice bucket, icehouse, refrigerator, refrigerator-freezer, refrigeratory

ice cream frozen yogurt, ice, ice milk, sherbet, sorbet

ice-cream maker ice-cream freezer

ice-cream scoop ice-cream dipper

ice-cube tray ice tray

ice pack cold pack, ice bag

idée fixe compulsion, fetish, fixation, fixed idea, infatuation, irresistible impulse, mania, monomania, obsession, obsessive compulsion, one-track mind, preoccupation

identification card ID, ID card, identity card

identity element unity

id est as it were, i.e., that is, that is to say

idiot box boob tube, television, television receiver, television set, telly, TV, TV set

igneous rock abyssal rock, felsitic rock, hypabyssal rock, mafic rock, magmatic rock, plutonic rock, ultrabasic rock, ultramafic rock

ill-advised foolhardy, foolish, half-baked, harebrained, ill-considered, ill-devised, ill-judged, impolitic, imprudent, inappropriate, misguided, not thought out, rash, reckless, shortsighted, stupid, thoughtless, unwise

ill at ease anxious, apprehensive, awkward, discomfited, edgy, fidgety, insecure, nervous, on edge, on pins and needles, restless, self-conscious, shy, uncomfortable, uneasy, unrelaxed, unsettled

illegal act illicit act, immoral act

illegal alien day-crosser, illegal immigrant, wetback

illegitimate child bar sinister,

bastard, bastard child, by-blow, child born out of wedlock, child born without benefit of clergy, love child, nullius filius, out-of-wedlock child, whoreson

ill-fated baleful, blighted, damned, dire, disastrous, doomed, hopeless, ill-starred, luckless, star-crossed, unfortunate, unlucky, unpromising

ill-mannered badly behaved, bad-mannered, beastly, boorish, coarse, crude, discourteous, disrespectful, ill-behaved, impolite, rough, rude, tacky, uncivil, unmannerly, unrefined, vulgar

ill-natured bad-tempered, cantankerous, contentious, crabby, crotchety, disagreeable, grouchy, ill-humored, ill-tempered, irritable, mean, moody, nasty, ornery, petulant, sour, sulky, surly, temperamental, touchy, unfriendly, unpleasant

ill-suited ill-fitted, ill-matched, improper, inappropriate, incompatible, malapropos, mismatched, out of its element, out of place, unfit, unfitting, unsuitable

ill-tempered annoyed, bad-tempered, cantankerous, crabby, crotchety, grouchy, grumpy, ill-natured, irascible, irritable, moody, nasty, quick-tempered, snappy, sour, surly, testy, touchy

ill will acrimony, animosity, animus, bad blood, bad will, bitter feeling, bitterness, dislike, enmity, feud, grudge, hard feelings, hate, hatred, hostility, malevolence, malice, no love lost, resentment, spite, spitefulness, venom

ill wind bad fortune, bad influence, evil dispensation, evil fortune, evil star, frowns of fortune, ill fortune, malevolent influence

image sensor OCR, optical character reader, optical scanner, reader, scanner

imaginary number pure imaginary {compare *complex number*}

improper fraction vulgar fraction

in a flash instantaneously, quickly

in agreement congruent, cooperative, corresponding, harmonious, like-minded, of one mind, parallel, unanimous, with one voice

inalienable right birthright, natural right, presumptive right
in a moment at once, in an instance, in a trice, in a wink, right away, very soon
in black and white in print, in writing
in brief in a few words, in short
in cahoots in conspiracy, in partnership
incandescent lamp candent lamp, candescent lamp, tungsten lamp
incidental music accompaniment
inclined plane chute, ramp, simple machine, slide
in cold blood calculatedly, callously, coldheartedly, coldly, cruelly, dispassionately, heartlessly, indifferently, intentionally, premeditatedly, unemotionally, unfeelingly, with full intent
income tax business income tax, personal income tax
in commission in service, into commission
in concert jointly, together
in conclusion lastly, to conclude
in consequence as a result, consequently
indecent assault acquaintance rape, date rape, grope, rape, ravishment, sexual assault, violation
indecent exposure exhibitionism, exposing oneself, flashing, public indecency
indentured servant articled servant, bond slave, bondsman, chattel, serf, servant, slave
Independence Day Fourth of July, July 4th, our nation's birthday
in depth extensively, thoroughly
index finger first finger, forefinger, index, indicator, pointer
index fossil guide fossil
index of refraction refractive index
India ink Chinese ink, printer's ink
Indian corn maize
Indian file row, single file
Indian meal cornmeal
Indian paintbrush Castilleja, painted cup
Indian pudding suet pudding
Indian red iron oxide
Indian summer warm autumn weather, warm spell
Indian wrestling arm wrestling
India paper Bible paper
indirect evidence collateral evidence, secondary evidence
indirect tax sales tax, value-added tax
individual retirement account 401(k), 401K, IRA, Keogh plan, pension

industrial arts applied science, industrialism, industrialization, manufacture, production
industrial park enterprise zone, factory belt, factory district, industrial area, industrial estate, industrial zone, manufacturing quarter
industrial relations labor relations, work relations
in effect basically, essentially
inert gas halogen gas, noble gas, rare gas
inertial guidance astro-inertial guidance, astronavigation, celestial guidance, celestial navigation, celo-navigation, inertial navigation system, INS
infantile paralysis polio, poliomyelitis
inferiority complex low self-esteem, personality disorder
infernal machine time bomb
inflationary spiral cost-push inflation, deficit finance, hot economy, inflation, inflationary pressure, inflationary trend, rising prices
information retrieval IR, search engine, searching
information science informatics, information processing, information services, information studies, information theory, library science
information superhighway cyberspace, data highway, I-bahn, infobahn, Infostrada, Internet, National Information Infrastructure, Net, Web, World Wide Web, WWW
information technology computerized information, data processing, IT
information theory communications theory, communication theory, information processing, information retrieval
informed consent voluntary medical consent
infra dig beneath one, beneath one's dignity, debasing, degrading, demeaning, inexpedient, infra dignitatem, unbecoming, unworthy of one
inheritance tax death duty, death tax, estate tax
initial public offering going public, IPO
inkblot test Holtzman technique, Rorschach test
inkhorn term inkhorn word, lexiphanic term, pedantic term, scholarly term
ink-jet printer bubble-jet printer, electronic printer, electrostatic printer, thermal printer

in-line skating blading, Rollerblading™

inner circle brains trust, brain trust, cadre, charmed circle, cohort, corps of advisers, in-crowd, infrastructure, in-group, inside, kitchen cabinet, we-group

inner city barrio, center city, central city, city center, condemned buildings, core, core city, downtown, ghetto, public housing district, skid row, slum, slums, urban city, urban ghetto

inner joy bliss, inner light

inner man bosom, breast, cockles of the heart, core, deepest mind, ego, heart, heart of hearts, inmost heart, inmost mind, inmost soul, innermost being, inner self, inner woman, mind's core, soul, spirit, subconscious

inner planet Earth, Mars, Mercury, Venus

inner product dot product, scalar product

inner tube bladder

inner voice categorical imperative, code of honor, conscience, inner guide, moral code, sense of duty, sense of obligation

insane asylum asylum, bedlam, booby hatch, bughouse, funny farm, laughing academy, loony bin, lunatic asylum, madhouse, mental health institution, mental home, mental hospital, mental institution, nuthouse, padded cell, psychiatric hospital, psychiatric ward, rubber room, sanatorium, sanitarium, snake pit

insane person dement, fruitcake, head case, lunatic, madman, madwoman, maniac, mental defective, neurotic, non compos, non compos mentis, nutter, raving lunatic

inside information confidence, exclusive, hot news, lowdown, poop, private source, reliable source, scoop, secret, state's evidence, undisclosed source

inside job cabal, conspiracy, insider dealing, insider trading

insider trading cabal, insider dealing, rigged market

inside track advantageous position, commanding lead, connections, control, flying start, head start, lead, mastery, networking, right people, winning position

installment plan borrowing,

consumer credit, deferred payment plan, hire purchase plan, installment buying, installment credit, layaway plan, store credit, time payment plan

instant camera Polaroid™

instant replay playback, replay

instrument flying blind flying

instrument landing blind landing, dead-stick landing

instrument panel cockpit console, console, control board, control desk, control panel, dash, dashboard, instrument board, jack field, master control desk, mixer

insulin shock hypoglycemia

integrated circuit chip, circuitry, computer chip, IC, logic circuit, microchip, microcircuit, microelectronics, microprocessor, microprocessor chip, semiconductor chip, silicon chip, transputer

intellectual property copyright, patent, trademark, trade secret

intelligence quotient caliber, compass of mind, IQ, mental age, mental caliber, mental capacity, mental ratio

intelligence test intelligence quotient test, IQ test, psychological measurement, psychometric test

intensive care unit ICU, incubator

interactive fiction computer fiction

intercontinental ballistic missile guided missile, ICBM, missile weapon

interest group lobby, political action committee, pressure group, single-interest group, special-interest group, special interests

interest rate annual percentage rate, bank rate, borrowing rate, interest, lending rate, price of money, prime interest rate, prime rate, rate of interest

interior decoration feng shui, furnishing, interior decorating, interior design, room decoration

interior monologue soliloquy, stream of consciousness

intermediate school junior high, junior high school, middle school

internal ear inner ear, labyrinth

internal revenue inland revenue, tax assessment

International Date Line date line, demarcation line

international law law of nations

international Morse code continental code, cryptanalysis, cryptography, Morse code

international pitch concert pitch

international relations comparative government, foreign affairs, geopolitics, geopolitik, international affairs, public administration, statesmanship

International Standard Book Number ISBN

International System of Units SI

international waters high seas, open sea

interrogation point interrogation mark, question, question mark

intestinal fortitude backbone, balls, brass balls, chutzpah, courage, endurance, energy, fitness, fortitude, guts, gutsiness, heart, moxie, spunk, stamina, staying power, stick-to-itiveness, strength, strength of will, toughness, vigor, wind

intestinal gas breaking wind, fart, flatulence, flatulency, flatuosity, flatus, gas, passing gas, wind

in the ballpark close to, near

in the black at a profit, gainfully, making money, operating at a profit, profitable, profitably, realizing net profit

in the dark ignorant, unaware, uniformed, unknowing

in the family way anticipating, carrying, expecting, gestating, heavy with child, knocked-up, pregnant, with child

in the meantime for the time being, sometimes, temporarily

in the nick of time at the last minute, at the last possible moment, eleventh hour, under the wire

in the red at a loss, bankrupt, behindhand, defaulting, delinquent, in arrears, in dire straits, insolvent, in the hock, in the hole, losing money, nonpaying, operating at a loss, to the bad, unprofitably

in the stars appointed lot, destined, destiny, doomed, fate, fated, foreordained, fortune, God's will, karma, kismet, predestination, predestined, predetermined, preordained, what is fated, what is in the books, what is written

intrauterine device Dalkon Shield™, IUD, Lippes loop

in turn consecutively, following, in order, in sequence, one after another, orderly, sequential, succeeding

invalid argument fallacy, incorrect reasoning

investment company closed-end investment company, holding company, investment firm, investment house, investment trust, trust

invisible ink sympathetic ink

in vitro in an artificial environment

in vogue à la mode, all the rage, avant-garde, chic, chichi, craze, dernier cri, fad, fashionable, happening, hip, in, in fashion, in style, in the latest style, in thing, in with it, latest fad, latest fashion, latest thing, latest wrinkle, mod, modern, modish, new look, on the cutting edge, smart, stylish, swank, trendsetting, trendy

ionic bond electrovalent bond

ipso facto actually, by that very fact, by the fact itself

iron hand big stick, control, firm hand, grip, hard line, heavy hand, high hand, iron boot, iron fist, iron rule, jackboot, mailed fist, strong hand, tight grasp, tight hand, tight rein, tight ship

iron horse locomotive

iron(s) in the fire fish to fry, matter(s) at hand, matter(s) in hand, project(s) in progress, things to do

iron lung life-support system, oxygen tent, respirator

iron maiden instrument of torture, the rack, thumbscrews, treadmill, triangle, wheel

irrational fear anxiety, aversion, fear, hang-up, irrationality, mania, neurosis, obsession, phobia

irrational number irrational, pi

irritable bowel syndrome IBS, spastic colon

isometric exercise isometrics, no-movement exercise

isotopic spin isospin

itching palm avarice, covetousness, cupidity, itchy palm, moneygrubbing, sticky fingers

item veto line-item veto, selective veto

ivory tower halls of ivy, hermitage, intellectual isolation, study

Ivy League Brown, Columbia, Cornell, Dartmouth, Harvard, Princeton, University of Pennsylvania, Yale

Jj

Jack Frost cold weather, frost, frostwork, touch of frost

jam session impromptu gathering, impromptu music

Jane Doe average man, average person, common man, Jane Q. Public, Joe Blow, Joe Six-Pack, John Doe, John Q. Public, lowest common denominator, man in the street, ordinary Joe, woman in the street

jaundiced eye bias, biased judgment, favoritism, green-eyed monster, jaundice, partiality, warped judgment

Jaws of Life™ pneumatic tool

jean jacket denim jacket

Jekyll and Hyde ambiguity, double life, dual personality, duplicity, Proteus, split personality, two-facedness

jester's cap dunce cap, fool's cap

Jesus Christ Christ, God the Son, Good Shepherd, Jesus, King of Kings, Lamb of God, Lord, Lord of Lords, Messiah, Prince of Peace, Redeemer, Savior, Son of God, Son of man

jet engine fan-jet, pulse-jet, ramjet, reaction engine, rocket, rocket motor, turbofan, turbojet, turboprop

jet plane blowtorch, business jet, Concorde, jet, jetliner, jumbo jet, multijet, pulse-jet, ramjet, single-jet, supersonic jet, supersonic transport, turbojet, twin-jet

jet propulsion jet power, pulse-jet propulsion, ramjet propulsion, reaction propulsion, resojet propulsion, rocket power, rocket propulsion, turbojet propulsion

jet set beau monde, beautiful people, café society, country-club set, cream of society, crème de la crème, elite, fashionable society, gentlefolk, glitterati, haut monde, high life, high society, in-crowd, privileged class, salon, smart set, the privileged, upper class, upper crust, wealthy people

jet stream air stream, geostrophic wind, gradient wind, high-altitude wind, high-speed wind stream, prevailing wind, upper-atmosphere wind, upper-atmospheric wind

jet wash prop wash, slipstream

jewel box jewel case

job action blue flu, industrial action, sick-in, slowdown, stickout, strike, tie-up, walkout, work stoppage

job bank employment agency, temp agency, temporary agency

job lot grab bag, inventory, miscellanea, miscellaneous merchandise, mixed bag, ragbag

jog trot amble, cross-country run, dogtrot, extended trot, lope, trot

John Doe average Joe, average person, common man, everyman, Jane Doe, Joe Blow, Joe Doakes, Joe Six-Pack, John Q. Public, John Smith, man in the street, Mr. Brown, Mr. Nobody, ordinary Joe, Richard Roe

John Hancock authorization, autograph, endorsement, hand, initial, inscription, mark, name, OK, signature, subscription, X

Johnny Reb Confederate soldier, Rebel

joint resolution concurrent resolution, resolution

joint return joint tax return

Jolly Roger black flag, jack, pirate flag, pirate ship flag, skull and crossbones

joss house Chinese shrine, Chinese temple, idolatry, teocalli

joss stick censer, incense, sulfur, thurible

journal box axle box, journal

judge advocate attorney general, district attorney, JA, public prosecutor

judge advocate general JAG

judgment call exercise of judgment

Judgment Day court of conscience, crack of doom, Day of Judgment, day of reckoning, doomsday, the Judgment, tribunal of penance

jug wine inexpensive table wine, plonk, table wine

juke joint bar, club, disco, discotheque, nightclub, night spot, pool hall, roadhouse, tavern

jump bail go AWOL, run away, skip bail, take French leave

jumper cable booster cable

jumping-off place beginning of venture, beginning point, jumping-off point, springboard, starting blocks, starting gate, starting line, starting post

jump shot jumper

jump the gun beat someone to the punch, beat the gun, get a head start, preempt

junior college two-year college

junior high eighth grade, intermediate school, junior high school, middle school, seventh grade

junior varsity jayvee, JV, second team

junk bond high-risk bond, high-yield bond

junk food candy, canned food, convenience food, dehydrated food, fast food, frozen food, prepackaged food, processed food, snack food, snacks, unhealthy food

junk mail circular, direct mail, spam, third-class mail, unsolicited mail

just deserts comeuppance, desert, deserts, dose of one's own medicine, dueness, meed, punishment, reward, what is due, what is merited, what's coming to one

justice of the peace JP, judicial officer, magistrate

justification by faith justification, justification by works

juvenile delinquent criminal, delinquent, first offender, gangbanger, hood, hoodlum, hooligan, JD, punk, punk kid, troublemaker, youthful offender

juvenile-onset diabetes insulin-dependent diabetes, insulin-dependent diabetes mellitus, Type I diabetes

Kk

kangaroo court impromptu court, mock court

keep one's nose to the grindstone hammer away, plug away, put one's nose to the grindstone, struggle on, wade through, work hard

keep the peace pour oil on troubled waters, practice nonviolence, wage peace

kettle of fish another can of worms, another tune, bird of another feather, different breed of cat, horse of a different color, piece of business

key card smart card

key club private club

keynote address keynote, keynote speech, main speech

key signature key, measure signature, sharps and flats, time signature, tonality

kick the bucket bite the dust, buy the farm, cash in one's chips, cease living, croak, die, expire, go belly up, go to the wall, go west, meet one's maker, pass away, pass on, shove off, succumb

kick upstairs advance, promote

kid gloves delicacy, fastidiousness, gentle handling, gentleness, good taste, kid-glove treatment, leniency, light hand, light rein, refinement, tact, tolerance, velvet gloves

kidney stone renal calculus

kid stuff easy thing, no-brainer

kill time amuse oneself, consume time, fritter away time, have leisure, idle away time, pass the time, sit on one's hands, summer, waste time, while away the time, winter

kinetic energy actual energy, motive power, motivity

kingdom come afterlife, heaven, hereafter, next world; end of time

Kingdom of God Abraham's bosom, City of God, city of light, heaven, kingdom come, Kingdom of Heaven, Land of the Leal, New Jerusalem, nirvana, paradise, Promised Land, Shangri-la, upstairs, utopia

king of arms earl marshal, herald, king at arms

King's English Received Standard English

king-size bed king bed, large-size bed, large-sized bed, man-sized bed, very large bed

king's ransom El Dorado, end of the rainbow, Golconda, good sum, land of milk and honey, large sum, pot of gold, pretty penny, riches of Solomon, tidy sum, weight in gold

kissing cousin blood relation

kiss of death clincher, coup de grâce, deathblow, end-all, finishing stroke, knockout, mortal blow

kiss of peace pax

kit bag ditty bag, duffel bag, knapsack, traveling bag

kitchen cabinet camarilla, charmed circle, inner circle, privy council, shadow cabinet, unofficial advisers

kitchen gods lares and penates

kitchen midden compost heap, kitchen refuse, midden, refuse heap, shell mound

kitchen police detail, KP

kitchen scissors kitchen shears

kitchen table dinette

kitchen towel dish towel, paper towel

kith and kin acquaintances, consanguinity, family, kin, kindred, kinfolk, kinsfolk, kinsmen, relations, relatives

kitty litter cat litter

klieg light arc light, carbon arc lamp, floodlight, footlights, house lights

knee breeches knickers

knee jerk automatic response, involuntary impulse, knee-jerk reaction, reflex

knee-jerk reaction absence of thought, automatic reaction, automatic response, gut reaction, Pavlovian response

knight-errant Don Quixote, knight

knock for a loop clobber, deck, knock cold, punch out, sandbag, wallop

knock off blow away, bump off, chill, dispatch, dispose of, do away with, do in, dust, grease, hit, ice, kill, murder, off, rub out, snuff out, stretch out, waste, wax, whack, zap

knock out coldcock, do in, hamstring, kayo, knock senseless, KO, lay out

knockout drops chloral hydrate, joy juice, mickey, Mickey Finn

knockout punch Sunday punch

knock up get pregnant, impregnate, inseminate, procreate, spermatize

know by heart know backwards

and forwards, know by rote, know inside out, know like a book, know one's stuff

know-how ability, adeptness, capability, capacity, competence, experience, expertise, flair, knack, knowledge, mastery, proficiency, skill, talent, touch

know-it-all brain, intellectual; smart aleck, smart-ass, walking encyclopedia

knowledge base database, expert system

knowledge engineer artificial-intelligence scientist, expert system programmer

know the ropes know the ins and outs, know the score

knuckle sandwich blow, punch in the mouth

K ration emergency field ration, military ration, prison fare, short commons, short rations

Krebs cycle citric acid cycle, tricarboxylic acid cycle

Kriss Kringle Father Christmas, Saint Nicholas, Saint Nick, Santa, Santa Claus

Ll

labor camp chain gang, corvée, forced labor, gulag, hard labor, prison camp, rock pile, servitude, slavery

labor dispute lockout, protest, shutdown, strike, walkout

labor force crew, factory floor, labor pool, manpower, personnel, proletariat, shop floor, workforce, working classes

labor of love act of grace, courtesy, good deed, good offices, good turn, good work, kindly act, kind offices, mitzvah

labor union craft union, industrial union, local, organized labor, trades union, trade union

ladies' man Casanova, cocksman, Don Juan, lady-killer, Lothario, philanderer, seducer, sheik

ladies' room girls' room, little girls' room, powder room, restroom, women's room

lady bountiful benefactor, distributor of largesse, fairy godmother, generous giver, good giver

Lady Day Annunciation, March 25

lady-in-waiting abigail, lady of the bedchamber, lady's maid, maid-in-waiting, soubrette, waiting maid, waiting woman

Lady Luck Chance, Dame Fortune, fate, Fortuna, Fortune, Lady Fortune, Luck, wheel of fortune

lady of the evening call girl, fallen woman, hooker, prostitute, scarlet woman, streetwalker, whore

lady of the house feudatory, householder, lady of the manor, landlady, mesne, mesne lord

lady's maid abigail, companion, confidante, domestic, lady-in-waiting, lady's attendant, waiting woman

laissez-faire delay, do-nothing policy, free hand, inaction, laissez-aller, laisser-faire, laissez-faire, laissez-passer, latitude, let-alone policy, live and let live, mañana, noninterference, nonintervention, nonrestriction, overindulgence, permissiveness, procrastination, spoiling

lake dwelling crannog, lacustrine dwelling, lake house, lakeside home, lakeside village, palafitte, pile dwelling, pile house, stilt house

Lamb of God Jesus, Son of man

lame duck crumbling power, holdover, incumbent, loser, weak administration, weakling

land bridge isthmus

landing field air base, air harbor, airfield, airstrip, aviation field, field, flight deck, flying field, landing, landing deck, port

landing gear undercarriage

landing strip aerodrome, air base, airfield, airport, airstrip, flight strip, runway, strip, takeoff strip, taxiway

land mine acoustic mine, antipersonnel mine, booby trap, claymore mine, ground mine, limpet, magnetic mine, mine, pressure mine

land-office business boom, bullish market, bullishness, bull market, heavy demand, roaring trade, seller's market, strong demand

land of milk and honey Beulah, Beulah Land, desired object, El Dorado, end of the rainbow, happy valley, over the rainbow, promised land

land of Nod dreamland, sleepland, slumberland

land of plenty Canaan, Goshen, land of milk and honey, land of promise, the promised land

landscape architecture landscape gardening

lap belt seat belt

lap dance striptease

lap dog instrument, minion, puppet, small dog, teacher's pet

lapel mike lavaliere microphone

laptop computer laptop, microcomputer, minicomputer, notebook computer, palmtop, portable computer {compare *desktop computer*}

lares and penates Hestia, household effects, household gods, household possessions, Vesta

larger than life awesome, big, colossal, epic, extraordinary, gigantic, great, heroic, imposing, impressive, legendary, mighty, mythical, titanic, towering

laser disc laser disk, optical disc, optical disk

last breath death rattle, death song, death throes, dying breath, dying moment, final twitch, final words, last gasp, last hurrah, last legs, last words, swan song

last chance desperation, final proposal, last offer, ultimatum, warning

last-ditch attempt improvised attempt, last try, old college try

last laugh ultimate success, ultimate victory

last minute eleventh hour, high time, nick of time, under the wire

last name byname, cognomen, family name, surname

last resort ace in the hole, card up one's sleeve, dernier ressort, desperate remedy, last expedient, last hope, last resource, pis aller, recourse, resort, trump card

last rites burial service, exequies, extreme unction, funeral ceremony, funeral rites, funeral service, last duty, last honors, last offices, memorial service, obsequies, sacrament of the sick, viaticum, visitation of the sick

last straw affront, breaking point, final stroke, indignity, last lick, limit, match in the powder barrel, overload, provocation, straw that broke the camel's back

Last Supper Communion, Eucharist, Holy Communion, Holy Sacrament, Lord's Supper, Sacrament

last word dernier cri, in thing, latest thing, new wrinkle; clincher, final say, point well taken, valid point, veto power

latchkey child unsupervised schoolchild

late bloomer naive person, sleeper, slowpoke, up-and-comer

latent heat heat of transformation, specific heat

lateral axis pitch axis

lateral pass lateral

lateral thinking association of ideas, idea association, intuition, intuitive reason, meditation, word association

latest thing current fashion, dernier cri, fad, in thing, latest wrinkle, newest wrinkle, the last word, the rage, the thing

Latter-day Saints Church of Jesus Christ of Latter-day Saints, Mormon Church, Mormons

laughing gas anesthetic, nitrous oxide

laugh track recorded laughter

launch pad Cape Canaveral, firing table, launching pad, launching platform, launching rack, rocket platform

launch vehicle launcher, launching rocket, multistage rocket

laundry list agenda, enumeration, shopping list, to-do list, want list, wish list

laundry room laundry, utility room

law enforcement peace enforcement, police, police force, policing

lawn bowling bowling on the green, bowls, green bowling, lawn bowls

lawn chair camp chair, folding chair, patio chair

lawn mower cutter, grass cutter, mower, push mower, riding mower, trimmer

lawn tennis court tennis, tennis

law of averages actuarial calculation, probability, statistical probability, stochastics, theory of probability

law of dominance law of independent assortment, law of segregation, Mendelism, Mendel's law, Mendel's rule

law of large numbers Bernoulli's law

Law of Moses Bible, Five Books of Moses, Jewish Law, Koran, Mosaic Law, Pentateuch, Qur'an, Ten Commandments, the Law, Torah

law of nations international law

law of parsimony economy of assumption, economy of means, Occam's razor, Ockham's razor

layaway plan credit plan, deferred payment plan, installment plan, layaway purchase, payment plan

lay eyes on catch sight of, notice, perceive, recognize, see, set eyes on, spot

laying on of hands Christian rite, faith healing, gift of healing, imposition

lay of the land how the land lies, lay, lie, orientation

lay one's cards on the table put one's cards on the table

lay to rest bury, entomb, hold a funeral, inter, lay in the grave, put six feet under; abolish, annul, bring to a close, bring to an end, cancel, invalidate, negate, nullify, put an end to, put to rest, revoke, undo, void

lazy eye amblyopia, defective eye, swivel eye

lazy Susan dumbwaiter, revolving tray, trolley

lead down the garden path deceive, lead astray, lead down the primrose path, mislead, seduce

leader board top competitors

leading edge cutting edge, forefront, front, front edge, point, state-of-the-art, van, vanguard

leading lady fat part, heroine, leading role, leading woman, lead role, starring role

leading light choice spirit, leader, luminary, master spirit, one in a million, sage, shining light, star, superstar

leading man fat part, hero, lead, leading role, lead role, starring role

leading question clue, feeler, fishing question, hint, indirect question, leader, poser, prompt, prompting, reminder, stumper, suggestion, trial balloon, trick question

lead poisoning saturnism

lead singer frontman, frontperson, frontwoman

leap of faith act of trusting, instance of trusting, trusting moment

leap year bissextile year, defective year, intercalary year

learn by heart commit to memory, learn by rote, learn verbatim, learn word for word, memorize

learned person bibliophile, bookman, bookwoman, brain, educated person, erudite person, intellectual, know-it-all, man or woman of learning, man or woman of letters, sage, savant, scholar, walking encyclopedia

learning disability LD, learning deficit, learning disorder, learning impairment

learn the ropes get the hang of, get the knack of, learn something new, learn the ins and outs

least common denominator LCD, lowest common denominator

least common multiple LCM, lowest common multiple

leave alone let alone, let well enough alone

leave in the lurch betray, leave holding the bag, let down, play one false

leave of absence busman's holiday, furlough, leave, liberty, sabbatical, shore leave

left-handed abusive, backhanded, degrading, insolent, insulting, offensive, sinister, sinistral, sinistrous

left-handed compliment aspersion, backhanded compliment, damning with faint praise, home truth, insult, no compliment, slap in the face, slight, snub, uncomplimentary remark

left wing left, leftism, leftist, left-winger, liberal, liberalism, on the left, progressive, progressiveness, progressivism, radical

legal action court case, lawsuit, legal proceedings, litigation, trial

legal age adultness, age of consent, drinking age, driving age, full age, full growth, legalis homo, majority, man's or woman's estate, maturation, mature age, matureness, voting age

legal eagle fixer, lawyer, shyster

legal guardian guardian, keeper

legal holiday bank holiday, business holiday, national holiday

legal tender circulating medium, cold cash, currency, hard cash, honest money, medium of exchange, money, sound currency, valid currency

Legionnaires' disease (or Legionnaire's) Legionella pneumophila

leisure suit zoot suit

lending library bookmobile, circulating library, county library, mobile library, municipal library, public library, school library, state library, town library

lethal gene lethal factor, lethal mutation

letter bomb package bomb

letter box letter drop, mailbox, mail drop, pillar-box, postbox

letter carrier bicycle messenger, courier, mail carrier, mailman, mailperson, mailwoman, postal carrier, postman, postwoman, special messenger

letter of credit banker's credit, circular note, credit memorandum, credit slip, LC, lettre de créance

letter of the law constitutionality, due process, form of law

leveling rod leveling pole, leveling staff

level playing field equal rights, equity, justice, proportion, symmetry

leveraged buyout buyout, LBO, takeover

liberal arts general education, history, language, liberal studies, literature, mathematics, philosophy, science, trivium and quadrivium

liberty cap Phrygian cap

library science cybrarian services, information science, librarianship, library and information services, library and information studies, library services

license plate number plate, vanity plate

lick and a promise Band-Aid™, cosmetic measure, short measure, superficial effort, wash

lie detector polygraph, polygraph machine, psychogalvanic skin response, psychogalvanometer

life-and-death all-important, consequential, critical, crucial, earthshaking, earth-shattering, essential, important, indispensable, life-or-death, of vital importance, vital, vitally important

life and death emergency, heavy scene, necessity, need, no laughing matter

life belt buoy, life preserver

life cycle biological clock, biorhythm, circuition, life process, wheel of life

life expectancy all one's natural life, expectation of life, life cycle, life's duration, life span, lifetime, longevity, period of existence

life force brio, élan vital, joie de vivre, life, spirit, vital force, vitality, vital principle

life history bio, biography, curriculum vitae, CV, life story, résumé

life instinct Eros, id, libido, pleasure principle, primitive self, sexual urge

life insurance credit life insurance

life jacket buoy, cork jacket, flotation device, life belt, lifeline, life net, life preserver, life vest, Mae West, swimmies

life list bird-watcher list

life of Riley bed of roses, clover, easy street, Fat City, gravy train, hog heaven, lap of luxury, life of ease, luxury, the good life, velvet

life of the party comic, cutup, fun maker, funnyman, humorist, jokester, life

life peer aristocrat, blue blood, Brahman, hereditary peer, person of rank, silk stocking, swell, upper-cruster

life preserver buoy, cork jacket, flotation device, life belt, life jacket, lifeline, life net, life vest, Mae West, swimmies

life science animal biology, anthropology, biological science, biology, bioscience, botany, ecology, environmental science, medicine, science of life, study of living things, zoology

life span life cycle, life expectancy, lifetime

life-threatening capital, dangerous, deadly, hazardous, mortal, threatening, touch and go, unsafe

lift the curtain on disclose, make public

light being discarnate being, disembodied being, immaterial being, saint, spirit guide

light breeze fresh breeze, gentle breeze

light chatter banter, persiflage

light-emitting diode LED, photoemission

light meter actinometer, ASA scale, exposure meter, photometer, radiometer, Scheiner scale

lightning bug candle fly, fire beetle, firefly, fireworm, glowworm, lampyrid, lantern fly, Noctiluca

lightning rod ground, lightning arrester, lightning conductor

light pen absolute pointing device, electronic stylus, light stylus

light quantum phonon, photon, quantum

light show phantasmagoria, play of light, shifting scene, son et lumière, sound-and-light show

light-year astronomical unit

like-minded agreeing, compatible, in accord, in agreement, of like mind, of one mind, of the same mind, similar, together, unanimous, united

limited edition special edition

limited war localized war, small war

linear accelerator linac, microwave linear accelerator, synchrotron

linear measure length, linear dimension, long measure, measurement of length, metrology, micrometry

linear momentum momentum

line drawing black-and-white, delineation, drawing, illustration, pen-and-ink, pencil drawing, picture, sketch

line drive clothesline, liner, line shot, rope

line engraving black-line engraving, engraving, halftone, plate engraving

line-item veto budget-item veto, budget-line veto, item veto

line of credit borrowing capacity, borrowing limit, credit line

line of demarcation bisector, boundary, divider, halfway mark, partition

line of duty assignment, call of duty, duties and responsibilities, workload

line of scrimmage flat, imaginary line, line, LOS, scrimmage line

line of sight beeline, line of vision, optical axis, sight line, straight shot, unobstructed path, view, visible horizon

line of work business, calling, career, department, employment, field, job, life's work, line, line of business, occupation, practice, profession, pursuit, trade, vocation, walk of life, work

line one's pockets clean up, coin money, feather one's nest, fill one's pockets, get rich, have one's ship come in, have the golden touch, make a bundle, make a fortune, make a mint, make a wad, make money, put money in one's pocket, strike it rich

line squall squall, squall line, storm, tempest, tropical storm, wind-shift line

linguistic atlas dialect atlas, isogloss

linoleum cut linecut

lint screen lint trap

lion's share advantage, better part, biggest slice of the cake, body, bulk, chief part, gist, main part, mass, meat, most

lip balm Chap Stick™

lip service empty talk, hollow words, hypocrisy, hypocritical respect, insincerity, jive, lie, lip devotion, lip homage, lip praise, lip reverence, lip worship, mouth honor, mouthing, sham, smooth talk, sweet talk, tokenism, tongue in cheek, unctuousness

liqueur glass brandy balloon, brandy snifter, cordial glass, highball glass, martini glass, pony, rocks glass, tumbler, wineglass

liquid assets assets, available means, available resources, balance, black-ink items, capital, cash flow, estate and effects, financial resources, means, pluses, stock in trade, wealth

liquid measure British imperial liquid measure, cup, gallon, gill, pint, quart, US liquid measure {compare *dry measure*}

list price market price, retail price, sale price, selling price, standard price, sticker price

list server LISTSERV, mailing list manager

litmus paper indicator, reagent, testing agent

litmus test acid test, base test, test with single indicator

little finger minimus, pinkie

little people common people, laborers, small businesspeople, small merchants, the unremarkable; dwarfs, midgets; small children; dwarfs, elfenfolk, elves, fairies, fairyfolk, imaginary beings, leprechauns

little theater community theater

little woman ball and chain, helpmate, old lady

liver spot lentigo

live together cohabit, live as man and wife, set up house together, share bed and board

live wire danger, electrical wire

living death death in life, fate worse than death, hell, hell on earth, purgatory, suffering

living room best room, common room, drawing room, foreroom, front room, LR, parlor, parlour, salon, sitting room, withdrawing room

living wage adequate income, competence, income, minimum wage

living will last will and testament

loaded dice crooked dice, false dice, unfair advantage

loaded question catch, cross-question, trick question

load line legal limit, load waterline, Plimsoll line, Plimsoll mark

loan shark moneylender, shylock, Shylock, usurer

loan translation borrowing, calque

loaves and fishes milk and honey

local area network communications network, computer network, LAN, workgroup computing

local color ambience, color, evocation, feel, note, regional character, regional detail, sense of place, vibes

local government city government, municipality, town government

local time apparent time, correct time, exact time, right time, true time

lock horns clash, collide, come to grips, contend, grapple, meet head-on

locking pliers Vise-Grips™

lock nut self-locking nut

lock, stock and barrel bag and baggage, inventory, provisions, stores, supplies, whole

loco disease loco, locoism

lodging house rooming house

logical positivism empiricism, logical empiricism, naturalism, positive philosophy, positivism

logic bomb computer virus, computer worm, electronic virus, logic error, phantom bug, Trojan horse

lone wolf hermit, independent, individualist, lone hand, loner, nonconformist, odd man out, outsider, pariah, rogue elephant, separatist, solitary

long dozen baker's dozen, thirteen

long face black look, dejected look, face as long as a fiddle, frown, gloom, glumness, hangdog look, sullen face, sullen look

long green big money, gigabucks, mint, nice hunk of change, packet, paper money, serious money

long haul hard labor, hard way, hard work, interminability, labor, long distance, long period of time, long wait, uphill work

long in the tooth aging, getting on, getting up in years, gray-haired, senescent, white-haired

long johns flannels, long underwear, thermals, thermal underwear, woolens

long jump broad jump, running broad jump, standing broad jump

long-nose pliers needle-nose pliers

long run distant future, long duration, long haul, long period, long term, remote future, whole

long shot chance hit, fluke, long odds, lucky shot, one in a million, outside chance, poor bed

long-standing deeply rooted, fixed, long-established, long-lasting, long-lived, permanent, rooted, time-honored, traditional

long suit forte, good points, likable trait, métier, redeeming feature, redeeming quality, specialty, strength, strong point, strong suit

long-winded dragged-out, drawn-out, endless, lengthened, loquacious, overlong, prolix, protracted, rambling, talkative, tedious, verbose, voluble, wordy

look-alike carbon copy, clone, dead ringer, double, duplicate, mirror image, spitting image, twin

looking back hindsight, reexamination, reflection, remembering, reminiscence, retrospect

loony bin bedlam, booby hatch, bughouse, funny farm, insane asylum, laughing academy, lunatic asylum, madhouse, mental health institution, mental hospital, mental institution, nuthouse, padded cell, psychiatric hospital, psychiatric ward, psycho ward, rubber room, sanatorium, sanitarium, snake pit

loose cannon powder keg, time bomb, unpredictable person

loose end job half-done, noncompletion, unresolved problem, work undone

loose-leaf binder spiral notebook, trapper

loose-leaf paper holed paper

loose talk blue story, double entendre, impure talk, locker-room humor

Lord's Prayer Our Father, Paternoster

Lord's Supper Communion, Eucharist, Holy Communion, Holy Sacrament, intinction, Last Supper, Sacrament

lose face give in, have egg on one's face, stultify oneself

lose ground fall away, fall farther behind, run out of gas, slump

lose one's mind crack up, flip, flip out, go bananas, go crazy, go insane, go nuts, lose one's marbles, lose one's reason, lose one's senses, lose one's wits

lose one's shirt fail at business, make a bad investment

lose one's temper become irate, blow one's top, blow up, boil over

loss leader bargain, feature, lead item, special

lost soul âme damnée, backslider, damned, fallen angel, lost sheep, recidivist, sinner

lotus position cross-legged sitting, half lotus

Lou Gehrig's disease amyotrophic lateral sclerosis

lounge car club car

lounge lizard cadger, freeloader, idle man, moocher, social parasite, sponger

love affair adultery, affair, affaire de coeur, affair of the heart, amour, courtship, dalliance, entanglement, fling, flirtation, forbidden love, hanky-panky, illicit love, infidelity,

intrigue, involvement, liaison, relationship, romance, romantic affair, seduction, tryst
love apple tomato
love child bar sinister, bastard, bastardy, by-blow, child born out of wedlock, fruit of adultery, illegitimate child, natural child, nullius filius, spurious offspring, whoreson
love feast agape, communion, ritual act
love handles fat, flab, middle-age spread, spare tire
love knot badge of loyalty, lover's knot, rosette, true lovers' knot, truelove knot
love life sex life
love nest abode of love, assignation house, bower, bower of bliss, lovers' lane, meeting place, place of assignation, trysting place
love potion aphrodisiac, love philter, magic instrument, magic potion, philter, stimulant, Viagra™
love seat courting chair, two-seater
loving cup cup, pot, trophy
low blood pressure hypotension
low blow insult, unscrupulous attack
low comedy burlesque, horseplay, light comedy, slapstick
low country lowland
lower chamber lower house
lower class commonalty, hoi polloi, lower orders, lower ranks, lowlife, masses, other half, plebeians, plebs, proletariat, rank and file, working class, working people
lower criticism critical study
lowest common denominator everyman, Joe Blow; least common denominator
low frequency LF, lower frequency, very low frequency, VLF
low-key mellow, quiet, restrained, subdued, subtle, toned down, understated
low profile inconspicuousness, latency, low key, low visibility, reluctance, reticence, secrecy, semivisibility
low relief bas-relief, basso-relievo, basso-rilievo, cavo-relievo, cavo-rilievo, rilievo stiacciato, sunk relief
low tide dead low tide, dead low water, ebb tide, low ebb, low water, mean low water
lucky break blessing, bonanza, break, fluke, good break, jackpot, luck of the draw, luck of the Irish, lucky strike, mere luck, stroke of good fortune, stroke of luck

luggage rack roof rack

luminous flux candlepower, flux, intensity, luminous intensity, luminous power

lunar eclipse eclipse of the moon

lunar month lunation, synodic month

lunar rock moon rock

lunar year synodic year

lunatic fringe aficionados, energumen, extremists, fanatical group, fanaticos, fanatics, nuts, nympholepts, zealots

lunch counter cafeteria, canteen, deli, delicatessen, diner, dog wagon, drive-in restaurant, fast-food restaurant, hamburger stand, hot-dog stand, ice-cream parlor, quick-lunch counter, sandwich shop, snack bar

lunch meat bologna, cold cuts, cold meat, ham, luncheon meat, salami, turkey

luxury items ego goods, frills, luxury articles, nonessentials

lynch law criminal syndicalism, gang rule, kangaroo court, mob law, mobocracy, mob rule, ochlocracy, reign of terror, syndicalism

Mm

Ma Bell AT&T

macaronic verse cento, fescennine verse, Hudibrastic verse, macaronicism, macaronics, nonsense verse

machine gun Gatling gun, MG, mitrailleuse, submachine gun, tommy gun, Uzi™

machine language assembler, assembly language, machine code, programming language

machine screw machine bolt

machine tool borer, broaching machine, drill, facing machine, grinder, lathe, mill, planer, precision tool, press drill, saw, shaper, tapping machine, threading machine

Mach number Mach, Mach one, Mach two, sonic speed, speed of sound

mad cow disease loco disease

made-up concocted, contrived, cooked-up, dreamed-up, fabricated, fictional, fictitious, invented, manufactured, trumped-up

mad money contingency money, petty cash, pin money, pocket money, small change, spending money

magic bullet miracle drug, wonder drug

magic carpet flying carpet

magic lantern film projector, overhead projector, projector, slide projector, stereopticon

magic spell abracadabra, chant, conjuration, hex, hocus-pocus, incantation, jinx, magic charm, magic formula, magic words, mumbo jumbo

magic wand fairy wand, wand, wish-bringer, wish-giver

magna cum laude honors, with great praise, with high honors

magnetic disk diskette, floppy disk, hard disk, hard drive, magnetic drum, magnetic tape, magnetic tape unit, magneto-optic disk, optical disk, primary storage

magnetic equator aclinic line

magnetic field electromagnetic field, magnetic field of currents

magnetic flux gilbert, maxwell, weber

magnetic flux density gauss, magnetic induction, magnetic intensity, oersted

magnetic needle compass needle, direction finder, indicator, needle

magnetic north compass point, magnetic pole, MN

magnetic pickup cartridge, magnetic cartridge, pickup

magnetic resonance imaging diagnostic radiology, MRI, MRI scan, scanning

magnetic storm electrical storm, geomagnetic storm

magnetic tape cassette, eight-track, magnetic drum, magnetic tape unit, mag tape

magnetomotive force magnetomotivity, mmf

magnifying glass eyeglass, hand lens, lens, loupe

magnum opus chef d'oeuvre, crowning achievement, greatest single work, great work, jewel, major work, masterpiece, masterstroke, masterwork, monumental work, pièce de résistance, showpiece, tour de force

maiden name family name, surname

mail bomb letter bomb, package bomb

mail carrier letter carrier, mailman, postal worker, postman, postwoman

mail drop letter box, letter drop, mailbox, postbox

mailed fist big stick, brute force, iron hand, military threat

mailing label address label

mailing list distribution list

mail order catalog buying, shopping by mail, teleordering, teleshopping

main dish entrée, main course, pièce de résistance

main drag main road, main street, principal street

main memory main storage, main store, primary storage

main squeeze honey, lover, mate, spouse, sweetie

Main Street center city, city center, principal street, urban center

maître d'hôtel headwaiter, maître d', majordomo

majority leader floor leader

major league big league, bigs, big time, majors

major orders apostolic orders, holy orders

major party political party

major prophet Ezekiel, Isaiah, Jeremiah

make a mistake blow it, blunder, err, goof, miscalculate, misconstrue, misestimate, misjudge, misread, misstep, misunderstand, muff, slip up

make-believe dream, fantasy, fiction, figment of the imagination, imagination, invention, pretending

make believe bluff, fake, feign, let on like, make a show of, make as if, playact, play the part, pretend

make concessions accommodate, agree, bargain, compromise, find a happy medium, find the middle ground, give and take, go fifty-fifty, make a deal, meet halfway, reach an agreement, settle, split the difference, strike a deal, trade off

make fun of burlesque, deride, heckle, kid, lampoon, make sport of, mock, parody, poke fun at, ridicule, satirize, tease

make love be intimate, breed, copulate, fool around, fornicate, fuck, go all the way, go to bed with, have sex, have sexual intercourse, have sexual relations, lay, make out, mate, procreate, screw, sleep together

make restitution atone, compensate, indemnify, make amends, make good, pay back, pay damages, recompense, refund, reimburse, repay, square

make the cut cut the mustard, hack it, make it, make the grade

make worse add insult to injury, aggravate, exacerbate, fan the flames, intensify, irritate, rub salt into the wound, twist the knife in the wound, worsen

male alto countertenor

male chauvinist bigot, chauvinist, female chauvinist, jingoist, male chauvinist pig, manist, masculist, MCP, misanthrope, racist, sexist, supremacist

male chicken chanticleer, rooster

male pattern baldness alopecia, baldness, hair loss, male pattern hair loss, MPB

malice aforethought by design, deliberate malice, full intent, in cold blood, malice prepense, with intent

malpractice insurance physician liability

malted milk malt, malted, milk shake

malt liquor ale, beer, John Barleycorn

mama's boy baby, big baby, crybaby, gutless wonder, lightweight, Milquetoast, mollycoddle, mother's boy, mother's darling, namby-pamby, pansy, sissy, softy, teacher's pet

man-about-town citizen of the world, city slicker, cosmopolitan, fashionable man, man of the world, mondain, mondaine, sophisticate

management information system MIS

managing editor editorial director, editor in chief, executive editor, senior editor, supervising editor

man and wife bride and groom, cohabitants, husband and wife, man and woman, married couple, Mr. and Mrs., wedded pair

mandarin collar banded collar, stand-up collar

man Friday assistant, gal Friday, girl Friday, right arm, right-hand man, second self

manic depression bipolar disorder, clinical depression, psychotic

manifest destiny colonialism, expansionism, imperialism, neocolonialism

manila folder file folder, manila paper

man in the street average Joe, everyman, John Doe, Mr. Average, ordinary citizen

man-made artificial, ersatz, fabricated, fake, imitation, manufactured, substitute, synthetic, unauthentic, unnatural

manna from heaven blessing, boon, gift from on high, godsend, loaves and fishes, manna

manner born blue-blooded, highborn

man of God clergyman, man of the cloth, minister, reverend, servant of God, shepherd, sky pilot, woman of God

man of letters belletrist, brain, educated person, intellectual, literary craftsman, literary scholar, litterateur, man of learning, savant, scholar, walking encyclopedia, wordsmith

man of means baron, fat cat, magnate, man of wealth, moneyed man, Mr. Moneybags, rich person, wealthy individual, wealthy person, woman of means

man of straw cipher, figurehead, insubstantial thing, jackstraw, nobody, nonentity, nonperson

man of the cloth clergyman

man of the house father, goodman, husband, lord and master, master of the house, paterfamilias, patriarch, provider

manor house estate, hall, main house, manor, mansion, palatial residence, stately home

manual alphabet American

Sign Language, dactylology, deaf-and-dumb alphabet, finger alphabet, sign language

manual labor common labor, handiwork, handwork, manual work, physical work, sweat of one's brow, unskilled labor, unskilled work

marching orders boot, bounce, chuck, drumming out, elbow, gate, heave-ho, orders to move on, pink slip, sack, walking papers

Mardi Gras carnival, Carnival, celebration, festival, Pancake Day, parade, revels, Shrove Tuesday

mare's nest can of worms, dog's breakfast, gallimaufry, hash, mess, patchwork, rat's nest, salmagundi

marine architecture underwater architecture

mariner's compass pyxis

maritime law admiralty law

market basket grocery cart

market price flash price, list price, quoted price, retail price, selling price, standard price

market research census, consumer research, inquiry, market survey, opinion research, poll, public opinion research, statistical study

mark time abide, bide, bide one's time, cool one's heels, pass time, queue up, tread water, wait, wait around

marriage ceremony betrothal, wedding, wedding bells

marriage of convenience arranged marriage, arranged match, mariage blanc, mariage de convenance

marsh gas methane, poison gas, swamp gas

marshmallow cream Marshmallow Fluff™

martello tower column, martello, round tower

martial arts aikido, judo, jujitsu, karate, kendo, kick boxing, kung fu, sumo wrestling, tae kwon do, t'ai chi, wrestling

martial law army rule, imperium in imperio, iron rule, military government, rule of the sword, stratocracy, suspension of civil rights

Mary Jane grass, hemp, marijuana, pot, reefer, weed

masked ball bal costumé, bal masqué, mask, masque, masquerade, masquerade ball

mason jar canning jar

massage parlor bawdy house, bordello, brothel, cathouse, den of vice, house of ill fame, house of ill repute, house of prostitution, joy house, whorehouse

mass-energy equation mass-energy equivalence

mass media broadcasting, communications industry, electronic media, information media, media, press, radio, television

mass meeting demonstration, gathering, meet, protest meeting, rally, sit-in

mass murder bloodbath, butchering, carnage, ethnic cleansing, extermination, final solution, genocide, holocaust, massacre, mass destruction, mass execution, mass extermination, mass killing, pogram, race extermination, race murder, Roman holiday, slaughter, wholesale murder

mass noun count noun

mass number atomic mass, atomic number, atomic volume, atomic weight, nucleon number

mass production assembly-line production, automation, productiveness, reduplication, volume production

mass spectrometer mass spectrograph

mass transit public transportation

master bedroom bedchamber, bedroom, boudoir, main bedroom, sleeping chamber

master craftsman master, master carpenter, master workman

master key opener, passe-partout, passkey, skeleton key

master of arts A.M., artium magister, M.A., master, master's degree

master of ceremonies compere, emcee, host, marshal, MC, mistress of ceremonies, moderator, toastmaster

master of science master, master's degree, M.S., S.M.

master plan approach, big picture, blueprint, detailed plan, five-year plan, map, plan, plan of attack, prototype, schedule, scheme

matador pants toreador pants

matched siding drop siding

match point game point, set point

maternity clothes maternity wear, mother-to-be wear, pregnancy clothes

mathematical logic logistic, symbolic logic

matinee idol box office gold, favorite, film star, leading lady, leading man, star, star of stage and screen, superstar, tin god

matter of course logical outcome, natural outcome, nothing to wonder at, rule, usual, usual course, usual practice

matter-of-fact businesslike, direct, down-to-earth, dry, dull, literal, literal-minded, nonchalant, pedestrian, plain, plain-speaking, prosaic, sober, straightforward, straight-thinking, unemotional, unexciting, unimaginative, unimpassioned, unromantic

matter of life and death case of emergency, case of need, emergency, exigency, grave affair, matter of necessity, necessitude, urgency, vitalness

matzo ball dumpling, knaydlach, matzo

Maundy Thursday Holy Thursday

mazel tov best wishes, congratulations

mea culpa acknowledgment of error, confession, my fault, penance, repentance

meal ticket cash cow, financial support, grubstaker, patron, staker, supporter

mean business be in earnest, be resolute, mean what one says, stick at nothing

mean solar day mean solar time, mean time, twenty-four-hour day

mean square root mean square

measure for measure amends, atonement, compensation, eye for an eye, indemnification, indemnity, lex talionis, meed, payback, quid pro quo, reciprocity, recompense, rectification, reparation, restitution, retaliation, tit for tat, tooth for a tooth

measuring stick barometer, benchmark, criterion, frame of reference, gauge, guide, guideline, referral, standard, standard of comparison, test, touchstone, yardstick

meat and potatoes ball game, basis, bottom line, essence, fundamental parts, gist, gravamen, guts, name of the game, nitty-gritty, nuts and bolts, score, substance

meat-eating cannibalistic, carnivorous, flesh-eating, omophagous, predacious

meat hooks fists, hands

meat market family butcher

mechanical advantage fulcrumage, leverage, mechanical power

mechanical drawing computer graphics, drafting, draftsmanship, graphic arts, graphics, technical drawing

mechanical pencil lead holder

media center library, reference center

media event media happening, nonevent, photo op, photo opportunity, pseudoevent

median strip boulevard, boulevard strip, center strip, divider, island, jersey barrier, medial strip, median, meridian, neutral ground

medical examination checkup, health examination, physical, physical examination, yearly checkup

medical examiner coroner, ME, mortality committee, pathologist

medicine ball conditioning ball, exercise ball

medicine man faith healer, healer, idolater, isangoma, mundunugu, shaman, shamanist, sorcerer, witch doctor

medium frequency MF

medium of exchange cash, circulating medium, currency, legal tender, money

meet halfway come to terms, compromise, forgive and forget, settle one's differences, shake hands

meeting of the minds agreement, concord

meeting place confluence, focus, gathering place, meeting house, meeting point, rendezvous

meeting room boardroom, conference room

meet one's maker bite the dust, buy the farm, cash in one's chips, cease living, croak, die, expire, go to glory, go to one's reward, kick the bucket, pass away, pass on, succumb

meet one's Waterloo get the worst of it, lose, lose out

melting point boiling point, ebullition, flash point

melting pot America, conflation, ethnic diversity, fusion, multiculturalism, multiculturism, pluralism, United States; crucible

memento mori death's-head, memoirs, memorial, memories, reminder of death, reminder of human failure, reminder of mortality, skull

Memorial Day Decoration Day, May 30

memory cell bit

memory trace engram, traumatic memory, traumatic trace

Mendel's law law of independent assortment, law of segregation, Mendelian, Mendelism

mend fences improve poor relations, make peace

men's room little boys' room, men's, restroom

mental age intelligence quotient, IQ, MA, mental ratio

mental health mental hygiene

mental hospital mental institution, psychiatric hospital, psychiatric unit, psychiatric ward, psychopathic hospital, sanitarium

mental illness craziness, delusions, depression, derangement, disturbed mind, emotional disorder, insanity, loss of mind, lunacy, madness, mania, mental disease, mental disorder, mental sickness, nervous breakdown, nervous disorder, neurosis, paranoia, personality disorder, phobia, psychopathy, psychosis, schizophrenia, sick mind, troubled mind, unbalanced mind, unsoundness of mind

mentally ill cracked, crazed, crazy, cuckoo, daft, demented, deranged, insane, loco, loony, lunatic, mad, not of sound mind, nuts, nutty, off one's rocker, out of one's mind, paranoid, psycho, psychopathic, psychotic, schizophrenic, touched, unbalanced

mental retardation amentia, brain damage, dementia, mental defect, mental deficiency, mental handicap, subnormality

mental state frame of mind, humor, mental processes, mindset, mood, morale, state of mind

merchant marine commercial ships, marine, mercantile marine, merchant fleet, merchant navy, naval militia, naval reserve, shipping line

merchant prince merchant venturer

merci beaucoup je vous remercie beaucoup, many thanks, thank you very much

mercury-vapor lamp mercury-vapor light, neon light, sodium lamp, streetlight

mercy killing assisted suicide, euthanasia, negative euthanasia, passive euthanasia, playing God, pulling the plug

mescal button peyote

Mesozoic era Cretaceous period, Jurassic period, Triassic period

mess jacket monkey jacket, shell jacket

mess kit cooking kit

metamorphic rock gneiss, marble, multiform rock, schist

meter maid traffic control, traffic officer

method acting character acting, playacting, the Method

metric system metrication, metrology, weights and measures

Mexican standoff collision, cross-purposes, dead heat, deadlock, even money, impasse, showdown, standoff, wash

Mexican wave coordinated crowd wave, successive crowd wave

Mickey Finn knockout drops, mickey, somnifacient, tranquilizer

Mickey Mouse chintzy, glitzy, in poor taste, rinky-dink, tacky

microwave oven microcooker, microwave

microwave-safe microwaveable

Midas touch golden touch, philosophers' stone

middle age middle years, midlife, the wrong side of forty

Middle Ages Dark Ages, medieval times

Middle America bourgeoisie, silent majority, subtopia, suburbia, the burbs

middle class bourgeois, bourgeoisie, burgherdom, common people, educated class, hoi polloi, Middle America, middle-income group, middle order, ordinary people, plain folks, proletariat, working class

middle distance equidistance, middistance, middle ground

middle ear tympanic cavity, tympanum

middle ground center, centrism, golden mean, happy medium, interface, meeting ground, middle of the road, neutral ground, neutral territory, straddling the fence

middle-of-the-road bland, centrist, fair, inoffensive, mild, moderate, neutral, noncommittal, nonpartisan, reasonable, temperate

middle of the road center, centrism, middle course, middle ground, middle way, midway, moderate position, via media

middle school intermediate school, junior high, junior high school, secondary school

middle term intermedium, medium, serial place

midlife crisis change of life, climacteric, menopause, midlife depression

migrant worker agricultural laborer, agricultural worker, casual laborer, day laborer, emigrant, émigré, farm laborer, farm worker, migrant, rover

military academy general staff school, military college, military school, naval academy, officer candidate school, service academy, service school

military affairs art of war, military arts, military operations, military science, military strategy, military tactics, rules of war, science of war

military hospital base hospital, field hospital

military-industrial complex arms industry, arms maker

military police constabulary, gendarmerie, MP

military post bastion, bunker, command post, fort, fortress, garrison, post, stronghold, troop station

military school military academy

military store post exchange, PX

military weapons engines of war, military weaponry, weapons of mass destruction

milk shake cabinet, frappé, shake, velvet

milk sugar lactose

milk tooth baby tooth, deciduous tooth, primary tooth

Millenial Church Shakers, United Society of Believers in Christ's Second Appearing

mime show pantomime

mind-blowing amazing, breathtaking, eye-opening, hallucinatory, hallucinogenic, heart-stirring, impressive, mind-altering, mind-bending, mind-expanding, psychedelic, staggering, striking, stunning

mind-boggling amazing, astonishing, astounding, baffling, bewildering, confounding, eye-opening, fantastic, incomprehensible, inconceivable, mysterious, numbing, overwhelming, perplexing, puzzling, spectacular, startling, stunning, surprising, unexplainable, unfathomable, unheard of, unknown, unthinkable

mind mapping thought association, word association

mind reader clairvoyant, mentalist, mental telepath, psychic, telepath, thought reader

mind reading mental telepathy, telepathic transmission, telepathy, thought transference

mind's eye eye of the mind, fancy, fantasy, imagination, inward eye, mirror of the mind, tablets of the memory, visualization

mineral spring hot spring, spa, warm spring, watering place

mineral water carbonated water, designer water, spring water, tonic water

mineral wax ozokerite

mineral wool rock wool

miner's lung black lung, pneumoconiosis

miniature golf mini golf, par-three golf, peewee golf, putting

minimal art ABC art, conceptual art, minimalism, reductivism, rejective art

minimum wage base pay, living wage, lowest wage

minor detail formality, minor point, technicality

minor league bushes, bush league, junior league, junior varsity, minors, triple-A

minor orders holy orders, orders

minor party third party

minor scale harmonic minor, melodic minor, natural minor

minstrel show minstrel, raree-show, review, revue

minute hand needle

miracle drug panacea, synthetic drug, wonder drug

Miranda rule reading of rights, reading of rules

mirror image carbon copy, copy, dead ringer, doppelgänger, eidetic image, exact counterpart, exact duplicate, facsimile, living image, living picture, look-alike, spit and image, spitting image, very image

MIRV multiple independently targetable reentry vehicle, multiple independently targeted reentry vehicle

missing link broken thread, lost connection, omission; prehuman, protohuman

Mister Nice Guy good egg, good guy, living doll, Mr. Nice Guy, nice guy

mitigating circumstances diminished responsibility, extenuating circumstances, palliative, partial excuse, qualification

mitral valve bicuspid valve, left atrioventricular valve

mixed bag all sorts, assortment, conglomerate, hodgepodge, jumble, medley, mélange, miscellany, mishmash, montage, odds and ends, patchwork, potpourri, smorgasbord, sundries

mixed blessing double-edged sword, doubtful advantage, pis aller, two-edged sword

mixed drink alcoholic drink, cocktail, concoction, punch, spritzer

mixed marriage interfaith marriage, intermarriage, interracial marriage, miscegenation

mixed media multimedia

mixed-up befuddled, confounded, confused, disorganized, disorientated, disoriented, flustered, foggy, fouled up, jumbled, lost, muddled, perplexed, puzzled, rattled, ruffled, scatterbrained, scramble-brained

mobile home camper, house trailer, motor home, recreational vehicle, RV, trail car, trailer

mobile phone car phone, cell phone, cell telephone, cellular phone, digital phone, mobile telephone, radiotelephone

modal auxiliary auxiliary, auxiliary verb, can, may, must, ought, shall, should, will, would

modeling clay clay, plasticine, Plasticine™, Play-Doh™, sculptor's wax

modus operandi approach, manner of working, means, method, method of functioning, method of operating, MO, modus vivendi, procedure, process, system, technique

modus vivendi lifestyle, manner of living, way of life

Mohs' scale mineral classification

Molly™ bolt toggle bolt

Molotov cocktail homemade bomb, makeshift bomb

moment of truth charged moment, climax, critical moment, crucial moment, crunch, decisive moment, defining moment, fated moment, fateful moment, kairos, kairotic moment, pregnant moment, turning point, when push comes to shove

mommy track householding, housekeeping

Monday-morning quarterback armchair quarterback, hindsight critic

monetary award monetary gift
monetary unit monetary denomination
money box safe, strongbox, vault
money market exchange, money market fund
monkey bars jungle gym
monkey business antics, buffoonery, clowning around, foolishness, hanky-panky, high jinks, hokeypokey, horseplay, misbehavior, mischief, monkeyshines, prank, shenanigans
monkey jacket mess jacket
monkey on one's back incubus, jones, Mighty Joe Young, Old Man of the Sea, onus
monkey wrench obstruction wrench, pipe wrench, spanner, Stillson™ wrench
Montezuma's revenge Aztec two-step, dysentery, flux, GI's, loose stool, runs, tourista, traveler's diarrhea, trots, turista
month of Sundays ages, blue moon, dog's age, eternity, indefinitely long period, lifetime, time immemorial, when pigs fly
moon blindness moon-blind, moo-neye
moot court mock court
moot point arguable point, debatable point, debating point, moot case, point at issue; irrelevant point
moral code code of conduct, ethicalness, ethics, good morals, ideology, morality, moral philosophy, morals, principles, standards, value system, values
moral fiber fortitude, good character, good conscience, honesty, incorruptibility, moral courage, moral excellence, morality, moral rectitude, moral virtue, scruples, strong-mindedness
moral philosophy ethical philosophy, ethics, moral science
more or less about, approximately, generally, in the ballpark, nearly, roughly, thereabouts
Mormon Church Church of Jesus Christ of Latter-day Saints, Latter-day Saints, Mormons
morning-after pill abortion pill, Brompton, Brompton's mixture, RU 486
morning dress dressing gown, formal dress, morning coat, robe de chambre, yukata
morning sickness nausea, vomiting

morning star daystar, Lucifer, Phosphor, Phosphorus, Venus

Morse code cryptanalysis, cryptography, Morse alphabet, telecommunication

mortal remains ashes, cadaver, corpse, dead body, dead man, relics, reliquiae, remains, stiff

mortal sin atrocity, cardinal sin, deadly sin, disgrace, unforgivable sin, venial sin, vice

mortise joint dovetail joint, miter joint

mother country homeland, motherland, native land, native soil, the old country

Mother Earth earth mother, Gaea, Gaia, Ge, Great Mother, Magna Mater, mother goddess, Tellus, Terra

mother lode abundant source, bonanza, El Dorado, gold mine, lode, main vein, pot of gold, rich lode, rich source

Mother Nature Dame Nature, Great Mother, Natura, Nature

Mother of God Blessed Virgin Mary, Madonna, Mater Dolorosa, Our Lady

mother superior abbess, ecclesiarch, holy mother, lady superior, prioress, reverend mother, superior, superioress

mother tongue first language, natal tongue, native language, native speech, native tongue, parent language, vernacular

mother wit common sense, faculties, innate common sense, innate intelligence, intellectual gifts, nous, senses, wits

motion picture cinema, film, flick, flicker, movie, moving picture, photodrama, photoplay, picture, picture show, talkie

motion sickness airsickness, car sickness, mal de mer, nausea, queasiness, seasickness, travel sickness, vomiting

motive power driving force, electromotive force, kinetic energy, locomotion, means of propulsion, motivity, prime mover, propulsion

mot juste aptness, right word at the right time, the right word

motley crew crowd, omnium-gatherum

motor home camper, camp trailer, caravan, house trailer, mobile home, recreational vehicle, RV, trailer

motor lodge auto court, motel, motor court, motor hotel, motor inn

motor scooter dirt bike, motorbike, motorcycle, scooter, scrambler, trail bike

motor torpedo boat gunboat, MTB

motor vehicle auto, automobile, bus, car, motorcar, motorized vehicle, truck, van, voiture

mountain bike mountain bicycle, off-road bicycle

mountain cat mountain lion

mountain climber alpinist, climber, mountaineer, rock climber, rock-jock

mountain climbing alpinism, bouldering, climbing, mountaineering, rock climbing, scaling

mountain dew bathtub gin, bootleg liquor, corn liquor, home brew, hooch, illegal liquor, moonshine, white lightning

mountain man backwoodsman, frontiersman, hinterlander, mountaineer, ridge runner

mountain oyster prairie oyster, testis

mountain range Alps, Andes, chain, cordillera, cordilleran belt, fold belt, Himalayas, massif, mountain chain, mountain system, range, Rockies, Rocky Mountains, sierra

mountain sickness altitude sickness

mouth organ French harp, harmonica, harmonicon, harp, kazoo, mouth bow, mouth harp, panpipe

mouth-to-mouth resuscitation artificial respiration, kiss of life

movable feast feast day

mover and shaker affluent, catalyst, doer, entrepreneur, go-getter, heavy hitter, heavyweight, leader, lightning rod, man of influence, palpable presence, pathfinder, player, presence, producer, spark plug, trailblazer, VIP, wheeler and dealer, whip

movie studio animation studio, back lot, dream factory, film studio, location, lot, motion-picture studio, sound stage

movie theater cinema, circuit theater, dream palace, drive-in movie, drive-in theater, film theater, fleapit, grind house, motion-picture theater, movie house, movie palace, multiplex, picture house, picture palace, picture show, picture theater, revival house

moving floor moving walkway, people mover

moving picture cinema, film, flick, motion picture, movie, picture, picture show, talkie

mud flap mud guard, splash guard

mud flat flat, marsh, tidal flat, wash, wetlands

muffin pan muffin tin

mug shot close-up, head shot, identification photo, identification photograph, mug, passport photo, police photograph

mulligan stew Irish stew, mulligan

multiple fruit aggregate fruit, composite fruit, fig, mulberry, pineapple

multiple personality alternating personality, dual personality, personality disorder, split personality

multiple sclerosis MS

multiplication sign raised dot, times sign

mumbo jumbo claptrap, double-talk, empty talk, gibberish, gobbledygook, hocus-pocus, hogwash, mere words, obscuration

mum's the word hold your tongue, hush, keep quiet, not another peep, say nothing, shut your mouth

municipal court city court

Murphy's Law axiom, humorous axiom

muscle spindle stretch receptor

muscular dystrophy Duchenne muscular dystrophy, MD

museum piece antique, classic, collector's item, collector's piece, curio, heirloom, masterpiece, old master, showpiece

mushroom cloud fallout, nuclear fallout, radioactive cloud

musical arrangement adaptation, composition, harmonization, musical notation, musical score, musical transcription, orchestration, score, setting, written music

musical chairs exchange, rearrangement, trade, trading

musical comedy comic opera, light opera, musical

musical saw viol

music box jukebox, musical box, orchestrina, orchestrion

music drama lyric drama

music hall amphitheater, auditorium, ballroom, concert hall, dance hall, hall, hippodrome, theater, variety theater, vaudeville theater

muster roll account, inventory, muster, roll call, roster

mutual friend friend of a friend, friend of the family, friend's friend

mutual fund bond fund, closed-end fund, investment fund, money market fund, no-load fund, open-end fund, stock fund

mutual understanding agreement, arrangement, compact, concord, consensus, contract, covenant, deal, entente, entente cordiale, good understanding, pact, rapport

Nn

nail down cinch, clinch, establish conclusively, lock in, pin down

nail file emery board, file

nail in the coffin deathblow, defeat, quietus

nail polish nail enamel

nail set nail punch

nail to a cross brutalize, burn at the stake, crucify, excruciate, hang, martyrize, persecute, put on the rack, put to death, torture

naked ape creature, flesh and blood, noble animal, ordinary clay

naked truth basic truth, honest truth, plain truth, straight truth, unqualified truth

namby-pamby baby, chicken, lightweight, mama's boy, milksop, mollycoddle, pansy, pantywaist, pushover, sissy, weakling, wimp, wuss, wussy

name day baptism day, birthday, red-letter day, special day

name of the game bottom line, chief thing, essence, main point, real issue, where it's at

nanny goat doe, female goat, nanny, she-goat

Napoleonic code civil code, Code Napoléon, penal code

narrow-minded biased, bigoted, closed-minded, illiberal, intolerant, myopic, nearsighted, one-sided, pigheaded, prejudiced, shortsighted, small-minded

national assembly assembly, chamber of deputies, congress, diet, federal assembly, general assembly, house of assembly, legislative assembly, parliament, soviet

national debt budget deficit, funded debt, government debt, public debt

national park national forest, national seashore, preserve, protected area, reservation, reserve

Native American American Indian, Amerind, Amerindian, Indian

native land birthplace, country of origin, fatherland, home, homeland, mother country, motherland, native soil, old country, old world, one's native soil, terra firma

natural environment domain, dwelling, habitat, home, home turf, native environment, natural element, natural surroundings, realm, stomping grounds

natural history anthropology, archaeology

naturalistic art lifelike art, realistic art, true-to-life art

natural language human language, lingua franca, NL, spoken language, tongue, written language

natural logarithm Napierian logarithm

natural number positive integer

natural resource mineral deposit, natural deposit, raw material, timber, water

natural science biology, chemistry, life sciences, physical science, physics, pure science, science of matter, social science

natural selection adaptation, artificial selection, biological evolution, Darwinism, evolution, law of the jungle, natural law, phylogeny, social Darwinism, social evolution, survival of the fittest, theory of evolution

natural theology physicotheology, revealed theology

nature worship druidism, naturism, plant worship, primitive religion, tree worship

nautical mile international nautical mile, knot, naut mi, NM, sea mile

naval architecture ship design

near miss close call, close shave, narrow escape, near hit, near thing, squeaker, tight squeeze

neck and neck close, deadlocked, drawn, nip and tuck, tied, too close to call

neck of the woods backyard, neighborhood, region, stamping ground, vicinage, vicinity

needle-nose pliers long-nose pliers

ne'er-do-well bum, do-nothing, failure, good-for-nothing, loafer, loser, scapegrace, slug, stiff, wastrel

negative attitude bad attitude, chip on one's shoulder, cynicism, defeatism, discouragement, gloomy outlook, hopelessness, lack of confidence, low spirits, negative thinking, negativism, pessimism

negative cash flow expenses greater than income

negative space air, white space

negotiable instrument bill, bill of exchange, commercial paper, negotiable paper, paper

neighborhood association home watch, neighborhood watch

neither here nor there beside the point, immaterial, impertinent, inapplicable, irrelevant, nonessential, not at issue, nothing to do with the case, off the subject, unessential

ne plus ultra extreme case, extremity, highest degree, highest point, limit, nth degree, perfection, ultimate, utmost, utmost extent, uttermost

nerve cell afferent neuron, sensory cell, sensory neuron

nerve center center of activity, command post, control center, epicenter, esoteric reality, ganglion, headquarters, hotbed, HQ, hub, inner reality, intrinsic reality, switchboard, vital center, vital principle

nerve gas asphyxiant, mustard gas, poison gas, tear gas, war gas

nervous breakdown burnout, clinical depression, collapse, crack-up, emotional collapse, nervous exhaustion, nervous prostration, neurasthenia, neurosis, shattered nerves

nervous Nellie a bundle of nerves, chicken, fraidy cat, nervous wreck, pantywaist, wimp, worrier, worrywart, wuss

nervous system central nervous system, nerve system, nerves, neurology, peripheral nervous system, sense organs, sensorium, sensory apparatus

nest egg backup, emergency funds, funds, investment, piggy bank, reserve, reserve fund, savings, savings account, sinking fund, something for a rainy day, something to fall back on, stash, stockpile, unexpended balance

net loss bottom line, deficit, diminishing returns, losses

net worth assets, available means, cash flow, means, pecuniary resources, resources, total assets, wherewithal, worth

neural network neural net, semantic net, semantic network

neutral ground center, gray area, happy medium, interface, meeting ground, middle ground, neutral territory

neutron bomb enhanced radiation bomb

never-never land cloud-cuckooland, Cockaigne, fantasyland, Fiddler's Green, Never Land

New Age new consciousness, new wave

New Age music ambient sound, fusion, grunge, new wave, punk rock

new blood fresh blood, new members, revitalizing force

New English Modern English

new kid on the block beginner, greenhorn, incomer, neophyte, new arrival, newcomer, new kid in town, nouveau arrive, nouvelle arrivée, novice, rookie, tenderfoot, tyro

new leaf clean slate, flip-flop, 180, reverse, U-turn

new moon crescent moon, wet moon

new morality sexual freedom, sexual revolution

news agency AP, news service, press agency, press association, Reuters, TASS, the press, wire service

news conference brief, briefing, press conference

news flash brief, bulletin, flash, newsbreak, news bulletin, news report, update

news gatherer newsmonger

newspaper article editorial, feature, newspaper account, notice, report, write-up

newspaper columnist commentator, editorialist, news analyst

news release communication, communiqué, dispatch, handout, press release

new wave new age, nouvelle vague

New World America, North America, Western Hemisphere

next of kin closest relative, heir, kinsman, near relative, relation, relative, sibling

nicad battery nickel-cadmium battery, rechargeable battery

nicotine addiction chain-smoking, heavy smoking, nicotinism, tobaccosis

night and day all the time, at all hours, continually, perpetually, round the clock

night blindness moon blindness, nyctalopia

night crawler angleworm, earthworm, fishworm, nightwalker

night letter overnight letter

night school evening school

night shift anchor watch, dogwatch, graveyard shift, lobster shift, swing shift, third shift

night table bedside table, nightstand

night terror bad dream, nightmare

night watch night patrol, sentry

night watchman Charley, lookout, security officer, sentry, watchman

nine days' wonder annus mirabilis, fifteen minutes of fame, flash in the pan, momentary success, nine day wonder, phenom, phenomenon, sensation, stunner, wonderment

900 number toll-call number, vanity number

nineteenth hole refreshment; cocktail lounge

nip and tuck abreast, deadlocked, drawn, level, neck and neck, parallel, tied, too close to call

nip in the bud abort, anticipate, cut off, cut short, put the kibosh on, stymie

nitrous oxide anesthetic, laughing gas

nitty-gritty bottom line, brass tacks, cold fact, core, essence, essential details, gist, hard fact, heart, heart of the matter, kernel, meat, meat and potatoes, name of the game, nuts and bolts, quintessence, reality, soul, substance, the facts, the name of the game

noble gas inert gas

noble savage child of nature, savage

no cigar close, no dice, refusal

no-fly zone forbidden ground, forbidden territory, no-man's-land

noise pollution contamination, environmental pollution, sound pollution

nom de guerre alias, anonym, assumed name, false name, fictitious name, pseudonym

nom de plume alias, allonym, ananym, anonym, assumed name, false name, fictitious name, pen name, professional name, pseudonym

nom de théâtre professional name, stage name

nominal wage minimum wage

nonaligned nation isolationist, neutralist nation, unaligned nation

nonce word invented word, neologism, new word, singleton

noncommissioned officer NCO, noncom

non compos mentis demented, deprived of one's wits, lunatic, non compos, not of sound mind, of unsound mind, unbalanced, unsound

nonstick surface Teflon™

nonvascular plant bryophyte

normal distribution Gaussian distribution

northern lights aurora, aurora borealis, aurora polaris, merry dancers, polar lights

North Star cynosure, guiding star, lodestar, Polaris, polar star, polestar

nose cone heat barrier, heat shield, thermal barrier, warhead

nose job cosmetic surgery, plastic surgery, rhinoplasty

Nosey Parker busybody, gossip, inquisitive person, meddler, Paul Pry, snoop, snooper, yenta

notary public commissioner for oaths, notary, NP

not-for-profit charitable, nonprofit, philanthropic

nothing to it a breeze, a snap, duck soup, easy, easy as ABC, easy as pie, effortless, piece of cake, simple

nouveau riche arriviste, newly rich, new money, nouveau arrive, nouveau roturier, parvenu, profiteer, self-made man, upstart

nouvelle cuisine contemporary French cooking, designer food, haute cuisine

nouvelle vague new wave

NOW account interest-bearing savings

now and then at times, every now and then, every once in a while, every so often, from time to time, intermittently, not often, now and again, occasionally, once and again, once in a while, once or twice, periodically, sometimes, sporadically

no-win situation conundrum, dilemma, double bind, knot, quandary

nuclear bomb A-bomb, atom bomb, atomic bomb, atomic warhead, fission bomb, H-bomb, hydrogen bomb, neutron bomb, nuclear arms, nuclear warhead, nuke, plutonium bomb, thermonuclear bomb

nuclear chemistry atomic theory, radiochemistry

nuclear energy atomic energy, atomic power, fission power, fusion power, nuclear power, thermonuclear energy, thermonuclear power

nuclear equation strong-force equation

nuclear family children, family, father, household, mother

nuclear fission atom chipping, atom smashing, atom splitting, fission, fission reaction, nucleonics, splitting

nuclear force strong force, strong interaction, strong nuclear force

nuclear fusion atomic fusion, cold fusion, fusion, fusion reaction, laser-induced fusion, thermonuclear fusion, thermonuclear reaction

nuclear magnetic resonance Mossbauer effect, NMR, nuclear resonance

nuclear membrane nuclear envelope

nuclear physics atomic physics, atomics, atomic science, atomistics, atomology, nucleonics, particle physics, quantum mechanics, quantum physics

nuclear reaction fission, fusion, radioactive decay, thermonuclear reaction

nuclear reactor atomic furnace, atomic pile, atomic reactor, breeder reactor, chain reactor, core reactor, fast breeder reactor, neutron factory, nuclear furnace, pile, plutonium reactor, reactor, reactor pile, uranium reactor

nuclear weapon atomic weapon, A-weapon, strategic nuclear weapon, tactical nuclear weapon, theater nuclear weapon, thermonuclear weapon, weapon of mass destruction

nuclear winter China Syndrome, fallout

null and void annulled, no longer law, null, nullified, of no effect, void

number cruncher accountant, actuary, bean counter, bookkeeper, calculator, certified public account, CPA, statistician

number one champion, hero, leader, master, numero uno, winner

number sign crisscross, pound sign

numbers pool Chinese lottery, number lottery, numbers, numbers game, numbers policy, numbers racket

numerical taxonomy taximetrics

nursery rhyme nursery tale

nursery school day care, day-care

center, day nursery, infant school, play group, play school, preschool

nursing home assisted-living facility, convalescent home, convalescent hospital, nursing home, old folks' home, old soldiers' home, rest home, retirement facility

nuts and bolts basics, innards, inner workings, no frills, no-nonsense, workings

Oo

objective correlative metaphor, symbol

object lesson concrete illustration, deterrent example, example, lesson, practical demonstration, proof, visible evidence, warning example

objet d'art artistic production, art object, artwork, collector's piece, composition, curio, design, knickknack, object of art, piece, piece of art, study, work of art

objet trouvé found art, found object

obstacle course training course

obstacle race hurdle race, slalom

Occam's razor law of parsimony, Ockham's razor, premise

occupational therapy physiotherapy

ocean liner cruise ship, floating hotel, floating palace, liner, luxury liner, ocean greyhound, passenger steamer

octane number octane rating

odd job chore, exercise, labor, piece of work, set task, stint, task

odd lot fractional lot

odd number impair

odds and ends assortment, bits and pieces, hodgepodge, knickknacks, leftovers, miscellany, mishmash, mixed bag, notions, novelties, oddments, patchwork, rags, refuse, remainder, remains, scraps, sundries

odds-on favorite best bet, chalk horse, favorite, front-runner, public choice, top horse

Oedipus complex narcissism, parent complex

off and on alternately, at irregular intervals, fluctuating, hardly, infrequently, intermittent, irregularly, not often, on and off, scarcely, sometimes, sporadically, vacillating, variable, very seldom, when the mood strikes

off base badly mistaken, off balance, offside, out of line

off-color dirty, gross, improper, inappropriate, indecent, lewd, offensive, racy, raunchy, risky, risqué, salty, spicy, suggestive, tasteless

off duty at liberty, on furlough, on holiday, on leave, on one's own time, on sabbatical, on vacation

off guard asleep, asleep at the switch, derelict, flat-footed, napping, negligent, not on the job, unalert, unguarded, unprepared, unready, unwatchful

office boy boy Friday, copyboy, errand boy, gofer, messenger boy, office girl, page

officer of the day OD, orderly officer

officer of the law constable, cop, deputy, detective, flatfoot, fuzz, law enforcement agent, lawman, lawwoman, marshal, meter maid, military police, mounted police officer, MP, patrolman, patrolwoman, peace officer, policeman, police officer, policewoman, sheriff, the man, traffic officer, trooper

off-key flat, inharmonious, off-pitch, off-tone, out of pitch, out of tune, sour, unmusical, untuned

off-limits banned, barred, forbidden, illegal, illicit, not allowed, not permitted, outlawed, out of bounds, prohibited, restricted, taboo, unlawful

off-line disconnected, logged off

off the beaten path not well-known, offbeat, off the beaten track, out of the ordinary, unfrequented, unusual, unvisited

off-the-cuff ad-lib, by ear, extemporaneously, impromptu, improv, improvised, makeshift, offhand, off the hip, off the top of one's head, spur of the moment, unrehearsed

off-the-record between us, confidential, eyes only, for no other ears, in confidence, not for publication, not for the record, not to be quoted, on the QT, sensitive, unofficial, within these four walls

off-the-wall crazy, curious, daft, different, eccentric, flaky, kinky, kooky, nonconforming, not tightly wrapped, nuts, nutty, odd, off-center, outlandish, peculiar, queer, schizo, schizoid, strange, unconventional, unpredictable, weird, wigged out

off year contretemps, evil hour, inopportune moment, poor timing, unfortunate time, unlucky day, unlucky hour, unsuitable time

oil paint oil color, oils

oil well gusher, oiler, oil field, oil rig, wildcat

old age elderliness, geriatrics, longevity, oldness, retirement age, senescence, seniority, winter of life

old bag battle-ax, old bat, old battle-ax, old dame, old girl, old prune, old witch

old-boy network age group, freemasonry, networking, old-girl network, peer group

old college try all-out effort, best effort, college try, serious effort, valiant effort

old country birthplace, country of origin, fatherland, homeland, mother country, motherland, native country, native land, native soil, old world, Old World, one's native soil

Old English Anglo-Saxon

old-fashioned antiquated, antique, behind the times, dated, obsolete, of the old school, old, oldfangled, outdated, outmoded, out-of-date, out of style, passé

old fogy diehard, fogy, fossil, has-been, mossback, old poop, stick-in-the-mud

Old Glory Star-Spangled Banner, Stars and Stripes

Old Guard conservative group, diehards, veterans, warhorse

old hand experienced person, expert, old soldier, old-stager, old-timer, veteran, warhorse

old hat back-number, behind the times, has-been, old-fashioned, old school

old lady granny, mother, old dame, old maid, old woman

old maid bachelor girl, lone woman, maiden, single woman, spinster, unmarried woman; fuddy-duddy, fussbudget, goody-goody, prig, prude

old man father, genitor, grandfather, pater, patriarch

old money inherited wealth

old news stale news

old school backward-looking, conforming, conservative, earlier generation, leftovers, old-fashioned, old line, past, traditional, unprogressive

old school tie club tie, regimental tie

old soldier old trooper, vet, veteran, warhorse

old wives' tale allegory, fable, fallacy, false belief, false knowledge, folklore, legend, lore, moral, myth, parable, popular belief, story, superstition, superstitious belief, tale, tradition, yarn

Old World Eastern Hemisphere, Europe

olive branch dove of peace, friendliness, hand of friendship, offer of peace, outstretched hand, overture, parley, peaceful approach, peace offer, peace offering, peace pipe

on and off alternately, at irregular intervals, fluctuating, inconstantly, infrequently, intermittently, irregularly, not often, now and then, off and on, sometimes, sporadically, uncertainly, variable, very seldom, when the mood strikes

on and on constantly, continuously, forever, never-ending, relentless, time after time, time and time again, uninterruptedly, unremitting, without a break, without stopping

on a roll cooking, hot, hot-handed, in a groove, in a zone, on fire, on one's game, smoking

on behalf of in behalf of, in support of, on the side of

on call accessible, at hand, at one's beck and call, at one's disposal, available, handy, on alert, on deck, standing by

once and for all at long last, conclusively, decisively, finally

once in a while every now and then, every once in a while, every so often, from time to time, infrequently, irregularly, now and again, now and then, occasionally, once and again, periodically, sometimes, sporadically

on cloud nine carried away, ecstatic, entranced, euphoric, filled with joy, in seventh heaven, overjoyed, transported

on duty at work, clocked in, on the job, punched in, working

one-armed bandit fruit machine, gaming machine, slot, slot machine, the slots

one by one individually, in succession, one at a time, separately, singly

on edge anxious, edgy, fidgety, high-strung, hyper, impatient, in suspense, jittery, jumpy, nail-biting, nerves on edge, nervous, skittish, uneasy, wired

one-horse town hick town, jerkwater town, jumping-off place, one-gas-station town, one-stoplight town, tank town, whistle-stop, wide place in the road

one-liner crack, gag, joke, wisecrack, witticism, witty comment, witty remark, zinger

one-night stand casual sex, one-nighter, quickie, tryst; one-night engagement, one-nighter, road gig, stand

one-of-a-kind distinctive, in a class by itself, special, unique, unparalleled, unprecedented

one-piece suit bathing suit, jumpsuit, maillot, maillot de bain, swimsuit, tank suit

one-sided biased, influenced, narrow-minded, partial, partisan, prejudiced, slanted, swayed, unfair, unobjective

one-track mind compulsion, fixation, fixed idea, idée fixe, monomania, obsession, passion, preoccupation, prepossession, ruling passion, single-mindedness

one-two punch jab and cross, the old one-two, the one-two

one-upmanship artfulness, bettering, caginess, canniness, competition, competitive advantage, competitive edge, cunning, cutthroat, gamesmanship, outfoxing, outsmarting, outwitting, rivaling

on fire afire, burning, ignited; ardent, eager, zealous; feverish

on guard alert, careful, cautious, defensive, guarded, heedful, mindful, observant, on one's guard, on one's toes, on the lookout, on the watch, vigilant, wary, watchful

on-line accessible, connected, hooked up to the Internet, linked, networked, onstream, operative, plugged in, wired

on-line magazine electronic magazine, e-zine, webzine

on one's guard alert, careful, cautious, defensive, guarded, heedful, mindful, observant, on guard, on one's toes, on the lookout, on the watch, vigilant, wary, watchful

on paper hypothetically, in theory, theoretically

on purpose by design, consciously, deliberately, in cold blood, intentionally, knowingly, of one's own free will, premeditatedly, purposefully, willfully, with full intent, wittingly

onside kick free kick, squib kick

on tap accessible, at hand, at

one's fingertips, available, convenient, handy, on deck, ready

on the ball alert, alive, attentive, awake, on one's toes, on the job, on top of, ready, sharp, vital, wide-awake, with it

on the blink bonkers, broken, faulty, haywire, in disrepair, inoperable, kerflooey, not working, on the fritz, out of commission, out of kilter, out of order, out of whack

on the brink at the limit, at the threshold, on the borderline, on the edge, on the point, on the verge

on the double chop-chop, double time, fast, hastily, hurried, in double time, in high gear, lickety-split, promptly, pronto, quickly, rapidly, snappily, speedily, swiftly

on the fence divided, fifty-fifty, impartial, indifferent, in the middle of the road, neutral, nonaligned, noncommitted, nonpartisan, passive, torn, unaligned, uncommitted, undecided

on the fritz bonkers, broken, faulty, haywire, in disrepair, inoperable, kerflooey, not working, on the blink, out of commission, out of kilter, out of order, out of whack

on the house complimentary, compliments of the house, for free, for nothing, free, freebie, free of charge, free of cost, gratis, gratuitous, no charge

on the level aboveboard, authentic, fair, fair and square, for real, honest, legitimate, on the up-and-up, right as rain, square, straight, straight-shooting

on the nose accurate, bull's-eye, exactly, on target, on the mark, on the money, precisely, well-aimed

on the wagon abstinent, dry, free of alcohol, period of abstinence, sober, stone-cold sober, sworn off, unintoxicated

on time dependable, on schedule, prompt, punctual, reliable, timely

on trial before the court, in litigation, under examination, under suspicion

op art pop art

open admissions open enrollment

open air alfresco, great outdoors, open, outdoors, out-of-doors, outside

open-and-shut apparent,

assured, cinched, clear-cut, conclusive, cut-and-dried, easy, evident, glaring, guaranteed, iced, indisputable, in the bag, nailed down, obvious, sewn up, simple, unmistakable

open door equal admission, free access, generosity, open-door policy, smiling reception, warmheartedness

open-ended hanging, loose, not restrained, undetermined, unlimited, unrestricted

open house entertaining, hospitality

opening night debut, first appearance, first night, first performance, first showing, gala opening, gala performance, opener, premiere, preview, sneak preview, world premiere

open letter published letter

open market common market, competitive market, free enterprise, free market, free port, free trade, free-trade area, open trade

open marriage companionate marriage, temporary marriage, trial marriage

open-minded amenable, broadminded, impartial, liberal-minded, open, persuadable, reasonable, receptive, tolerant, unbiased, understanding

open primary nonpartisan primary, preference primary

open question anybody's guess, loose end, question, toss of a coin, undecided issue

open sea high seas, international waters, ocean blue, the briny deep

open season hunting season, legal hunting period, period of attack, piling on, unrestrained attack

open secret common knowledge, no secret, public knowledge

open sesame abracadabra, abraxas, access, key, key word, magic formula, opener, password, paternoster, secret sign, watchword

open shop nonunion shop

open universe expanding universe, inflationary universe, pulsating universe

opéra bouffe comic opera, farcical opera, opera buffa, opéra comique

opera glasses binoculars, field glasses, lorgnette, pince-nez, prism binoculars

opera hat silk hat, stovepipe hat, top hat, topper

opera house concert hall, music hall, opera

operating expense business expenses, general expenses, operating budget, operating costs, operating expenses, overhead

operating room operating table, operating theater, OR, surgery

operating system disk operating system, DOS, executive, MacOS, MS-DOS, OS, OS/2, system software, systems program, UNIX, Windows

operations research business management, management study

opposite number correlation, counterpart, equipollent, vis-à-vis

optical art op art

optical character recognition OCR, OCR device, optical character reading, optical scanning, scanner

optical disk compact disc, laser disc, magneto-optical disk

optical glass eyeglass, eyepiece, lens, magnifying glass

optical illusion apparition, fata morgana, hallucination, illusion, mirage, phantasm, phantasmagoria, specter, trick of eyesight, trick of light, trick of the eyesight, vision, visual fallacy

oral contraceptive abortion pill, birth control pill, Brompton, Brompton's cocktail, morning-after pill, RU 486, the pill

oral history firsthand account, folk literature, narrative history, oral record, survivors' account, witnesses' account

oral hygiene dental hygiene

oral sex blow job, cunnilingus, fellatio, fellation, oral-genital stimulation, sixty-nine

oral surgery dental surgery

order blank order form, ordering form

order of business agenda, calendar, docket, frame, lineup, order of the day, program of operation, schedule, schedule of operation, schema, things to be done, time, time scheme, timetable, to-do list

order of the day agenda, business, day's business, directive

organ-grinder hurdy-gurdist, hurdy-gurdyist, hurdy-gurdy man

organic farming chemical-free farming, natural farming

organized crime Black Hand, Cosa Nostra, gangland, Mafia, the mob, the rackets, the syndicate, the underworld

organized labor industrial union, labor union, trades union, trade union

organized movement campaign, crusade, drive, grassroots movement, lobby, popular front

Oriental rug Persian rug

original sin carnal sin, disobedience, eating the apple, fall from grace, fall of man, inborn tendency, mortal sin, sinfulness, sin of Adam, wickedness

orphan drug specialized drug

otitis media middle-ear inflammation

out-and-out absolute, blatant, categorical, complete, downright, flagrant, flat-out, outright, stark, straight, straight-out, thorough, total, undeniable, unmitigated, unquestionable, utter

out box finished work, outgoing messages

out cold anesthetized, comatose, dead to the world, down for the count, fast asleep, oblivious, out like a light, out of it, sound asleep, unconscious, zonked out

outer ear external ear

outer limit ceiling, extreme, peak, top, ultimate, utmost

outer planet Jupiter, Neptune, Pluto, Saturn, Uranus

outer space celestial spaces, cosmic space, cosmos, deep space, empty space, ether space, infinite space, infinity, intercosmic space, intergalactic space, interplanetary space, interstellar space, metagalactic space, ocean of emptiness, pressureless space, the heavens, the universe, the void, the void above

out of bounds beyond the pale, forbidden, off-limits, prohibited, restricted

out of breath breathless, dyspneic, gasping for breath, panting, short of breath, short-winded, winded

out of business bankrupt, closed, defunct, extinct, no more, nonexistent

out of commission decommissioned, down, faulty, in repair, kaput, not in service, out of kilter, out of order, out of whack

out of control carried away, disorderly, out of hand, rebellious, uncontrollable, ungovernable, unmanageable, unruly, wild

out of hand beyond control, out of control

out of one's head crazy, delirious, insane, irrational, out of one's mind

out of one's mind around the bend, bananas, crazy, cuckoo, daffy, deranged, insane, irrational, off one's head, off one's rocker, out of one's head, out of one's tree

out of order bonkers, broken, faulty, haywire, in disrepair, inoperable, kerflooey, not working, on the blink, on the fritz, out of commission, out of kilter, out of whack

out of print no longer published, nonexistent, obsolete, out of stock, unattainable

out of sight hidden, invisible, lost to view, unseen

out of sorts below par, in a bad humor, out of humor, under the weather, unwell

out of the blue not predicted, surprising, unanticipated, unexpected, unforeseen, unplanned, unprepared for

out of the closet brought to light, disclosed, divulged, exposed, out, out into the open, revealed, uncovered, unveiled

out of the ordinary bizarre, exceptional, incredible, notable, odd, offbeat, off the beaten track, one of a kind, out of this world, special, strange, uncommon, unheard of, unique, unusual, wonderful

out of the question incomprehensible, inconceivable, unthinkable

out of this world alien, ethereal, extraterrestrial, ghostly, heavenly, otherworldly, strange, supernatural, unearthly, weird

out of touch inaccessible, out of contact, removed

out of work available for hire, jobless, laid off, unemployed

out on a limb chancy, dangerous, exposed, in trouble, liable, on the spot, open, perilous, precarious, risky, shaky, up a tree

Oval Office office of the president of the United States, presidency

ovarian follicle graafian follicle

oven mitt oven glove {compare *pot holder*}

over a barrel in a jam, in a mess, in an awkward position, in a pickle, without choices

overhand knot single knot

overnight bag carry-on, overnight case, overnighter, suitcase

over one's head baffling, bewildering, beyond comprehension, beyond one, complex, complicated, deep, hard to understand, incomprehensible, profound, unfathomable

overseas cap garrison cap

over the counter OTC, retail, without a prescription

over the edge gone crazy, lost one's mind

over the hill elderly, gray, past one's prime

over the top exaggerated, excessive

owner's manual instruction manual, machine instructions

oxygen debt oxygen deficiency

oxygen tent respirator

oxyntic cells parietal cells

ozone layer isothermal layer, ozone, ozonosphere

Pp

package deal all-in-one, compact, complement, package, set

package store liquor store, spirit shop, spirit shoppe, wine shop, wine store

pack ice bay ice, berg ice, field ice, floating ice, ice pack, sheet ice, shelf ice

packing tape sealing tape, strapping tape

pack rat accumulator, collector, gatherer, hoarder, magpie, saver, squirrel

paddle steamer paddleboat, paddle wheeler, riverboat, showboat, side-wheeler, sternwheeler

paddy wagon Black Maria, cruiser, panda car, patrol car, patrol wagon, police car, police van, police wagon, prowl car, squad car, wagon

pad of paper jotter, notebook, scratch pad, stationery, steno pad, tablet, writing pad

pain in the neck headache, nudnick, nudnik, nuisance, pain in the butt, pain in the rear, pest, schmo

painted cup Indian paintbrush

pajama party overnight party, sleep-over, slumber party

palace revolution bloodless revolution

pale horse death, grim reaper, pale rider

Palladian window Diocletian window

Palm Pilot™ Handspring Visor™, palmtop, PDA, personal digital assistant

palm reader chiromancer, palmist

pancake turner spatula

Pandora's box can of worms, confusion, evil, hornet's nest, ill, snake in the grass

panic attack anxiety attack, fit of terror, panic, panic disorder, scare, spasm

panic button alarm button, buzzer, emergency signal, 911, nurse's signal

panty girdle foundation garment, girdle, undergirdle

panty hose leggings, nylons, stockings, tights

paper clip gem clip, paper fastener

paper money bill of exchange, cash, dollar bill, fiat money, fiduciary currency, negotiable instrument, note

paper tiger empty suit, hollow man, man of straw, petty tyrant, straw man, tin god

paper tissue Kleenex™

paper trail documentary evidence

paradoxical sleep rapid eye movement sleep, REM sleep

parallel cable Centronics cable {compare *serial cable*}

parallel evolution biological evolution, convergent evolution, speciation

parallel parking curbside parking, street parking

parallel port {compare *serial port*}

parametric equation limiting equation

par excellence eminent, important, incomparable, preeminent, superior, supreme, the most

pari-mutuel betting system, gaming house, off-track betting, OTB, totalizator

parking brake emergency brake, hand brake

parking lot car park, garage, park, parking garage, stable

Parkinson's disease paralysis agitans, parkinsonism, shaking palsy

parliamentary law parliamentarian law

parlor car chair car, dining car

parlor game board game, indoor game, party game, role-playing game

parlor grand grand piano, piano

parochial school church-related school, church school, convent school, denominational school, religious school

part and parcel constituent, element, module, part

Parthian shot answer, last word, parting shot, stratagem

partial-birth abortion D&X, dilation and extraction, intact D&E

particle accelerator accelerator, atomic accelerator, atomic cannon, atom smasher, cyclotron, linear accelerator, synchrotron

particle physics atomics, atomic science, atomistics, atomology, nuclear physics, nucleonics

party line bandwagon, line, party doctrine, party ideology, party philosophy, party policy, party principle, platform, policy, position

party pooper grinch, grouch, killjoy, malcontent, sourpuss, spoilsport, wet blanket

party wall buffer, dividing line, garden fence, partition, property line, shared wall

Paschal Lamb Agnus Dei, Jesus, sacrificed lamb

pass away bite the dust, buy the farm, cash in one's chips, cease living, croak, die, expire, kick the bucket, meet one's maker, pass on, succumb

passed out anesthetized, asleep, blacked out, comatose, dead to the world, knocked out, out cold, out like a light, unconscious

passenger vehicle automobile, car, truck, van

passing note passing tone

passive resistance civil disobedience, nonresistance, nonviolent resistance

passive smoking involuntary inhalation, secondhand smoke

pass muster come through with flying colors, come up to scratch, come up to snuff, cut the mustard, do credit to, fill the bill, find favor with, get by, keep up to standard, make it, make the cut, make the grade, measure up, meet with approval, pass, pass inspection, prove acceptable, recommend itself, satisfy requirements, stand the test, stand up, suffice

pass the buck cop out, dodge, duck, get out of, pass on, pass responsibility, relay, slide out of

past master cordon bleu, grand master, master

pastry bag decorating bag

pastry board pastry marble

pastry shop bakery, bread shop, cake shop, confectionery, patisserie

pastry tip icing tip

patch pocket flat pocket

patch test allergy test, scratch test, tuberculin test

patent leather shagreen, shiny leather

patent medicine ethical drug, medication, proprietary, proprietary drug, proprietary medicine

pathetic fallacy anthropomorphism, anthropomorphology, anthropopathism

patience of Job fortitude, self-control, stoicism

pat on the back blessing, compliment, congrats, congratulations, felicitation, flattery, stroke

patrol car cruiser, panda car, patrol wagon, police car, prowl car, squad car

patron saint beatified soul, canonized mortal, guardian angel, saint and martyr

patty shell puff pastry, vol-au-vent

Pauli exclusion principle exclusion principle

Pavlovian conditioning classical conditioning, conditioning, Pavlovian psychology

pax romana lasting peace, pax dei, peace of God, truce of God, universal peace

paying guest boarder, lodger, roomer

pay phone call box, coin telephone, pay station, public telephone, telephone booth, telephone box, telephone kiosk

pay television pay-per-view, pay TV, STV, subscription television

peace envoy peace emissary

peaceful coexistence coexistence, neutralism, nonresistance

peace negotiation mediation, peace conference, peacemaking, peace talk

peace offering dove of peace, eirenicon, expiatory offering, expiatory sacrifice, hand of friendship, heave offering, irenics, olive branch, outstretched hand, piacular offering, piaculum, present, sacramental offering, sacrifice, sin offering, whole offering

peace officer arm of the law, law enforcement agent, law enforcer, policeman, police officer

peace of mind bliss, calmness, cheer, clear conscience, comfort, composure, contentment, delight, ecstasy, elation, euphoria, exuberance, felicity, fulfillment, happiness, high spirits, joy, peacefulness, pleasure, quiet mind, satisfaction, serenity, soothingness, tranquility, well-being

peace pipe calumet, pipe of peace

peace treaty accord, arms agreement, cease-fire, concord, entente, entente cordiale, international agreement, mutual-defense treaty, nonaggression pact, nonaggression treaty, nonproliferation treaty, peace accord, peace agreement, suspension of hostilities, treaty of friendship

peaches and cream glowing, good, healthy, OK, okay, rosy

pea jacket double-breasted coat, peacoat
peanut gallery botherers, cheap seats, hecklers, interrupters, paradise
pearly whites choppers, dentition, ivories, pearly teeth, teeth
pea soup dense fog, pea-souper, pea-soup fog, thick fog
pecking order chain of command, class structure, corporate ladder, dominance, food chain, grouping, hierarchy, line of dominance, power structure, ranking, social hierarchy, social ladder, social pyramid, social stratification, social structure
pedal point organ point
pedal pushers breeches, calf-length slacks, capri pants, capris, cropped pants, jodhpurs, knickers, leggings, pegged pants
pedal steel guitar pedal steel
pedestrian walkway footbridge
Peeping Tom ogler, scopophiliac, voyeur, watcher
peep show cabaret, floor show, raree-show
peep sight leaf sight, open sight, rear sight
peer group age group, colleagues, compeers, fellowship, old-boy network
peg leg artificial leg
peg top humming top, spinning top
pell-mell carelessly, frantically, frenziedly, hastily, heedlessly, helter-skelter, hurriedly, impetuously, in disorder, madly, recklessly, wildly
penal institution brig, concentration camp, correctional facility, dungeon, house of detention, jail, labor camp, lockup, military prison, pen, penal colony, penitentiary, POW camp, prison, prison camp, prisoner-of-war camp, slammer, stockade
penalty area penalty bench, penalty box, penalty spot, penalty-kick mark
penalty shot foul shot, free throw, penalty kick
pencil pusher black-coat worker, clerical worker, desk worker, office worker, white-collar worker
pen name alias, allonym, ananym, anonym, assumed name, false name, fictitious name, nom de plume, professional name, pseudonym
penny-pincher cheapskate, miser, money-grubber, pinchpenny, scrooge, skinflint, tightwad

pen pal correspondent, epistoler, letter writer

pension plan retirement account

people mover automated monorail, monorail, moving sidewalk

pepper mill peppercorn grinder, pepper grinder, pepper shaker

pepper pot Philadelphia pepper pot

pep pill amphetamine, analeptic, benny, crank, restorative, speed, stimulant, tonic, upper

pep talk inducement, inspirational talk, rallying cry, trumpet call

per annum annually, by the year, per year

per capita per head, per person, per unit of population, proportionately

per centum per hundred, percent

percussion cap blasting cap, detonator, fulminating mercury

percussion hammer plessor, plexor

percussion instrument castanets, clappers, cymbals, drum, gong, maraca, piano, spoons, triangle, xylophone

per diem by the day, daily, daily expense allowance, per day

perfect participle past participle

perfect pitch absolute pitch

performing arts dance, drama, fine arts, music, theater

periodical cicada seventeen-year locust

periodic table periodic table of elements, table of elements

periodontal disease gum disease, periodontitis, pyorrhea

peripheral vision peripheral field

permanent press durable press, Perma-Prest™

permanent tooth adult tooth

Persian carpet Herez, Heriz, Kirman, Oriental rug, Persian rug, Tabriz

persona grata acceptable person, good fellow, welcome guest

personal care bathing, cooking, hygiene

personal computer computer, desktop computer, home computer, microcomputer, minicomputer, PC, workstation

personal digital assistant Handspring Visor™, Palm Pilot™, PDA, personal organizer

personal effects bag and baggage, impedimenta, personal estate, personal items, personal property, worldly goods

personal foul personal

personal identification number code number, ID, PIN, PIN number

personality trait personality tendency, personality type

personal organizer agenda book, Filofax™, PDA, personal digital assistant

personal property chattels personal, choses transitory, effects, personal effects

personal secretary personal assistant

personal stereo boom box, box, Discman™, ghetto blaster, portable, transistor, Walkman™

persona non grata bad news, bête noire, objectionable person, pet peeve, unacceptable person, undesirable

petite bourgeoisie lower middle class, petit bourgeois

petit four cookie, madeleine

petit jury petty jury, traverse jury, trial jury

pet name affectionate name, byname, diminutive, hypocorism, nickname, pretty name

pet peeve bête noire, bugbear, complaint, grievance, groan, hateful object, peeve, personal vexation, pet aversion

petri dish culture dish

petroleum jelly K-Y™, petrolatum, Vaseline™

petty cash fund, kitty, made money, pin money, pocket money, pool, spending money

petty officer noncommissioned officer, PO

phallic symbol fertility symbol, phallus

Philadelphia lawyer horse trader, shady character, shrewd attorney, shyster, trickster

philosophers' stone elixir

phone call buzz, long-distance call, ring, telephone call, toll call, toll-free call, trunk call

phone company communications corporation, communications provider, long-distance service, telephone company, telephone firm

phonetic alphabet code words, International Phonetic Alphabet, IPA, phonetic transcription

photo-essay photographic story

photo finish blanket finish, close finish, dead heat, even money, Garrison finish, neck-and-neck race

photograph album album, scrapbook

photo opportunity media event, media happening, nonevent, photo op, press opportunity, pseudoevent, staged media event, staged public event

phrase book dictionary, foreign language dictionary

physical anthropology anthropogeny, anthropography, biological anthropology, human geography, somatology

physical chemistry physicochemistry

physical disability handicap, hearing impairment, learning disability, speech impairment, visual impairment

physical education athletics, calisthenics, fitness education, gym class, gymnastic, PE, phys ed, physical culture

physical examination checkup, health examination, medical examination, physical, physical checkup, physical exam

physical fitness aerobic fitness, agility, anaerobic fitness, cardiovascular fitness, condition, coordination, endurance, fitness, flexibility, physical conditioning, shape, strength

physical geography physiography

physical science astronomy, biology, chemistry, geology, natural science, physics

physical therapist occupational therapist, physiotherapist, speech therapist

physical therapy acupressure, healing arts, physiotherapy, shiatsu

physiological psychology physiologic psychology, psychophysiology

piano accordion accordion, concertina

piano bar cocktail bar, lounge bar, piano lounge

pick and roll pick, screen, screen play

picket fence paling fence

picket line demonstrators, picketers

pick of the litter apple of one's eye, champion, choice, cream, cream of the crop, crème de la crème, darling, dearest, favorite, lap dog, pet, preference, prime, prize, the best, the top of the heap

pickup truck panel truck, pickup

picnic basket hamper

picture frame canvas, mount

picture tube cathode-ray tube, kinescope, projection tube

picture writing cuneal writing, cuneiform, curiologics, curiology, hieroglyphics, ideography, phonographic writing, runes, script, symbolical writing, symbology

pièce de résistance centerpiece,

chef d'oeuvre, culinary masterpiece, dish fit for a king, dish of the day, feature, great performance, highlight, magnum opus, main attraction, main dish, masterpiece, masterwork, outstanding accomplishment, plat du jour, prize, specialty

piece goods dry goods, textiles, yard goods

piece of cake a snap, breeze, cakewalk, chicken feed, child's play, cinch, duck soup, easy thing, kid stuff, nobrainer, no problem, peanuts, picnic, pie, snap

pie chart circle graph, histogram, scatter diagram

pie in the sky air castle, castle in the air, empty promise, empty wish, end of the rainbow, Xanadu

pie pan pie plate, pie tin

pie server cake server

piggy bank penny bank

pig in a poke blind bargain, blind date, foolishly accepted deal, grab bag, green cheese, leap of faith, random shot, shot in the dark, sight-unseen transaction, uncertainty

pig Latin jargon, rhyming slang

pig out overeat, overindulge, pork out, scarf, stuff oneself, wolf down

pillow talk intimate conversation

pilot jacket aviator's jacket, bomber jacket

pilot light Bunsen burner, burner, element, gas jet, heating element, jet, pilot burner

pinch bar claw bar, crow, crowbar, iron crow, ripping bar, wrecking bar

pinch-hit fill in, hit for, stand in for, substitute hit

pinch hitter alternate, backup, designated hitter, DH, fill-in, proxy, replacement, stand-in, sub, substitute, understudy

pink elephant blue devil, delirium tremens, DTs, heebie-jeebies, jimjams, pink spider

pink slip ax, boot, gate, notice of dismissal, sack, termination notice, walking papers, walking ticket

pin money change, mad money, part-time job earnings, petty cash, pittance, pocket money, spending money

pins and needles deadness, formication, sensation, tingle, tingling, tingling sensation

pipe bomb plastic bomb, plastique bomb
pipe cleaner reamer
piped music canned music, elevator music, musical wallpaper, Muzak™, wall-to-wall musical
pipe dream airy hope, castle in the air, castle in the sky, chimera, daydream, false hope, fantasy, fool's paradise, golden dream, pie in the sky, unrealistic hope, wishful thinking
pipe of peace calumet, peace pipe
pipe organ calliope, church organ, Hammond organ, organ, steam organ
pitched roof angled roof, gable roof, gambrel roof, hipped roof, hip roof, lean-to roof
pitch in chip in, contribute work, help, lend a hand
pit stop brief stop, call of nature, refueling stop, rest stop, service stop
pizza cutter pizza wheel
place-name toponym
place of worship cathedral, church, holy place, house of worship, mosque, shrine, shul, synagogue, tabernacle, temple
place setting table service
plain sailing easy going, easy progress, easy ride, smooth sailing, straight sailing
plain text ASCII, unencrypted text
plane geometry planimetry
planned obsolescence obsolation, superannuation
plant kingdom flora, plant life, plants, vegetable kingdom
plant pathology phytopathology, plant physiology, vegetable pathology
plasma cell plasmacyte
plasma membrane cell membrane
plaster cast cast, image, model, plaster of paris
plastic art modeling, sculpture
plastic surgeon cosmetic surgeon, face-lifter
plastic surgery cosmetic surgery, face-lift, nose job, prosthetics, reconstructive surgery, rhinoplasty, tummy tuck
plastic wrap cellophane, clingfilm, Saran Wrap™
plate armor body armor, suit of armor
plate glass sheet glass
plate tectonics continental drift
platform car flatcar
platinum blonde ash-blonde, bleached blonde, honey blonde, silver blonde

platonic love friendship, spiritual love

play ball collaborate, cooperate, reciprocate, work together

player piano keyboard instrument, piano organ

playing card deck, face card

playing field arena, athletic field, field, playground, recreation ground, sports field, stadium, turf

play it by ear improvise, make it up as one goes along, think on one's feet

play on words equivocalness, jeu de mots, pun, wordplay

play possum bluff, pretend to be dead, pretend to sleep, put up a bluff, roll over and play dead

play the field flirt, gallivant, philander, play around, run around, sow one's oats

pleasure principle instant gratification, Lustprinzip

plenary indulgence forgiveness, grace

Plimsoll mark load line, load waterline, Plimsoll line

plug and play automatic configuration, plug-and-play, PNP

plumb bob bob, lead, plumb, plumb line, plumb rule, plummet

plumber's auger auger, plumber's snake, snake

plumber's helper plumber's friend, plunger

plus fours loose knickers

plus size large size, large women's size, size 16, size 16 and over, women's, XXL

plutonic rock hypabyssal rock, igneous rock

pocket billiards billiards, pool, snooker

pocket edition duodecimo, miniature, twelvemo

pocket money allowance, change, extra money, loose change, mad money, petty cash, pin money, small change, spending money

pocket park minipark

pocket veto absolute veto, countermand, indirect presidential veto, item veto, limited veto, suspensive veto, suspensory veto

poetic justice just punishment, Nemesis, punitive action, retribution, retributive justice, vice punished, virtue rewarded, warrantability

poetic license artistic freedom, artistic license, poetic freedom

poet laureate honored poet, laureate, major poet

point and shoot autofocus, automatic camera

point guard playmaker, point, point man, point player, swingman

point lace needlepoint

point man explorer, guide, pathfinder, player, playmaker, point, scout, trailblazer, trailbreaker

point of fact matter of fact, truth

point of honor code of honor, principle, punctilio

point of no return climax, crossroads, crunch, decisive moment, defining moment, match point, moment of truth, Rubicon, terminus, turning point, when push comes to shove

point of purchase point of sale, POP, POS

point of view angle, Anschauung, attitude, frame of reference, opinion, orientation, outlook, perspective, position, private opinion, slant, standpoint, two cents worth, viewpoint, way of thinking

point system evaluation system

poison gas marsh gas, mustard gas, swamp gas, war gas

poker face deadpan, deadpan expression, expressionless face, impassivity, inscrutability, mask, seriousness, straight face

polar circle Antarctic Circle, Arctic Circle

polar coordinate altitude and azimuth, latitude and longitude, ordinate and abscissa, right ascension and declension

polar front cold front, cold sector

polar molecule dipole

polar region Antarctica, Arctic

pole horse plow horse, shaft horse

pole position first chair, front position, front seat, inside position, lead, pole, starting grid

pole vault pole jump, vault

police action armed intervention, intervention, military action

police car Black Maria, cruiser, paddy wagon, panda car, patrol car, patrol wagon, police cruiser, police vehicle, police wagon, prowl car, squad car

police force force, highway patrol, law enforcement agency, long arm of the law, police, posse, security force, special police, SWAT team, tactical police

police officer arm of the law, carabiniere, constable, cop, deputy, detective, flatfoot, flic, fuzz, gendarme, law enforcement agent, law enforcer, lawman, lawwoman, marshal, meter maid, military police, mounted police officer, MP, officer, officer of the law, patrolman, patrolwoman, peace officer, policeman, policewoman, sheriff, the man, traffic officer, trooper

police procedural crime drama, crime story

police state brute force, despotism, rule of terror, totalitarian government, totalitarianism, totalitarian regime

police station calaboose, lockup, police headquarters

polio vaccine OPV, Sabin vaccine, Salk vaccine

polish off dispose of, finish off, finish up, put the kibosh on

political action committee influence peddlers, lobbyist, PAC, pressure group, special-interest group

political economy economic science

politically correct considerate, diplomatic, inoffensive, multiculturally sensitive, PC, politic, political correctness, sensitive, socially acceptable

political prisoner enemy prisoner of war, POW, prisoner of conscience, prisoner of war

political science art of the possible, civics, governance, government, poli-sci, political philosophy, political theory, politics, realpolitik, statesmanship

polling booth ballot box, balloting place, polling place, polls, voting booth, voting machine

poll tax capitation tax, tax on people

polo shirt golf shirt, knit pullover

polyvinyl chloride pipe plastic pipe, PVC pipe

pommel horse side horse

pond scum freshwater algae

pony express mail system, post, postal service

pool table billiard(s) table

poor box alms box

poor boy submarine sandwich

poor farm almshouse, poorhouse, workhouse

poor white white trash

pop art neosurrealism, op art

pop fly bloop, blooper, can of corn, looper, pop-up, Texas leaguer

pop music light music, pop, popular music, popular song

pop psychology pop psych, psychobabble

pop the question ask for the hand of, ask to marry, become engaged, court, plight one's troth, propose, propose marriage, sue for, woo

popular culture pop, pop culture, popular taste

popular front bloc, coalition, grassroots movement, groundswell, people's front

population explosion baby boom, boom, explosion, high birthrate

pork barrel back-scratching, favors of office, logrolling, melon, patronage, payola, perks, perquisite, plum, political favor, political patronage, pork, public crib, public till, public trough, spoils of office, taxpayer funds

pornographic film adult movie, blue movie, dirty movie, hard porn, porn, porno film, porno flick, pornographic movie, NC-17 movie, skin flick, soft porn, stag film, X-rated movie

portal vein hepatic portal vein, vena portae

portmanteau word blend, blend word, compound, counterword, merged word, portmanteau, portmantologism, telescope word

port of call harbor, home port, port, seaport, stopping place

port-wine stain birthmark, hemangioma, nevus, strawberry mark, vascular nevus

position paper manifesto, outline, plank, platform, policy report, prospectus, research paper, statement of belief, statement of principles

positive cash flow expenses less than income

positive thinking bright outlook, bullishness, cheerfulness, enthusiasm, great expectations, hopefulness, optimism, Pollyannaism, positive attitude, rosy outlook, silver lining

postage meter bulk-mail machine

postage stamp frank, postage, stamp

postal card card, letter card, picture postcard, postcard

postal code postcode, ZIP, zip code, zip plus four

post chaise diligence, omnibus, stagecoach

post exchange commissary, PX

postgraduate degree advanced

degree, doctoral degree, doctorate, master's, master's degree, PhD, postgrad degree

post-horse carriage horse, coach horse, draft horse

postmaster general PMG, postmistress general

postnasal drip runny nose

post office general post office, GPO, mail, PO, postal service, postal system, postmaster

post-traumatic stress disorder battle fatigue, shell shock, trauma

potential difference electromotive force, electromotivity, EMF, voltage

potential energy internal energy

pot holder hot pad, oven mitt

potluck supper buffet, BYO, casseroles, clambake, covered-dish supper, feast, harvest supper, potluck dinner

pot roast joint, roast, rôti, rump roast

potter's clay argil, china clay, clay, fireclay, potter's earth, pottery, refractory clay

potter's wheel hand-turned wheel, kick wheel, pedal wheel, power wheel, rotator, wheel

potty training toilet training

pouncet-box perfume box, pomander, potpourri, sachet, scent bag

pound net gill net, purse seine, seine

pound of flesh letter of the law

pound sign crisscross, number sign

pound the pavement count ties, hit the road, hit the trail, travel on foot, walk the tracks

poverty line bare existence, breadline, hand-to-mouth existence, mere existence, pauperism, poverty level, poverty trap, subsistence level

poverty-stricken broke, destitute, down-and-out, impoverished, indigent, miserably poor, needy, poor, strapped, suffering

powdered sugar confectioners' sugar

powder horn powder barrel, powder flask, powder keg, powder magazine

powder keg explosive situation, loose cannon, time bomb

powder puff makeup brush, puff

powder room bathroom, comfort station, girls' room, ladies' room, latrine, lavatory, rest room

power base backing, constituency, home turf, niche, stamping ground, support, territory, turf, vantage

power broker fixer, hand that rocks the cradle, influence peddler, kingmaker, latency, logroller, power behind the throne, wire-puller

power line cable, cord, lead

power mower electric mower, gasoline mower

power of attorney agency, deputyship, executorship, PA, procuration, proxy, succession, supplantation, supplanting, trusteeship, warrant, writ, written authority

power pack amperage, commutator, transformer, wattage

power plant atomic power plant, generating station, hydroelectric plant, hydroelectric scheme, nuclear power plant, powerhouse, power source, power station, station

power play offensive maneuver, strategic maneuver

power politics bossism, machine politics, Machtpolitik

power shovel steam shovel

power structure class structure, corridors of power, establishment, hierarchy, interests, management hierarchy, managerial hierarchy, power elite, powers that be, ruling class, status system, stratification

power train drive train

practical joke antic, caper, escapade, espièglerie, fool's errand, frolic, gag, high jinks, mischievous trick, monkeyshines, prank, shenanigans, stunt, tomfoolery, trick

practical nurse licensed practical nurse, LPN

practice teacher apprentice teacher, pupil teacher, student teacher, teacher's aide

pragmatic sanction decree, edict

prairie oyster calf testis

prairie schooner Conestoga wagon, covered wagon, stagecoach

prairie wolf brush wolf, coyote, dingo, hyena, jackal, lobo, medicine wolf, timber wolf

prayer beads rosary

prayer book Book of Common Prayer, breviary, canon, lectionary, Mass book, missal book, prayers, psalmbook, Psalter, scripture

prayer rug prayer carpet, prayer mat

prayer shawl tallith

prayer wheel prayer machine
Precambrian era Archean era, Archeozoic era, azoic era, Proterozoic era
precious metal copper, electrum, gold, nickel, platinum, silver
precious stone diamond, emerald, gem, gemstone, ruby, sapphire, stone
preconceived notion assumption, preconceived idea, preconception, prejudgment, prejudice, presumption, something on the brain
preemptive strike preventive strike
prefer charges accuse, charge, indict, press charges, take one to court
preferred stock convertible preferred stock, cumulative convertible preferred stock, cumulative preferred stock, participating preferred stock, preference stock
première danseuse danseuse noble, prima ballerina, principal dancer
prenuptial agreement prenup, prenuptial contract
preparatory school prep school, private school
presence of mind calm, clear-headedness, confidence, cool-headedness, coolness, levelheadedness, poise, possession, sangfroid, self-control, self-possession
president pro tempore presiding senator
press agency news agency, news service, press association, publicity agency, public relations agency, wire service
press agent advance man, PA, PR consultant, press officer, publicist, publicity agent, public relations officer
press box press gallery, reporters' section
press conference interview, news conference, press opportunity
press corps fourth estate, media, news medium, the press
press of sail crowded sails, flank speed, forced draft, press of sail and steam, sails set
press release bulletin, handout, newsworthy item, notice, release
press the flesh give a high five, give one some skin, press one's hand, shake hands, squeeze one's hand
pressure cabin pressurized aircraft
pressure cooker airtight pot, autoclave

pressure gauge manometer, meter, pressure measure, vaporimeter

pressure group interest group, lobby, lobbyist, PAC, political action committee, single-issue group, special-interest group

pressure sore bedsore

pressurized suit aircraft suit, anti-G suit, G suit, pressure suit, space suit, spacecraft suit

previous question immediate vote, privileged question, question

price control credit squeeze, economic pressure, fixed price, price-fixing, price freeze, prix fixe, restraint, valorization

price-earnings ratio P/E

price hike abrupt hike, abrupt price rise

price index consumer price index, cost-of-living index, retail price index, stock price index, wholesale price index

price support depletion allowance, economic support, endowment, subsidization, subsidy, subvention, tax benefit, write-off

price tag cost, price sticker, price ticket, quotation, quoted price

price war price competition

prickly heat heat rash, miliaria

pride of place highest position, precedence, preeminence, seniority, superiority

prima ballerina ballerina, coryphee, leading woman dancer

prima donna diva, headliner, leading lady, lead vocalist, luminary, opera singer, principal female, star, superstar, superwoman

prima facie appearing, at first sight, at the first blush, evidential, on the face of it

primal therapy primal scream therapy

primary care health care, medical care

primary color blue, primary, primary pigment, primitive color, red, yellow

primary school elementary school, graded school, grade school, grammar school

prime cost cost, wholesale

prime meridian Greenwich longitude, zero meridian

prime minister chancellor, chief minister, chief officer, chief of state, dewan, doge, grand vizier, head of cabinet, head of state, premier

prime mover author, cause, creator, drive, initial force, instigator, motivator, motive force, mover, power source, primum mobile

prime rate bank rate, borrowing rate, interest rate, lending rate, lowest rate of interest, prime, prime interest rate, rate of interest, the price of money

prime rib beef ribs, standing rib roast

prime time evening television, prime-time attraction, prime-time show, prime-time television

primrose path garden path, life of ease, path of least resistance, slippery slope

Prince Charming Lothario, Romeo

prince consort queen's husband

Prince of Darkness Angel of Darkness, Archfiend, Ash-Shaytan, Beelzebub, Satan, the devil

Prince of Peace King of Heaven, King of Kings

printed circuit card, microcircuit, motherboard, PCB, printed circuit board

printed matter book, copy, literature, magazine, newspaper, print, printed material, reading matter, written word

printer's devil apprentice printer

printing press press, presswork, printing machine, printing works

print shop composer, composing room, pressroom, printer, printery, printing office, typesetter

priority mail airmail, domestic mail, express mail, first-class mail, special delivery

prison camp concentration camp, detention camp, gulag, internment camp, prison farm

prisoner of war captive, enemy prisoner of war, hostage, political prisoner, POW, prisoner

prison term slammer time, stretch, tour of duty

private detective beagle, detective, dick, eye, flatfoot, gumshoe, inquiry agent, inspector, investigator, operative, PI, private dick, private eye, private investigator, Sherlock Holmes, skip tracer, sleuth, sleuthhound, spotter, tec

private enterprise capitalism, capitalistic system, free economy, free enterprise, free-enterprise economy, free-enterprise system, private ownership, private sector

private law personal law

private parts genitalia, genitals,

meat, privates, privy parts, pudenda, reproductive organs, sex organs, sexual organs

private practice family practice

private school independent school, parochial school, preparatory school

private sector capitalism, economic sector, private ownership

privy council advisory council, British cabinet, council, council of state, presidium

privy purse private income

prix fixe fixed price, price control, price-fixing

prize money cash prize, door prize, jackpot, reward

probability density frequency distribution, probability distribution, probability function

probability theory game theory, theory of games

probable cause presumption, reasonable ground

probate court court of probate, surrogate court

problem drinker alcoholic, barfly, chronic alcoholic, chronic drunk, dipsomaniac, drunkard, hard drinker, heavy drinker, hooch hound, pathological drinker, soak

pro bono done without compensation, for the public good, free help, legal aid

processed cheese Cheez Whiz™, Velveeta™

process server catchpole, law officer, messenger, pursuivant, summoner

procrustean bed arbitrary standard, bed of Procrustes, instrument of torture

prodigal son lost lamb, magdalen, penitent, prodigal, prodigal returned, returnee

production line assembly line, assembly-line production, shop floor

profit and loss P&L, P and L

profit sharing copartnership, cosharing, partnership, pool, shared ownership, sharing

pro forma as a matter of form, done as a formality, for form's sake, perfunctory

programmed instruction computer-aided instruction, immersion method, induction

program music descriptive music, incidental music

program trading arbitrage, computer-assisted trading

progressive education coeducation, individual instruction, Montessori system

progressive taxation graduated taxation

projection printing contact printing

projection TV big-screen TV

promenade deck upper deck

Promised Land Abraham's bosom, Canaan, City of God, Goshen, heaven, Kingdom of God, Kingdom of Heaven, land of milk and honey, land of plenty, land of promise, Land of the Leal, New Jerusalem, upstairs

promissory note cosigned promissory note, IOU, note, note of hand, PN, written promise to pay

property tax personal property tax, real estate tax

prop-jet engine turboprop engine

proportional representation cumulative system, cumulative voting, hare system, list system, one man one vote, PR

pro rata according to the calculated share, ad valorem, in proportion, proportionately, prorate, prorated, respectively

pros and cons arguments, logomachy, pilpulistic, polemics, reasons

prosecuting attorney DA, district attorney, PA, prosecution, prosecutor

pro tempore for the moment, for the time, for the time being, pro tem, temporarily

Protestant ethic work ethic

proud flesh granulation tissue, swollen flesh, weal, welt

proving ground research center, testing ground, testing place

provost marshal military police head

prowl car Black Maria, cruiser, panda car, patrol car, patrol wagon, police car, squad car

p's and q's best behavior, good behavior, good example, manners

public-address system loudspeaker, PA, PA system

public assistance aid to dependent children, aid to the blind, food stamps, government aid, meal ticket, old-age assistance, public welfare, relief, relief payments, social welfare, welfare, welfare aid, welfare payments

public bathroom bathroom, comfort station, john, lavatory, rest room, toilet, water closet, WC

public debt national debt

public defender court-appointed lawyer

public domain government-owned property, public ownership, state ownership

public enemy common enemy, criminal, felon, gangster, lawbreaker, malevolent, outlaw, perpetrator, public enemy number one, racketeer, scofflaw, universal foe, villain

public eye exposure, limelight, public attention, public consciousness, public scrutiny, spotlight

public health epidemiology, hygiene, hygienics, sanitation

public house bar, beer parlor, hostelry, inn, pub, saloon, tavern, watering hole

public housing affordable housing, low-and-middle-income housing, low-cost housing, market-rate housing, public-sector housing

public land government land, national forest, national park, national wildlife refuge, nature conservancy land, unappropriated land

public law government law, public policy

public library bookmobile, book wagon, branch library, circulating library, city library, county library, lending library, local library, municipal library, national library, noncommercial library, state archives, state library, town library

public offering initial public offering, new securities issue

public opinion climate of opinion, common belief, community sentiment, consensus gentium, conventional wisdom, general belief, group pressure, popular belief, prevailing belief, prevailing sentiment, public belief, social pressure, special-interest pressure, vox pop, vox populi

public policy policy, polity, public law

public prosecutor attorney general, DA, district attorney, judge advocate

public relations hype, marketing, PR, promotions, propaganda, publicity

public safety safeguarding, security

public sale auction, auctioneering, Dutch auction, sale by auction

public school government-funded school

public servant civil servant, elected official, government employee, government worker, officeholder, official, public employee, public official

public service benevolences, civil service, good works, government employment, philanthropies, public life, works

public speaking art of speaking, declamation, elocution, oratory, rhetoric, speaking, speechification, speech making, stump oratory, tub-thumping

public television educational television, noncommercial television, PTV

public transportation bus line, light rail, LRT, mass transit, metro, rail rapid transit, railway, rapid transit, subway, urban transportation service

public utility communications company, electric company, telephone company, water company

public welfare public assistance, welfare, welfare expenditure

public works construction projects, publicly funded construction

puerperal fever childbed fever

pug nose upturned nose

pull-down menu drop-down menu

pulp magazine pulp fiction, rag

pump iron lift weights, work out

punch bowl flowing bowl, mixing bowl

punch card Hollerith card, punched card

punching bag crazy bag, heavy bag, speed bag

punch line gag line, joke climax, point, tag line

punctuation mark ampersand, apostrophe, braces, brackets, colon, comma, dash, ellipsis, exclamation point, guillemets, hyphen, interrobang, parentheses, period, question mark, quotation marks, semicolon, slash, virgule

punitive damages amercement, compensatory damages, damages, financial penalty

punk rock hard-driving rock

puppet show marionettes, Punch-and-Judy show, puppet play, puppetry

puppy dog pooch, pup, puppy, whelp

puppy love adolescent love, calf-love, crush, dawn of love, first love, infatuation, young love

pup tent canopy, shelter tent

purchasing power ability to purchase, buying power, earnings, real wages

purse strings almighty dollar, financial control, money belt, money power, power of the purse, wallet

push broom wide broom, wide sweeper

push button control, switch

push the envelope be the point man, blaze the trail, forge ahead, front, go to the limit, pioneer

put on an act bluff, fake, feign, invent, let on like, make up, play possum, play the part, pose, pretend, simulate

put paid to bring to a close, finish something, make an end of, put an end to

put something over on deceive, pull a fast one, put on, take in

putting green grass green

put together assemble, bring together, build, combine, compose, concoct, connect, construct, engineer, erect, form, gather, join, link, make up, mix, produce

put to shame bring shame upon, hold up to shame, humiliate, shame

Pyrrhic victory Cadmean victory, narrow victory, no-win situation, offset victory, victory at great cost

Qq

Quadragesima Sunday Quadragesima

qualitative analysis chemical testing

quality control cross-check, QA, quality assurance, review, survey, vetting

quantitative analysis chemical testing, gravimetric analysis, volumetric analysis

quantum leap breakthrough, giant strides, inspiration, leaps and bounds, quantum jump, radical change, sudden progress, transilience

quantum mechanics statistical mechanics, wave mechanics

quarter note crotchet

quartz glass fused quartz, fused silica

quartz lamp mercury-vapor lamp

Quaternary period Holocene epoch, Ice Age, Pleistocene epoch, postglacial epoch, recent epoch

queen consort king's wife

queen dowager dowager queen, queen mother

Queen Mab fairy queen

queen regent queen regnant

Queen's Bench criminal court, Queen's Counsel

Queen's English correct English, good English, King's English, Received Pronunciation, Received Standard, Standard English

que será será whatever happens, whatever may happen, whatever will be will be

quick-and-dirty ad hoc, cheaply done, cheaply made, crude but effective, improvised, jury-rigged, makeshift, offhand, off-the-cuff, of inferior quality, spur-of-the-moment

quick bread baking powder biscuits

quicken one's step accelerate, get a move on, quicken one's speed

quick fix hasty remedy, jury-rigged expedient, makeshift, stopgap

quick kick knuckler, squib kick

quick study mind like a sponge, quick mind, ready grasp, receptivity

quick-tempered cantankerous,

grouchy, hot-blooded, irritable, short-fused, short-tempered, testy, touchy, volatile

quick time double time, double-quick time, quick march, quickstep, quickstep march

quick-witted acute, alert, astute, bright, clever, intelligent, keen, nimble, on the ball, savvy, sharp, sharp-witted, shrewd, smart

quid pro quo equal exchange, equal substitution, equivalent, eye for an eye, like for like, measure for measure, something in return, substitute, tit for tat, trade-off

quinine water tonic water

Quinquagesima Sunday Shrove Sunday

quiz show game show, giveaway show, panel show, quiz program

quod erat demonstrandum it must follow, QED, which was to be proved

Rr

racial discrimination anti-Semitism, race discrimination, race prejudice, race snobbery, racialism, racism

racing boat cigarette boat, hydrofoil, speedboat

racing form daily racing form, form

rack and ruin blue ruin, destitution, destruction, rack, ruin, ruination, wreckage

rack of lamb crown roast, lamb ribs, roast lamb

rack railway cog railway

radar altimeter absolute altimeter

radar beacon racon, radar-marked beacon, ramark

radar detector Fuzzbuster™

radial engine pancake engine, piston engine, rotary engine

radial tire pneumatic tire

radiant heat convected heat, convector heat, induction heat, thermal radiation

radiation therapy adjuvant therapy, radiotherapeutics, radiotherapy

radioactive waste nucleonics, poison

radio announcer broadcaster, deejay, DJ

radio beacon radio beam, radio marker, radio navigation, radio-range beacon, radio-range station

radiocarbon dating carbon dating, carbon-14 dating, dating, half-life dating, radiometric dating, thermoluminescence

radio compass direction finder, navigational aid, radio direction finder, RDF, triangulator, wireless compass

radio frequency audio frequency, carrier frequency, extremely high frequency, high frequency, intermediate frequency, low frequency, medium frequency, RF, superhigh frequency, ultrahigh frequency, very high frequency, very low frequency

radio source quasi-stellar radio source, radio waves

radio spectrum electromagnetic spectrum, radio-frequency spectrum, visible spectrum

radio telescope dish antenna, parabolic reflector, radar telescope

radio wave electromagnetic radiation, frequency wave, microwave

rag doll Raggedy Andy, Raggedy Ann

ragged edge bedrock, brink, cliff's edge, edge, limit, precarious position

raglan sleeve dolman sleeve

rags to riches Horatio Alger story

ragtag and bobtail canaille, common ruck, everyman, lowest social class, rabble, ragtag, rank and file, riffraff

rag trade dressmaking, fashion design, garment industry, garment making, haute couture, Seventh Avenue, tailoring

railroad accident railroad disaster, railway accident, train accident

railroad flat railroad apartment

rain check assurance, postponement, promise, reserved ticket

rain forest jungle, tropical rain forest, tropical woods

rain gauge hygrometer, Nilometer, pluviometer, udometer

rainy day adversity, bad patch, trough

raise Cain cause trouble, raise a rumpus, raise hell, raise the devil, raise the dickens

raise one's voice assert oneself, shout, speak out, speak up, yell

raise the curtain ring up the curtain, shine some light on, take the lid off, unveil

raison d'être causa causans, justification for existing, reason for being, reason for existing, reason why

rake over the coals dress down, give a piece of one's mind, haul over the coals, reprimand

rammed earth pisé

ranch house country house, farmhouse

R&D experimentation, fieldwork, research and development

random access direct access

random-access memory RAM

random sample grab bag, sampling, straw vote

R and R downtime, R&R, reanimation, renewal, rest and recreation, rest and recuperation, rest and relaxation, reviviscence

rank and file common run, common soldiery, common sort, forces, grass roots, majority, plebeians, proletariat, ranks

rapid eye movement dreaming sleep, paradoxical sleep, rapid eye movement sleep, REM sleep

rapid transit elevated trains, underground trains, urban passenger transportation system
rap music hip-hop, rap
rap sheet arrest record, criminal record, police record
rapture of the deep nitrogen narcosis
rare bird oddball, odd fellow, queer duck, rara avis
rare book early edition, first edition, signed edition
rare earth element base metal, native metal, noble metal, oxide, precious metal, rare earth, rare metal, rare earth metal
raree-show peep show
ratchet wheel cog wheel, sprocket wheel
rate of exchange convertibility, currency exchange rate, exchange rate, foreign exchange
rat race battle of life, daily grind, hamster cage, survival of the fittest, treadmill, vicious circle
raw deal bad rap, bummer, drag, ill fortune, misfortune, pits, rotten hand, rotten luck, tough luck
raw material basic material, grist, natural resources, organic matter, primal matter, resources, staple, stock, unprocessed material
reading ability reading comprehension
reading desk ambo, desk, escritoire, lectern, reading stand, secretary
read-only memory CD-ROM, programmable read-only memory, PROM, ROM, small memory
real estate chattels real, freehold, immovables, land, land and buildings, landed property, landholdings, lot, plat, plot, real property, realty, territory
realistic art naturalistic art
real McCoy genuine article, goods, gospel, McCoy, no imitation, no joke, real thing, very thing
real time actual time, problem-solving time
real world actuality, here and now, natural world, physical world, things as they are, world of nature
rear end backside, behind, breech, hind end, hind part, posterior, stern, tail end
rear guard backyard, rear area
rear window defogger rear window defroster
receiving blanket baby blanket
receiving end receipt, receiving
receiving line line of greeters

rechargeable battery nicad battery

recommended daily allowance food pyramid, RDA, recommended daily vitamins and minerals

record album EP, 45, gramophone record, long-playing record, LP, platter, 78, 33

record player audio sound system, gramophone, hi-fi, high-fidelity system, phonograph, sound system, stereo, stereo set, Victrola™

recreational vehicle camper, camp trailer, house trailer, mobile home, motor home, RV, trailer, Winnebago™

recreation room basement, family room, game room, playroom, pool room, rec room, rumpus room

red apple Macintosh, Red Delicious

red blood cell erythrocyte, hemocyte, red cell, red corpuscle

red brick common brick

red carpet ceremony, red-carpet treatment, royal welcome, salutation, standing at attention, welcome mat

red cent cent, copper penny, farthing, hill of beans, insignificant value, penny

redeye gravy ham gravy

red flag casus belli, delicate subject, red light, red rag, sore point

red heat intense heat, oppressive heat, sweltering heat, torrid heat, tropical heat

red herring curve ball, distraction, distractor, diversion, diversionary tactic, false clue, false face, false trail, fool's errand, misleading clue, smoke screen

red-letter day anniversary, day to remember, gala day, holiday, special day

red light stop light, traffic signal

red man American Indian, Amerind, Amerindian, Indian, injun, Native American, Red Indian, redskin

red meat beef, flesh, mammal meat, meat, viande

red tape bureaucracy, bureaucratic paperwork, bureaucratic rules, city hall, official forms, officialism, official procedures, paper shuffling, proper channels

reduced hemoglobin deoxyhemoglobin

reductio ad absurdum disproof, reduction, ridicule

red wine burgundy, cabernet, cabernet sauvignon, claret, merlot, pinot noir, shiraz

reed instrument bass clarinet, basset horn, clarinet, double reed, reed, single reed, woodwind

reef knot square knot

reentering angle reentrant angle

refectory table board, heavy table

reference book almanac, atlas, dictionary, directory, encyclopedia, how-to book, sourcebook, thesaurus, wordbook, work of reference

reference mark asterisk, bullet, caret, dagger, diacritical mark, ditto, double dagger, leaders, punctuation, punctuation mark, reference

reflex action automatism, instinct, involuntariness, Pavlovian reaction, reflection, reflex

Reform Judaism Reconstructionism

reform school boot camp, Borstal, house of correction, military school, reformatory, training school

refractive index index of refraction

refresher course correspondence course, crash course, distance-learning course, elective course, further reading, further study, revision, seminar, summer course

registered nurse licensed practical nurse, LPN, nurse practitioner, RN

regulator gene cistron, operator gene, regulatory gene, structural gene

reign of terror brutal suppression, French Revolution, mob rule, period of suppression, terrorism

reinforced concrete ferroconcrete, prestressed concrete

rejection slip manuscript rejection, refusal slip

relate to comprehend, connect, empathize, have connection with, identify with, link with, stand in one's shoes, sympathize, understand

relational database database tables

relay race team race

relief map contour map, USGS map {compare *topographic map*}

relief pitcher bull pen, closer, fireman, inner reliever, long reliever, middle reliever, reliever, short reliever, stopper

religious ceremony celebration, circumcision, liturgy, marriage, observance, ritual, service, solemnization, sun dance

religious scholar theologian

Religious Society of Friends Friends, Quakerism, Quakers

remittance man defector, exile, expatriate, refugee, remittance woman

remote control clicker, push-button control, remote

REM sleep paradoxical sleep, rapid eye movement sleep

Renaissance man person of many parts, Renaissance woman

renewable energy geothermal power, hydroelectricity, renewable resource, solar energy, solar power, wave power, wind power

repeating decimal circulating decimal, recurring decimal

repertory company repertory theater, stock, stock company, strawhat, strawhat circuit, summer stock, summer theater, touring company

repetitive strain injury carpal tunnel syndrome, repetitive strain disorder, RSI, sprain, strain

report card grade card, progress report, transcript

Republican party GOP, Grand Old Party

requiescat in pace may he or she rest in peace, rest in peace, RIP

reserve bank central bank, federal reserve bank, reserve bank system, U.S. Federal Reserve Bank

res gestae acta, affairs, dealings, deeds, doings, things done

residential area community, residential district

respiratory distress syndrome hyaline membrane disease, respiratory disease, upper respiratory disease

respiratory system bronchi, epiglottis, lungs, trachea, windpipe

rest and recreation downtime, R and R, recreation, respite, rest and relaxation, revivification, time to chill

rest home assisted living facility, continuing care, convalescent home, convalescent hospital, nursing home, old folks' home, old soldiers' home, retirement community, retirement facility, retirement home, sailors' snug harbor, sanitarium

rest room bathroom, comfort

station, head, john, ladies' room, latrine, lavatory, men's room, outhouse, powder room, privy, public bathroom, toilet, urinal, water closet, WC

retail therapy home shopping, impulse buying, shopping, shopping spree, window-shopping

retaining wall abutment, breast wall, bulkhead, bulwark, embankment, piling

retirement home continuing-care community, life-care home, retirement community, retirement village

Revised Standard Version RSV

Revised Version American Revised Version, Authorized Version, King James Version

revolving door rolling stone, rotator

rhetorical question cross-question

rheumatoid arthritis rheumatism

Rh factor antigen, blood group, Rh antigen, Rh-negative, Rh-positive, Rh-type, rhesus factor

rhumb line compass point, loxadrome, loxodromic curve

rhyme royal ababbcc, tail rhyme

rhyming slang pig Latin

rhythm and blues R and B, the blues

rhythm method contraception by abstinence

ribonucleic acid RNA

rice paper onionskin, parchment

Richter scale earthquake scale

ride herd on drive, keep control over, keep watch, punch cattle, shepherd

ride shotgun fend, guard in transit, shelter, sit in the passenger seat

ridge beam ridgepole

riding breeches jodhpurs

rift valley midocean fracture, rift

right angle 90-degree angle

right ascension declination

right away at once, immediately, straightaway, without delay

right brain right hemisphere

right-hand man alter ego, fidus Achates, gal Friday, man Friday, right hand, right-hand woman, second self, strong right arm

right off the bat immediately, instantly, on the dot, without delay

right of way access, approach, inlet

right on the button correct, exact, on target, on the money, on the nose

right stuff abilities, bravery, courage, credentials, drive, experience, guts, qualifications, skills, talent, the goods, the makings, the stuff, what it takes

right up one's alley cut out for one, down one's alley, fits one like a glove

right wing conservative faction, extreme right, radical right, reactionary faction, right

rigor mortis death rattle, muscular stiffening, swan song

rime riche identical rhyme

ring binder trapper

ring down the curtain end a performance

ring finger annulary, third finger

ring mold Jell-O™ mold

ring road belt highway, beltway, circumferential

riot shield gas mask, protective clothing, safeguard

rip current riptide, tide rip, undertow

ripple effect causal sequence, chain of cause and effect, contagion effect, dispersion, dissemination, domino effect, knock-on effect, overspreading, slippery slope, sprawl

ripple mark corrugation, kink, rugosity

rise and shine arise, get going, get out of bed, get up, greet the day, pile out, roll out, shake a leg, turn out, up and at 'em, wake up

rising from the dead Lazarus effect, rebirth, regeneration, resurrection

rising rhythm ascending rhythm

risk capital venture capital

rite of passage baptism, circumcision, initiation, initiation rite, initiatory rite, rite de passage

road agent footpad, highwayman, highway robber, holdup man, robber

road hog hog, monopolist

road map itinerary, road book

road metal asphalt, blacktop, laterite, macadam, Tarmac™

road rage anger when driving, driver anger, driver rage

road test bench test, dry run, dummy run, practical test, practice run, trial run

road warrior bagman, commercial traveler, knight of the road, traveling man, traveling salesman, traveling woman

Roaring Twenties Age of the Red-Hot Mamas, Flapper Era, Golden Twenties, Jazz Age, Mad Decade

robber baron feudal lord, financial magnate, industrial magnate

robot bomb buzz bomb, doodlebug, flying bomb, P-plane, robomb, Vergeltungswaffe, V-weapon

rock and roll popular music, rock, rock music, rock 'n' roll, soft rock

rock bottom all-time low, base, bedrock, depths, nadir, record low, solid bottom, solid rock

rock candy hard candy, sugar candy

rock climber alpinist, climber, mountain climber, mountaineer, rock-jock

rock climbing ice climbing, mountain climbing, mountaineering, scaling, scrambles, walkups

rock crystal transparent quartz

rocker arm pivoted lever

rocket bomb cruising missile, flying bomb, flying torpedo

rocket engine reaction engine, rocket, rocket motor

rocket launcher bazooka, projector

rocket science rocket engineering, rocket research, rocketry, rocket technology

rocket scientist missile engineer, missile man, rocketeer, rocket engineer, rocketer, rocket man, rocket technician

rocket ship interplanetary rocket, manned rocket, space rocket, spaceship

rock garden rockery, Zen garden

rock hound earth scientist, geologist, geology enthusiast, mineral collector, rock collector, rock hobbyist, rock hunter

rocking chair cradle, rocker

rocking horse cockhorse, hobbyhorse

rock lobster crayfish, langouste, sea crayfish, spiny lobster

rock the boat challenge the status quo, complain, disturb, disturb the balance, make a stink, make waves, stir things up, upset the apple cart

rogues' gallery criminals' pictures, dossier

role model epitome, example, exemplar, good example, hero, heroine, idol, mentor, paragon, shining example, star, superstar, very model

roll bar roll cage

roll call census, head count, muster, roll, roster, rota, scroll, vote

roller bearing ball bearing

roller skate in-line skate, Rollerblades™

rolling boil full boil
rolling budget continuous budget, month-by-month budget
rolling paper cigarette paper
rolling pin flattener, roller
roly-poly big, dumpy, fat, full-faced, large, obese, overweight, plump, pudgy, rotund, soft in the middle, stout, tubby
roman à clef bildungsroman, historical fiction, roman-fleuve, saga
Roman alphabet Latin alphabet
Roman calendar lunar calendar
Roman candle Catherine wheel, rocket, signal rocket, skyrocket, sparkler
Roman Catholicism Catholicism, Catholicity, Church of Rome, papistry, popery, Romanism
Romance language Catalan, Continental, French, Indo-European language, Insular, Italian, Italic language, Latin, Portuguese, Provençal, Spanish
Roman collar clerical collar
Roman Empire Rome
Roman holiday duel, ethnic cleansing, final solution, gladiatorial combat
Roman nose hook nose
Roman numeral C, D, I, L, M, V, X
rood screen altar screen, chancel screen, gallery, jube, rood arch, rood loft
room and board bed and board, full board, lodging and meals
rooming house boardinghouse, lodging house, room rentals
room service delivery, free delivery
root cellar root-crop storage, underground cellar, underground pit
root crop cash crop, potatoes, turnips, yams
root directory highest-level directory
root of the matter casus belli, root of the trouble
rope tow lift, ski conveyor, ski lift, ski tow
Rorschach test inkblot test, personality test
rose-colored glasses dream world, hope, idealism, idealization, rosy picture
rotary beater eggbeater
rotary engine pancake engine, radial engine, turbine
rotary press cylinder press, platen press, web press
Rotisserie League fantasy baseball
rotten borough close borough, pocket borough

rough-and-ready ad-lib, crude, extemporaneous, improvised, jerry-built, makeshift, provisional, wild-and-woolly
rough cut unedited movie
rough diamond design, diamond in the rough, first draft, first stab, mock-up, raw material, rough copy, rough outline, rough sketch, study, unlicked cub
rough draft draft, outline, plan, sketch
rough endoplasmic reticulum granular endoplasmic reticulum, RER
rough up abuse, handle harshly, knock about, manhandle, roughen
round figure lump sum, round sum
round lot full lot
round number rough number
round sum lump sum
round table brainstorming, buzz session, conference, council, discussion group, forum, panel
round-trip big salami, circuit clout, circuition, closing the circle, dinger, full circle, home run, one you can hang the wash on, round-tripper, tater, there and back, tour
round window secondary eardrum
row house duplex house
rowing machine rower
RSVP please answer, reply, réspondez s'il vous plaît
rubber band elastic, elastic band, elastic loop, gum band
rubber check bad check, bounced check, bouncing check, bouncing paper, forgery, insufficient funds, kited check, not enough to cover, OD, overdraft, overdrawn account
rubber match tie-breaking game
rubber spatula rubber scraper
rubber stamp go-ahead, green light, notarization, seal, seal of approval, stamp, thumbs-up
rubbing alcohol isopropyl alcohol
rub elbows with interact, mingle with, mix with, rub shoulders with, socialize
rub out blow away, bump off, chill, deep-six, dispatch, dispose of, do away with, do in, dust, erase, grease, hit, ice, kill, knock off, murder, nuke, off, snuff, snuff out, stretch out, take care of, waste, wax, whack, zap
rub the wrong way annoy, bother, bug, irritate
RU 486 abortion pill

rugby shirt rugby jersey, Rugby jersey

rugged individualism individual freedom, individualism

rug rat carpet ape, carpet rat, crumb snatcher, curtain climber, rug ape, small child, tot

rule of the road customary practice, established practices, established rules

rule of thumb hit-and-miss, pragmatism, trial, trial and error, unwritten rule; criterion, standard

rules of conduct code of conduct, custom, decorum, diplomatic code, etiquette, formalities, guidelines, manners, protocol, social code, social procedures, standard procedure

rule the roost crack the whip, play first fiddle, ride herd, wear the pants

rumble seat backseat

rummage sale clearance sale, garage sale, tag sale, white elephant sale, yard sale

rumpus room family room, game room, party room, playroom, recreation room, rec room

runcible spoon three-pronged fork

runic character futhark, futhorc, futhork, ideograph, ogham, phonogram, rune, runic alphabet, runic symbol

running account checking account

running back blocking back, flanker back, fullback, halfback, offensive back, plunging back, slotback, tailback, wingback

running gear automobile's working parts

running head header, jump head, running title

running knot slipknot

running light sidelight

running mate companion candidate

running shoe sneaker, spikes

running water fresh water, stream, waterway

run-of-the-mill average, basic, common, everyday, fair, general, mediocre, normal, ordinary, regular, routine, so-so, standard, usual

run riot carouse, cut loose, debauch, insurge, insurrect, live hard, mutiny, revolt, riot, run amok, run wild

run the gauntlet be a target, be

a whipping boy, come to grips with, court disaster, face criticism, face one's punishment, go in harm's way, go through fire and water, march up to the cannon's mouth, meet head-on, take one's life in one's hands, take potshots, take the bull by the horns

rush candle rushlight

rush hour bottleneck, congestion, gridlock, heavy traffic, jam, road rage, traffic jam

Russian Revolution Russian Civil War

Russian roulette loaded pistol

rust belt industrialized area, Midwest

Rx cure, pharmaceutical prescription, remedy

Ss

sabbatical year breather, furlough, leave of absence, sabbatical, sabbatical leave, time off

sack race gunnysack race, potato-sack race, three-legged race

sacred cow god, goddess, golden calf, hero, idol, object of worship, protected interest, sensitive issue, tin god

sacrifice bunt sacrifice hit

sacrifice fly blooper, sac fly, sacrifice hit {compare *sacrifice bunt*}

saddle horse mount, palfrey, rider, riding horse, rouncy, saddler, steed

saddle stitch perfect binding, stapling, wire stitch

sad sack hard-luck guy, loser, schlemiel, unfortunate

safari jacket bush jacket

safari shirt bush shirt

safe-deposit box bank vault, personal vault, safe, safe-deposit vault, safety-deposit box, strong room

safe harbor asylum, haven, hiding place, port in a storm, protection, refuge, retreat, safe haven, safe house, sanctuary, security, shelter

safe house asylum, cloister, haven, hermitage, hiding place, port in a storm, protection, refuge, retreat, safe harbor, safe haven, sanctuary, secret place, security, shelter

safety belt lap belt, seat belt

safety curtain asbestos curtain, fire curtain, grand drape

safety glass laminated glass, laminated safety glass, tempered glass, tempered safety glass

safety island traffic island

safety lamp acetylene lamp, Davy lamp, miner's lamp

safety match friction match, matchbook

safety net insurance, parachute, precautions, preventive measure, protection, safeguard, safety plug, safety valve, sheet anchor

safety valve means of escape, outlet

Saint Elmo's fire corona discharge

Saint Vitus' dance chorea, rigor, Syndenham's chorea, tarantism, the jerks

salad days bloom, flower of life, heyday of youth, prime of life, school days, springtime of life, tender age, younger days, youth

salad dressing French dressing, Italian dressing, mayonnaise dressing, oil and vinegar, ranch dressing, Russian dressing, Thousand Island dressing, vinaigrette

sales slip proof of purchase, receipt, voucher

Salk vaccine OPV, polio vaccine, poliomyelitis vaccine, Sabin vaccine

Sallie Mae SLMA, Student Loan Marketing Association

sally forth emerge, go forth, launch, put forth, sally, set forth, start, strike out

salt flat alkali flat, badlands, Death Valley, salt marsh

salt water brine, saline, sea water

S&M algolagnia, algolagny, sadomasochism

sand trap beach, golf course hazard, sand green, sand hazard

sandwich board advertising placard, display board, notice board

sanitary landfill dump, dump site, garbage dump, junk heap, junk pile, junkyard, landfill, midden, scrap heap, toxic waste dump, wasteyard

sanitary napkin feminine napkin, sanitary pad

Santa Claus Father Christmas, Kriss Kringle, Saint Nicholas, Saint Nick, Santa

Saratoga trunk traveling trunk

saturated fat hydrogenated fat, saturated fatty acid

saturation point completeness, dew point, plenitude, satiety, saturation

Saturday night special cheap handgun, firearm, handgun, pistol, revolver, rod, sawed-off shotgun, six-shooter

save face preserve one's dignity, preserve one's honor

saving grace extenuation, good point, palliative, point of character, redeeming feature

savings account interest-bearing account, money market account, nest egg, provision

savings and loan association bank, building and loan association, building society, lending institution, S&L, S and L, savings bank, savings institution, thrift, thrift institution

savoir faire cultivation, diplomacy, graciousness, poise, savvy, social grace, social know-how, sophistication, suavity, worldliness

saw-toothed jagged, notched, serrated, zigzag

scalar product dot product, inner product

scandal sheet extra edition, rag, special edition, tabloid

scare tactics ambush, arm-twisting, bullying, coercion, duress, force, intimidation, persuasion, pressure, reign of terror, strong-arm tactics, terrorism, terrorization, threat

scarlet fever roseola, scarlatina

scarlet letter badge of infamy, bar sinister, mark of Cain

scarlet woman hooker, lady of the evening, painted woman, prostitute, streetwalker

scatter rug throw rug

scavenger hunt hare and hounds, treasure hunt

scene painter landscape painter, scenewright, scenic artist, scenographer

scenic railway scenic railroad

Schick test diphtheria test

school administrator school principal, superintendent of schools, vice principal

school age early years, juvenescence, juvenility, younger days, youth

school board board of education, board of trustees

school tie club tie, regimental tie, tie

school year academic year

science fiction futurism, sci-fi, sci-fi movie, SF, space fiction, space odyssey, space opera

scientific classification taxology, taxonomy

scientific name binomen, binomial name, binomial nomenclature, scientific epithet, taxonomic name, trinomen, trinomial name

scientific notation exponential notation, floating-point notation

scissors kick back kick, flutter kick, frog kick, wedge kick, whip kick

Scotch™ tape adhesive tape, sticky tape, tape

Scotch whisky scotch, whiskey

scot-free costing nothing, for free, free of charge, without making a payment, without penalty

scrap heap dump, dustheap, garbage dump, junk heap, junk pile, kitchen midden, landfill, midden, toxic waste dump, worthless material

scratch pad notepad, pad of paper, scrap paper

scratch sheet race card

scratch test allergy test

screen pass pitchout, quick release, short forward pass

screw propeller propeller, screw, twin screws

scrimmage line flat, imaginary line, line, line of scrimmage, LOS

scuba diving skin diving, snorkeling

scut work dirty work, donkey work, grunt work, thankless task

sea anchor anchor, bower, drift anchor, drogue, sheet anchor

sea breeze cat's-paw, cooling breeze, ocean breeze, onshore breeze

sea change break with the past, conversion, major change, marked transformation, metamorphosis, quantum jump, quantum leap, radical change, revolutionary change, sudden change, total change, transfiguration, transformation, upheaval

sea chest ditty box

sea dog barnacle-back, experienced sailor, mariner, master mariner, old salt, old sea dog, sailor, seafarer, shellback

sea king buccaneer, pirate, privateer, sea rover, Viking, Viking pirate chief

sea level mean sea level, ocean's surface, SL, water level

seal ring signet ring

sea power admiralty, naval strength

search engine browser, portal

search warrant discovery, summons

sea room elbowroom, leeway, open space, wide berth

sea rover buccaneer, corsair, picaroon, pirate, privateer, rover, sea robber, swashbuckler

sea scout sea explorer

sea serpent giant squid, hydra, kraken, leviathan, Loch Ness monster, oarfish

seasonal affective disorder melancholia, mild depression, SAD, seasonal depression

seasonal unemployment cyclical unemployment

seat belt lap belt, safety belt, safety strap

sebaceous cyst carbuncle, cyst, pimple, wen, zit

secondary cell storage cell

secondary school college-preparatory school, high school, intermediate school, junior high school, middle school, prep school, preparatory school, senior high school

secondary sex characteristic mons pubis, mons veneris

secondary stress weak stress

second banana assistant, chorus, deputy, runner-up, second fiddle, second string, second-rater, substitute, supporting role

second base keystone, keystone sack, second, second bag

second-best inferior, next best, next to best, nothing special, second-rate

second childhood anecdotage, dotage, dotardism, senile dementia, senilism, senility

second-class earthborn, lowborn, lowbred, lower-class, of humble birth, of secondary status, plebeian

Second Coming Advent, parousia, parousiamania, Second Advent

second estate aristocracy, better sort, cream, elite, gentry, patriciate, privileged, ruling class, upper class, upper crust

second fiddle backseat, benchwarmer, low man on totem pole, reserves, secondary role, second banana, second-string, second-stringer, second team, understudy

secondhand information buzz, gossip, grapevine report, hearsay, rumor, scuttlebutt, talk, unconfirmed report, word of mouth

secondhand smoke passive smoke

second mate second officer

second nature acquired behavior, custom, familiarity, force of habit, habit, habit pattern, matter of course

second person proximate

second-rate cheap, inferior, low-grade, mediocre, poor, second-best, second-class, shabby

second sight clairvoyance, ESP, extrasensory perception, feyness, inner sense, insight, lucidity, precognition, prescience, sixth sense, the force, third eye

second-story man burglar, cat burglar, cat man, housebreaker, robber, second-story thief, second-story worker

second-string bench, benchwarmers, reserves, second team, substitutes

second thought afterthought, arrière-pensée, better thoughts, disillusion, double take, esprit d'escalier, reconsideration, reservation, rethinking, review

second wind energy burst, refreshment, rejuvenation, renaissance, restored energy, restored strength, second energy burst

secret agent cloak-and-dagger man, double agent, informer, inside man, intelligence agent, mole, operative, scout, snoop, spy, undercover agent, undercover man

secret partner dormant partner, silent partner, sleeping partner

secret police gestapo, SWAT team

secret service intelligence agency, intelligence work, political police, secret police

secret society cabal, lodge, social club

Section Eight army discharge

section gang railroad work crew

secular humanism humanism, secularism

security blanket emotional support, psychological support, reassurance

security guard armed guard

security risk security threat, vulnerability

sedan chair palanquin

sedimentary rock chalk, chemical sedimentary rock, clastic rock, conglomerate, limestone, lithified sediment, mechanical sedimentary rock, nonclastic rock, sandstone, shale, stratified rock

seed money venture capital, venture money

Seeing Eye™ dog guide dog

seismic wave earthquake wave, shock wave

seize the day carpe diem, grab the chance, live for the day, seize the occasion, smell the roses, take the opportunity

selective service compulsory military service, national service

self-assured cocky, confident, full of oneself, secure, self-confident, sure of oneself

self-centered conceited, egocentric, egotistical, narcissistic, self-absorbed, selfish, self-serving

self-confidence aplomb, inner strength, positive self-image, self-assurance

self-conscious awkward, bashful, guarded, ill at ease, inhibited, reserved, sheepish, shy

self-control restraint, self-discipline, self-restraint, temperance, willpower

self-defeating defeating its own purpose

self-esteem belief in oneself, confidence, pride, self-assurance, self-regard, self-respect

self-evident apparent, clear, evident, obvious, plain, self-explanatory

self-important arrogant, bigheaded, conceited, egotistical, high-and-mighty, overbearing, pompous, smug, snobbish, snotty, swaggering

self-made man man to watch, nouveau riche, prosperous person, rising star, self-made woman, whiz kid

self-reliant autonomous, independent, self-sufficient

self-respect dignity, pride, self-esteem, self-regard, self-worth

self-righteous holier-than-thou, hypocritical, pious, preachy, sanctimonious, smug

self-satisfied arrogant, bigheaded, full of oneself, pleased with oneself, proud, smug

self-service buffet, self-serve, smorgasbord

self-sticking self-adhesive, self-stick

self-sufficiency autonomy, independence, self-reliance

seller's market bullish market, bull market, consumer demand, land-office business, roaring trade, short supply, steady demand

sell out betray, double-cross, stab in the back

seminal fluid milt, prostatic fluid, semen, sperm, spermatic fluid

semiprecious stone amazonite, opal

send packing discharge, dismiss, give walking papers, show the door

senile dementia Alzheimer's disease, presenile dementia, senile psychosis

senior citizen elderly person, geriatric, golden-ager, oldster, patriarch, pensioner, retiree

senior high school eleventh grade, gymnasium, high school, preparatory school, secondary school, tenth grade, twelfth grade

sense-datum color, elementary unit, smell, sound

sense organ ear, eye, mouth, nose, sensor, skin, throat, tongue

sense perception percept, perception, sense impression, sense-data, sense-datum

sensible horizon apparent horizon, local horizon, visible horizon

sentence structure syntax, word order

sentential calculus propositional calculus

sentential function open sentence, propositional function, truth function, truth table, truth-value

sentry box gatehouse, porter's lodge, tollbooth, tollhouse

separation energy binding energy

separation of powers executive branch, judicial branch, legislative branch

septic sore throat strep throat

septic tank catch basin, cesspit, cesspool, septic system, sewage-disposal tank, sewer, sump

serial cable {compare *parallel cable*}

serial number identification number, unique number

serial port serial interface {compare *parallel port*}

service break break point

service charge additional charge, corkage, cover charge

service line boundary line

service mark distinguishing mark, logo, logotype, registered trademark, trademark, trade name

service medal distinguished service medal, military medal, soldier's medal, war medal

service road frontage road, side road

service station filling station, gas station

service stripe epaulet, hash mark, Hershey bar, overseas bar

set piece ceremony, scenery, stage set, tableau

set sail dive in, go ahead, set out, start out

seven deadly sins anger, avarice, covetousness, envy, gluttony, lust, pride, sloth

seven seas Antarctic Ocean, Arctic Ocean, Indian Ocean, North Atlantic Ocean, North Pacific Ocean, South Atlantic Ocean, South Pacific Ocean

seventeen-year locust cicada, cicala, dog-day cicada, periodical cicada

seventh heaven celestial throne, cloud nine, empyrean, heaven of heavens, nirvana, throne of God

severance pay discontinuance wage, dismissal wage, golden parachute

sex appeal allure, animal magnetism, an indescribable something, charisma, charm, confidence, it, magnetism, pizzazz, presence, sexiness, sexual attractiveness, sexual magnetism, star power

sex cell gamete, germ cell

sex chromatin Barr body

sex chromosome heterochromosome, idiochromosome, sex chromatid, sex chromatin, X chromosome, Y chromosome

sex drive desire, horniness, libido, lust, sexual urge, urge

sex fiend nymphet, nympho, nymphomaniac, pervert, sex freak, sexual deviant, sexual pervert

sex kitten babe, bunny, centerfold, looker, pinup girl, pussycat, sex object, sex symbol, stunner

sex life love life

sex symbol Adonis, beefcake, dreamboat, Greek god, hunk, looker, sex object, stud

sexual assault carnal abuse, date rape, forcible intercourse, molestation, rape, sex crime, sexual offense, unlawful sexual intercourse

sexual deviation fetish, perversion

sexual harassment exploitation, impropriety, inappropriate behavior, intimidation, offensive sexual advances, unprofessional behavior, unwanted sexual advances

sexual intercourse cohabitation, coitus, consummation, copulation, going to bed with, making love, sex, sexual commerce, sexual congress, sexual relations, sleeping with

sexually active easy, fast, indiscreet, loose, of loose morals, promiscuous, wanton, whorish

sexually transmitted disease AIDS, chancroid, chlamydia, clap, crabs, gonorrhea, herpes, HIV, social disease, STD, syphilis, venereal disease

sexual maturity puberty, pubescence

sexual orientation sexual nature, sexual preference

sexual relations carnal knowledge, cohabitation, coitus, copulation, having sex, intercourse, intimacy, lovemaking, marital relations, mating, nooky, relations, screwing, sexual intercourse, sexual union, sleeping together, sleeping with

shadow play shadowgraph, shadow show

shady character shyster, smooth talker, trickster

shaggy-dog story exaggeration, tall story, tall tale

Shangri-la arcadia, Eden, Happy Valley, heaven on earth, New Atlantis, paradise, remote paradise, utopia, Xanadu

sharp-tongued biting, blunt, critical, cutting, frank, mean, negative, vitriolic

sharp-witted acute, alert, astute, bright, clever, intelligent, keen, nimble, on the ball, quick-witted, savvy, sharp, shrewd, smart

sheath knife bowie knife, case knife

sheep's eyes amorous glance, amorous look, bedroom eyes, come-hither look, doe eyes, fond look, glad eye, goo-goo eyes, longing eye, wistful eye

sheet glass plate glass

sheet lightning heat lightning, summer lightning

sheet music music paper, score, songbook, tablature, written music

shelf life mean life, serviceable life, service life, useful life

shell game bunco game, con game, thimblerig, thimblerigging

shell jacket mess jacket, monkey jacket

shell mound kitchen midden, midden

shell shock battle fatigue, combat fatigue, hysterical neurosis, post-traumatic stress syndrome

shelter tent pup tent

shield law journalist law

Shield of David Magen David, six-pointed star, Star of David

ship of the desert beast of burden, camel, dromedary

ship of the line battleship, line-of-battle ship

ship's papers bills of lading, docket, license, logbook, papers, registry

shirt jacket shirt-jac

shish kebab shish kabob, shish kebob, skewered food

shock absorber cushion, leaf springs, spring, suspension system, torsion bars

shock therapy convulsive therapy, ECT, electroconvulsive therapy, electrotherapy, EST, psychosurgery, shock treatment

shock troops crack troops, elite

troops, rapid-deployment troops, special troops, storm troops
shock wave compression wave, seismic wave
shooting gallery target range
shooting iron firearm, gat, handgun, heater, piece, rod
shooting script continuity, final script, photoplay, scenario, screenplay, script, storyboard, treatment
shooting star bolide, comet, falling star, fireball, meteor, meteorite, meteoroid
shoot the breeze chat, talk idly
shopping center arcade, mall, market, mini mall, plaza, shopping complex, shopping mall, shopping plaza, strip mall
shop steward bargainer, negotiator, walking delegate
Shop-Vac™ wet vac
shore leave furlough, leave, liberty
short and sweet brief, compact, concise, condensed, in a nutshell, succinct, summary, to the point
short list contenders, waiting list
short-lived brief, deciduous, ephemeral, evanescent, fleeting, fly-by-night, gone in a heartbeat, momentary, of short duration, over in a heartbeat, passing, quick, temporary
short notice unawares, without notice, without warning
short-order diner
short order flash, nothing flat, no time, twinkling
short paint thick paint
short ribs beef ribs, rib ends
short shrift kick in the teeth, no pity, no quarter, pitilessness, quick work, small end of the deal, small portion, tender mercies
short story account, narrative, novelette, novella, tale, yarn
short subject brief film, short, short movie
short-tempered cantankerous, crabby, cranky, fiery, grouchy, hot-blooded, hot-tempered, irritable, quick-tempered, short-fused, snappy, temperamental, testy, touchy, volatile
shotgun wedding compulsory marriage, forced marriage, forcible wedlock, shotgun marriage
shot in the arm energizer, incentive, jolt, motive, pick-me-up, stimulant, stimulus, upper
shot in the dark bet, chance, fall of the cards, flip of the coin,

gamble, guess, leap in the dark, long shot, luck of the draw, matter of chance, outside chance, risk, risky thing, speculation, throw of the dice, toss of the dice, turn of the wheel, wild guess

shoulder bag handbag, pocketbook, purse, reticule, tote, tote bag

shoulder blade scapula

shoulder board shoulder mark

shoulder knot braided cord, ornamental ribbon

shoulder patch epaulet, organization insignia, patch, unit insignia

shoulder strap purse strap

shouting distance hailing distance, short distance

show-and-tell public display, public presentation, sharing

show bill advertising poster

show business Broadway, entertainment industry, footlights, Hollywood, motion picture industry, show biz, television industry, theater, theater world, the boards, the bright lights, the footlights, the stage, the theater, TV industry

shrinking violet modest violet, mouse, retiring person, shy person, shy thing

Shrove Tuesday Carnival, Mardi Gras, Pancake Day

sick bay dispensary, hospital, isolation ward, sick berth, sickroom

sick building syndrome Legionnaires' disease

sick day sick leave

sick headache cephalalgia, hemicrania, megrim, migraine, misery in the head, sinus headache, splitting headache

sick leave authorized leave, excused absence

sickle-cell anemia sickle-cell disease

side by side abreast, alongside, beside, cheek by jowl, cheek to cheek, juxtaposing, next to each other, parallel, shoulder to shoulder

side dish antipasto, entremets, relish, salad, soup, vegetable

side drum snare drum

side effect aftereffect, aftermath, aftertaste, by-product, carryover, concomitant, corollary, leftover, offshoot, reaction, secondary response, sidebar, side issue, spinoff

side rail bed rail

sidereal time sidereal day, sidereal month, sidereal year

sidestream smoke secondhand smoke

side street backstreet, bylane, bypath, byroad, bystreet, byway, side road

sidewalk superintendent bystander, eyewitness, innocent bystander, kibitzer, passerby, spectator, witness

side whiskers burnsides, sideburns

side with agree with, support

sight gag visual joke

sight rhyme eye rhyme

sight-seeing tour bus tour, rubberneck tour, sight-seeing, sight-seeing excursion, tour, walking tour

signet ring seal ring

significant digit significant figure

significant other boyfriend, girlfriend, husband, live-in lover, lover, mate, spouse, wife

sign language American Sign Language, ASL, chironomy, dactylology, deaf-and-dumb alphabet, finger alphabet, finger spelling, gesture language, manual alphabet, nonverbal communication, signing, signing alphabet

sign manual autograph, hand, John Hancock, signature

sign of the cross cross, crossing oneself, gesture, signation, signing oneself, signum crucis

sign of the zodiac Aquarius, Aries, astrological sign, Cancer, Capricorn, Gemini, horoscope sign, Leo, Libra, Pisces, Sagittarius, Scorpio, Taurus, Virgo, zodiac sign

sign of things to come danger sign, foreshadowing, handwriting on the wall, harbinger, omen, portent, prediction, preindication, premonition, sign, signal, warning, warning sign

silent majority grassroots movement, groundswell, Middle America, suburbia

silent partner dormant partner, secret partner, sleeping partner, special partner

silent performer mime, pantomime

silent treatment blackballing, cold shoulder, ignore someone, ignoring, ostracism, ostracization, sending to Coventry

silicon chip board, chip, gallium arsenide chip, hybrid chip, microchip, microcircuit, motherboard, neural network chip, PCB, printed circuit board, semiconductor chip, superchip, transputer, wafer chip

silicon dioxide insulator, quartz, silica

Silicon Valley Bay Area, Palo Alto, San Francisco Bay, San Jose, southeast San Francisco

silk cotton kapok

silly season high summer, silliness

silver lining blue sky, break in the clouds, bright side, comforting prospect, good side, hopeful prospect, positive side

silver medal red ribbon, runner-up, second place

silver screen big screen, cinema, filmdom, films, Hollywood, motion pictures, motion picture screen, moviedom

silver spoon inherited wealth, lucky star

silver standard monetary standard, standard of value

Simon Legree brutal taskmaster, oppressor, slave driver

simple fruit orange, pea pod, tomato, true fruit

simple interest interest on principal

simple life plain living, self-sufficiency, simplicity

simple machine inclined plane, lever, pulley, wheel and axle

simple Simon foolish person, ninny, simpleton

sine curve sinusoid

sine wave Lissajous curve, Lissajous figure, sine curve

single file chain, column, Indian file, line, queue

single-handed alone, independent, left in the lurch, on one's own, unaided, unassisted

single knot overhand knot

singles bar dating bar, lounge, meat rack, meeting place, pickup joint, singles club

sin tax alcohol tax, cigarette tax, luxury tax

sit-down strike called strike, outlaw strike, refusal to work, sit-down, walkout, wildcat strike, work stoppage

sit-in demonstration, passive resistance, peaceful protest, protest, rally, sit-down, strike

sitting duck babe in the woods, dead duck, dead meat, easy pickings, easy target, easy victim, lamb, pushover, sinecure, soft touch, toast, vulnerable

sitting pretty ahead of the game, going places, on cloud nine, on top, on top of the heap, on top of the world, prosperous

sitting room drawing room, foreroom, front room, living room, salon, withdrawing room

situation comedy humorous series, sitcom

sitz bath hip bath, therapeutic bath

six feet under dead, deep-sixed, done for, eighty-sixed, gone to Davy Jones's locker, in the grave, on ice, pushing up daisies

six-shooter firearm, gun, pistol, revolver, six-gun

sixteenth note demiquaver, semiquaver

sixth sense clairvoyance, ESP, extrasensory perception, feeling, feeling in one's bones, foresight, gut feeling, hunch, insight, instinct, intuition, intuitiveness, keen intuition, perception, premonition, second sight, telepathy, vibes

sixty-four-thousand-dollar question burning question, crucial question, million-dollar question

skeletal muscle voluntary muscle

skeleton in the closet disgrace, misconduct, scandal, secret, shocker, sin, unmentionable thing, wrongdoing

skid row bowery, favela, ghetto, red-light district, skid road, squalid district, tenderloin

ski jump gelände jump, geländesprung, jump turn, ski leap, steeplechase

skin-deep shallow, superficial, surface

skin diving deep-sea diving, scuba diving, snorkeling

skin effect surface resistance, volume resistance

skin flick adult movie, blue movie, dirty movie, porno flick, pornographic movie, stag film, X-rated movie

skin game bunco game, confidence game, con game, fraudulent gambling, swindle

skin test patch test, prick, scratch test

ski pants snow pants

ski run course, mogul, racecourse, ski slope, ski trail

ski tow chairlift, J-bar, lift, poma, rope tow, ski lift, T-bar

skull and crossbones death's-head

skull session policy meeting, skull practice, strategy meeting

sky pilot Holy Joe, military chaplain, minister, parson, pastor, preacher, rector, reverend, servant of God

slack water half tide, still water

slam dunk dunk, dunk shot

slap on the wrist nominal punishment, token punishment
slap shot flick, wrist shot
slash mark diagonal, oblique, solidus, virgule
slave driver disciplinarian, hard master, oppressor, overseer of slaves, Simon Legree, taskmaster, tyrant
slave labor forced labor, slave trade, sweatshop labor, unwilling servant
sled dog dogsled dog, husky, malamute, police dog
sleep apnea apnea, Cheyne-Stokes respiration, dyspnea
sleep around fool around, fornicate, have sex, have sexual intercourse, make love, screw
sleeper sofa pullout sofa, sofa bed
sleeping bag bedroll, sleep sack
sleeping car Pullman car, roomette, sleeper, wagon-lit
sleeping gown bed gown
sleeping pill barbiturate, bromide, hypnotic, nightcap, soporific
sleeping sickness African sleeping sickness, encephalitis, encephalitis lethargica, narcolepsy, trypanosomiasis
sleight of hand conjuration, deception, escamotage, hocus-pocus, legerdemain, magic, prestidigitation, smoke and mirrors, trickery
slice of life episode of actual experience, faithful rendering, graphic account, lifelikeness, naturalistic description, photographic realism, realism, realistic description, realistic representation, tranche de vie, vraisemblance
slide fastener zipper
slide rule sliding scale
slings and arrows calamity, inauspiciousness, misfortune, outrageous fortune
slip of the tongue lapsus linguae, mistake, slip of the pen, solecism, spoonerism
slipped disk herniated disk
sloppy joe barbecued beef
slot machine coin machine, coin-operated machine, fruit machine, gaming machine, one-armed bandit, slots, vending machine
slow cooker Crock-Pot™
slow match fuse
slow-motion funeral pace, slow-mo, snail's pace, turtle's pace
slow virus lentivirus
slugging average batting average, slugging percentage
slumber party overnight party, pajama party, sleep-over

slush fund boodle, graft, hush money, inducement

sly dog charmer, cool customer, fox, slyboots, smoothie, smoothy

small arm handgun

small beer inferior beer, weak beer

small calorie calorie, gram calorie

small change chicken feed, coinage, coppers, peanuts, small beer, small potatoes

small-claims court court of claims

small fry lightweight, nobody, nonentity, tike

small hours midnight hours, wee hours, wee small hours

small intestine duodenum, ileum, jejunum, villus

small-minded biased, bigoted, closed-minded, illiberal, intolerant, myopic, narrow-minded, nearsighted, one-sided, petty, prejudiced, short-sighted

small of the back coccyx, dorsal region, lower back, lumbar region

small potatoes unimportant amount

small print escape clause, exception, fine print, proviso, saving clause, strings

small screen boob tube, television, telly, tube

small talk beauty-parlor chitchat, blather, chat, chatter, chitchat, conversation, gab, gossip, idle chat, idle chatter, idle talk, light talk, pleasantry, polite remark, prattle, rumors, table talk, trivial conversation

small-time bush-league, minor, piddling

smart aleck know-it-all, smart alec, smart-ass, smarty, smarty-pants, swellhead, wise-ass, wise guy, wisenheimer

smart bomb guided bomb

smart card supersmart card

smear campaign character assassination, defamation, defamation of character, dirty politics, dirty pool, injury of reputation, malicious defamation, mudslinging, negative campaign, negative campaigning, personal attack, slander

smelling salts ammonium carbonate, hartshorn, methamphetamine hydrochloride, methedrine, salts, sal volatile, spirits

smoke and mirrors crap, flimflam, hokum, legerdemain, sleight of hand, snow job

smoke detector emergency alarm, fire alarm, fire detector, heat sensor, smoke alarm

smoking car smoker, smoking compartment, smoking room

smoking gun absolute indication, clue, conclusive evidence, corroboration, damning evidence, documentation, evidence, incontrovertible evidence, indisputable evidence, proof, straw in the wind, substantiation, support, sure sign, telltale, tip-off, unmistakable sign, verification

smoking jacket lounge coat

smoke screen cover, false colors, false front, masquerade, red herring, screen

smokestack industry manufacturing industry

smooth endoplasmic reticulum agranular endoplasmic reticulum, SER

snack bar buvette, cantina, concession, concession stand, drive-in, fast-food restaurant, hamburger stand, hot-dog stand, lunch counter, sandwich bar, sandwich shop

snack table tray table

snail fever schistosomiasis

snail mail general delivery, s-mail, surface mail, USnail, USPS mail

snail's pace crawl, creep, footpace, lumbering pace, slow motion, slow pace, tortoise's pace, turtle's pace

snake dance Hopi ceremonial dance

snake doctor hellgrammite

snake eyes craps, deuce, Dolly Parton, doubleton, pair, two

snake fence Virginia fence, Virginia rail fence, worm fence, zigzag fence

snake in the grass back stabber, Pandora's box, pitfall, rat, scoundrel, snake, sneak, trap, villain, viper, weasel

snake oil nostrum, quack remedy, worthless preparation

snake pit can of worms, chaotic place, mare's nest, place of disorder, rat's nest

snappy comeback comeback, rebuttal, repartee, retort, riposte, snappy answer, witty comeback, zinger

snare drum side drum

sneak attack ambush, Pearl Harbor, shock tactics, surprisal, surprise attack, unforeseen attack

sneak preview command performance, first night, first performance, premiere, preview, sneak, world premiere

sneak thief prowler, shoplifter

snow blindness niphablepsia, ophthalmia nivialis

snow job bill of goods, con, conning, flattery, flimflam, hosing, rip-off, scam, smoke and mirrors, soft sell, soft soap, song and dance, the business

snuff out blow away, bump off, chill, dispatch, dispose of, do away with, do in, dust, grease, hit, ice, kill, knock off, murder, off, rub out, stretch out, waste, wax, whack, zap

soapbox oratory rabble-rousing, ranting, stump oratory, tub-thumping

soap opera daytime drama, daytime serial, daytime soap, melodrama, nighttime soap, serial, soap

sob sister sentimental author, sentimental journalist

sob story emotional appeal, hard-luck story, hardship tale, heartbreaker, human interest, maudlin plea, pathos, schmaltz, sentimentalism, tale of woe, tearjerker

so-called alleged, professed, supposed

social climber climber, name-dropper, social animal, status seeker, tuft-hunter

social Darwinism adaptation, Darwinism, evolution, law of the jungle, natural law, natural selection, phylogeny, social evolution, survival of the fittest, theory of evolution

social disease Cupid's itch, sexually transmitted disease, STD, VD, venereal disease, Venus's curse

social engineering social planning, social work, sociology

social gathering affair, function, get-together, party, social, social affair, soiree

social graces breeding, civility, consideration, courtesy, decorum, elegancies, etiquette, formalities, good manners, manners, mores, polished manners, politeness, proper conduct, protocol, savoir-vivre, table manners, tact

social insurance government insurance program, government-mandated insurance, social security

socialist realism literalism, Marxist aesthetic doctrine

socialized medicine government-provided health care, health insurance, Medicaid, Medicare, sickness insurance, state medicine

social life communion, community, fellowship, social intercourse, socializing

social psychology animal behavior, sociology

social science anthropology, archaeology, economics, history, political science, psychology, sociology

social security disability insurance, economic assistance, retirement income

social services casework, community service, free school lunch, good works, government-provided services, relief, social welfare, social work, support services, welfare, welfare work

social studies civics, geography, government, history, sociology

social work community service, good works, social service

Society of Friends Quakerism, Quakers

Society of Jesus Jesuits

Socratic method catechetical method, confession of ignorance, Socratic elenchus, Socratic induction, Socratic irony, Socratic philosophy, Socratism

soda biscuit soda cracker

soda bread Irish soda bread

soda fountain ice-cream parlor

soda jerk soda-fountain worker

soda pop carbonated beverage, carbonated soft drink, Coke™, pop, soda, soft drink, tonic

soda water carbonated water, club soda, effervescent water, seltzer, seltzer water, sparkling water

sod house adobe house

sodium bicarbonate baking soda, bicarbonate of soda

sodium carbonate sal soda, soda, soda ash, washing soda

sodium thiosulfate fixer, fixing bath, hypo, hyposulfite, sodium hyposulfite

sofa bed daybed, futon, pullout sofa, sleeper sofa

soft chancre chancroid

soft coal bituminous coal

soft drink carbonated beverage, carbonated drink, carbonated water, cola, pop, soda, soda pop, soda water, tonic

soft focus blur, blurriness, defocus, dimness, filminess, fogginess, fuzziness, indistinctness, lack of definition

soft goods clothing, dry goods, linens, textiles, white goods, yard goods

soft lens disposable lens, extended-wear lens

soft line line of least resistance

soft market declining market, off market, retreating market, sagging market, weak market

soft money tax-deductible donation

soft news unserious news

soft palate velum

soft-pedal blue-pencil, euphemize, hush, mitigate, moderate, palliate, play down, put on the soft pedal, shush, subdue, tone down

soft pedal damper, muffler, mute pedal, noise queller, silencer, sordine, sordino, sourdine

soft sell blandishment, low-pressure salesmanship, low-pressure selling, soft soap, sweet talk {compare *hard sell*}

soft soap blarney, cajolery, flattery, praise; fluid soap, liquid soap, semifluid soap

soft-spoken gentle, low-key, mild, quiet, smooth, well-spoken

soft spot exposed nerve, in the gut, nerve ending, raw, raw nerve, sore point, sore spot, tender spot, the quick, weakness, where it hurts, where one lives

soft touch bleeding heart, easy pickings, easy touch, prize sap, pushover, softie, softy, sucker

soil layer horizon

solar battery solar cell, solar collector, solar panel

solar cell photovoltaic cell, solar collector

solar eclipse eclipse, eclipse of the sun

solar energy insolation, solar power, solar radiation, sun energy

solar flare corona, facula, solar prominence, sunspot, tongue, tongue of flame

solar plexus pit of the stomach, plexus

solar ray ray of sunlight

solar system Copernican system, Earth, heliocentric system, Jupiter, Mars, Mercury, Neptune, planetary system, Pluto, Saturn, Uranus, Venus

solar year astronomical year, tropical year

soldering iron blowpipe, welding torch

soldier of fortune condottiere, free companion, freelance, hired gun, hireling, legionnaire, mercenary, professional soldier, soldier for hire

solemn mass high mass

solicitor general assistant attorney general

solitary confinement holding cell, isolation, lockdown, solitary, the hole

song and dance bill of goods, bull, con, elaborate explanation, jive, line, number, rip-off, scam, snow job, story, the business

song cycle round

sonic barrier sonic wall, sound barrier, transonic barrier

sonic boom burst of sound, loud report, Mach wave, shock wave

son of a gun rascal, rogue

Son of God Christ, Emmanuel, God the Son, Good Shepherd, Jesus, Jesus Christ, King of Kings, Lamb of God, Light of the World, Lord, Lord of Lords, Messiah, Prince of Peace, Redeemer, Savior, Son of man

sooner or later eventually, in time, one fine day, someday, sometime, sometime or other, somewhen, when all is said and done

sore throat septic sore throat

sorry sight depressant, memento mori, object of pity, painful sight, pathetic sight, sad spectacle

SOS international distress signal, save our ship, save our souls

so-so average, fair, fair to middling, mediocre, not bad, OK, okay, passable, run-of-the-mill, tolerable

SOS™ pad scouring pad

sotto voce barely audible, between the teeth, in an undertone, in a whisper, in soft tones, under one's breath, with bated breath

soul food collard greens, ham hocks

soul kiss French kiss

soul mate alter ego, companion, confidant, confidante, friend, heart's desire, helpmate, kindred soul, kindred spirit, lover, one's promised, partner, truelove

soul-searching consciousness-raising, contemplation, examination of conscience, introspection, reflection, self-analysis, self-examination, self-reproach

sound-and-light show son et lumière

sound barrier sonic barrier, sonic wall, transonic barrier

sound bite adage, brief broadcast statement, excerpt, maxim, motto, quotation, quote, slogan, snippet

sound effect electronic sound

sounding board sound box, soundboard

sounding line lead line, plummet

sound judgment analysis, deduction, discretion, discrimination, good judgment, good sense, logic, prudence, rationale, reasoning, sense

sound spectrograph sonogram

sound track movie album, movie music, soundstripe

sound wave acoustic wave, radio wave, sound propagation

soup du jour featured soup, flavor of the month, specialty of the house, today's special

source language SL, source code

sour grapes bad-mouthing, derogation, disappointment, disparagement

southern lights aurora australis

space age computer age, machine age, science fiction

space being alien, E.T., extraterrestrial, extraterrestrial visitor, little green man, man from Mars, Martian, visitor from another planet

space biology astrobiology, bioastronautics, exobiology, space bioscience, xenobiology

space cadet spacey person

space capsule ballistic capsule, capsule, command module, exploratory ship, lunar module, module, space shuttle, spacecraft, spaceship

spaced-out in a fog, out of touch with reality, out to lunch, spacey, zoned-out

space lattice crystal lattice

space medicine aerospace medicine

space opera space odyssey

space platform launching base, space airport, space dock, space laboratory, space observatory, spaceport, space station

space probe geo probe, interplanetary explorer, probe, space satellite, spy satellite

space science aerospace science, aerospace technology, astrionics, planetary science, rocket science, space engineering, space research, space technology

space shuttle lifting body, orbiter, shuttle, space capsule

space station advance base, astro station, cosmic steppingstone, island base, manned station, space airport, space island, space platform, spaceport, spaceport station

space-time continuum continuum, four-dimensional space, fourth dimension, spatiotemporal continuum

spaghetti western horse opera, low-budget Western

Spanish fly blister beetle, cantharides, cantharis

spare tire bay window, beer belly, breadbasket, corporation, love handles, potbelly, potgut; extra tire, spare

sparkling water carbonated water, fizzy water, mineral water, seltzer water, spring water

sparkling wine Asti Spumante, bubbly, champagne, Spumante

spark plug ball of fire, detonator, fuse, human dynamo, ignition system, sparker

sparring partner boxer, handler, palooka, practice partner, second

spastic colon irritable bowel syndrome

speaking engagement speaking appointment

speaking in tongues gift of tongues, glossolalia

speaking tube speaking pipe

spear side spear kin, sword kin, sword side

special delivery express, express mail, first class, hand to hand, messenger, package express, priority mail, special handling

special education compensatory education, learning-disability education, remedial education, special ed, special-needs education

special effects animation, FX, mechanical effects, optical effects, process photography

special favor indulgence, rare delight, rare pleasure, treat

special forces commandos, elite troops, Green Berets, guerrilla troops, paratroops, rangers, rapid deployment force, shock troops, storm troops

special interest group interest group, lobby, PAC, political action committee, pressure group, SIG, single-issue group, vested interest

special pleading hairsplitting, rationalization, sophism, sophistical reasoning

special relativity special theory of relativity

specific gravity relative density

specific heat blood heat, body heat, heat of transformation, latent heat

specific impulse specific thrust

speech community ethnic

group, isogloss, linguistic ambience, linguistic community, linguistic island, relic area, society, speech island

speech form linguistic form

speech sound affricate, click, consonant, fricative, implosive, liquid, phone, phonetic entity, phonetic unit, plosive, sibilant, sonant, spirant, syllable, vocable

speed bump sleeping policeman

speed limit maximum speed

speed of light terminal velocity

speed of sound Mach 1.0, 1108 ft/second, 741 mph, 658 knots, sonic barrier, 1215 km/hour

speed skating race skating

speed trap radar trap, VASCAR

spell checker spell check, spelling checker

spelling bee spelldown, spelling contest, spelling game, spelling test

spelling book casebook, speller

spelling pronunciation respelling pronunciation

spending money mad money, petty cash, pin money, pocket money, small change

sperm cell antherozoid, male gamete, spermatozoid, spermatozoon

sphere of influence ambit, bailiwick, mandate, mandated territory, niche, orbit, power base, territory

spick-and-span brand-spanking new, clean, clean and tidy, cleaned, cleaned-up, fresh, immaculate, neat, spic-and-span, spotless, spruce, tidy

spike heel stiletto heel, thin high heel

spill the beans divulge a secret, leak, let slip, let the cat out of the bag, sing, spill, squawk, tell a secret

spinal anesthesia epidural, spinal block

spinal canal vertebral canal

spinal column backbone, myel-, myelo-, spine, vertebrae, vertebral column

spin casting spin fishing

spin control disinformation, spin

spin doctor brainwasher, mouthpiece, persuader, salesperson, troubleshooter

spinning frame bobbin and fly frame, jenny, mule, mule-jenny, spinning jenny, spinning machine, spinning reel, spinning wheel

spin-off follow-up, offshoot, offspring, outgrowth, part two, sequel

spiral galaxy barred spiral galaxy, spiral, spiral nebula

spiritual teacher adviser, guru, maharishi, master, mentor, mystic, spiritual guide, spiritual leader, swami, teacher

spit and polish cleanly habits, daintiness, discipline, fastidiousness, punctilio, regimentation, rigorousness

spitting image carbon copy, copy, dead ringer, doppelgänger, duplicate, eidetic image, exact counterpart, exact duplicate, exact likeness, facsimile, image of, living image, living picture, look-alike, mirror image, picture of, replica, spit and image, twin, very image

splash guard mud flap, mud guard

splinter group breakaway party, dissenting group, faction, groupuscule, offshoot, political faction, religious sect, schismatic, seceder

split hairs cavil, chop logic, make a fine distinction, nitpick, pick nits, quibble, refine a distinction, sharpen a distinction, subtilize

split personality alternating personality, bipolar disorder, dissociative identity, dual personality, multiple personality, personality disorder

split second bat of an eye, blink of an eye, flash, fraction of a second, half a second, heartbeat, instant, jiffy, microsecond, millisecond, moment, nanosecond, nothing flat, twinkling

spontaneous abortion miscarriage

spontaneous combustion combustibility, thermogenesis

spontaneous generation abiogenesis, autogenesis

spontaneous reaction gut reaction, knee jerk, Pavlovian response, reflex, unthinking response

spoon-feed baby, coddle, indulge, mollycoddle, overindulge, pamper

sport fish game fish

sporting chance betting proposition, flip of the coin, gambler's chance, good chance, good possibility, hazard of the die, luck of the draw, matter of chance, throw of the dice, toss of the coin, toss-up

sporting goods athletic equipment

sports apparel activewear, athletic clothes, casual wear, playwear, sport clothes, sportswear

sports arena amphitheater, athletic field, ballpark, bowl, coliseum, dome, field, gymnasium, hippodrome, playing field, rink, sports dome, sports ground, sports venue, stadium, track, turf

sports car convertible, coupe, two-seater

sport shirt golf shirt, polo shirt, T-shirt

sports jacket blazer, reefer, sport coat, sports coat

sports star superstar, the franchise

sport suit town-and-country suit

sport utility vehicle SUV

spot announcement commercial, commercial announcement, commercial message, plug, spot

spot check check, random investigation, random sampling, test

spotted fever Kews Garden spotted fever, Rocky Mountain spotted fever, typhus; cerebrospinal fever, cerebrospinal meningitis

spray can aerosol, atomizer, concentrate sprayer, mist concentrate sprayer, spray

spring chicken young chicken

springform pan springform mold

sprinkler system automatic sprinkler, fire-extinguishing system, lawn sprinkler, sprinkler, sprinkler head, sprinkling system

spring tide flood tide, high tide, high water

spun glass fiberglass, filigree glass, fine blown glass, glass thread

spun sugar cotton candy

spun yarn continuous filament yarn, hank, skein, yarn

spur of the moment brainstorm, fly, impulse, inspiration, run, sudden impulse, top of the head

spy plane high-altitude military reconnaissance plane, reconnaissance plane, stealth bomber

squad car cruiser, paddy wagon, patrol car, police car, police cruiser, police vehicle, prowl car

squad room briefing room

square away make good, make right, rectify, set straight, straighten

square dance barn dance, country dance, hoedown, quadrille

square knot common double knot

square meal full meal, healthy

meal, hearty meal, heavy meal, large meal, man-sized meal, sit-down meal, substantial meal, three-course meal

square measure acreage, acres, rods

square one beginning, clean slate, fresh start, new beginning, outset, starting point

square root cube root, root-mean-square

square sail four-sided sail, lugsail, square rig

square shooter honest person, square dealer

squeaky clean above suspicion, beyond reproach, blameless, ethical, faultless, full of integrity, highly respectable, honest, immaculate, innocent, irreproachable, reputable, spotless, stainless, unblemished, uncorrupt, unimpeachable, upstanding, virtuous

squeeze play hit-and-run play, pickoff, pickoff play, pitchout

squirrel away accumulate, amass, assemble, collect, garner, gather, harvest, hoard, pack away, put away, reap, save up, sock away, stock up, store

squirt gun spray gun, water gun, water pistol

stab in the back back-stab, betray, double-cross, sell down the river, sell out

staff of life bread, bread and butter, daily bread, meat, necessary food, pain, pane, staple, staple food, vital necessity

stage business acting device, jeu de théâtre, stage directions

stage fright aphonia, aphonia clericorum, aphonia paralytica, aphonia paranoica, bashfulness, buck fever, butterflies, flop sweat, freeze, hysterical aphonia, loss of speech, mike fright, mutism, spastic aphonia

stage setting backdrop, film set, flats, location, mise-en-scène, scenery, set, setting, stage, stage set, trompe l'oeil

stage whisper aside, breathy voice, loud whisper, sotto voce, whisper, whispering

staging area assembly area, preparation area

stag party bachelor party, partie carree, stag

stained glass colored glass, mosaic

stamp collecting philately

stamping ground backyard, customary territory, favorite gathering place, habitat, hangout, haunt, native environment, neck of the woods, purlieu, stomping ground, turf

stamp out crush, extinguish, kill, put an end to, put out, snuff out, squelch, stop

standard deviation deviation, normal deviation, predictable error, probable error, range of error, SD, standard error

Standard English correct English, good English, King's English, Queen's English, Received Pronunciation, Received Standard

standard of living level of material comfort, standard of comfort, standard of life

standard operating procedure established procedure, modus operandi, set form, SOP, standing order

standard time mean solar time, zone time

standard transmission manual, manual transmission, standard, stick shift {compare *automatic transmission*}

stand for indicate, mean, represent, signify, symbolize

standing army active forces, career soldiers, permanent army, professional army, professional soldiers, regular army, regulars

standing committee subcommittee

standing eight-count mandatory eight-count

standing order house rule, military order, parliamentary procedure rule, party line, regulation, routine, rule of business

standing wave antinode, node, stationary wave

stand pat hold out, resist, stand one's ground, stay put, stick to one's guns

star-crossed cursed, damned, doomed, ill-fated, unfortunate, unlucky

Star of David estoile, hexagon, hexagram, hexahedron, Jewish star, Magen David, six-pointed star, star of Bethlehem

starry-eyed idealistic, impractical, optimistic, romantic, unrealistic

Stars and Bars Confederate flag

Stars and Stripes Old Glory; red, white and blue; Star-Spangled Banner; US flag

starting gate control gate, open gate, starting post

Star Wars nuclear deterrent, SDI, Strategic Defense Initiative

state-of-the-art advanced, latest,

modern, most recent, new, newest, ultramodern, up-to-the-minute

state of the art cutting edge, forefront, highest development, leading edge, modernity, modernization, updating

state's evidence evidence for prosecution, inside information, private source, singing, squealing, tattling, tergiversation

States of the Church Papal States

state trooper highway patrolman, mounted policeman, state police, trooper

static tube electrostatic tube

stationary bicycle exercise bicycle, exercise bike, stationary bike

stationary wave standing wave

station break intermission, pause for station identification, station identification

station house fire station, police headquarters, police station, precinct house

status quo current situation, existing condition, how things stand, no change, parameters, present state of affairs, situation, size of it, standing, state of affairs, status, status in quo, usual

status symbol prize possession

statute book codification, codified law, law book, legal code, statute law, written law

statutory offense statutory crime

statutory rape deflowerment

stave off avoid, block, fend off, hold off, repel, ward off

staying power conditioning, endurance, energy, fitness, fortitude, grit, heart, indefatigability, intestinal fortitude, perseverance, stamina, strength, survivability, vigor, wind

stay of execution delay, postponement, reprieve, stay, suspension

steady state theory continuous creation theory

stealth bomber stealth fighter

steam bath Finnish bath, hot tub, hummum, Jacuzzi™, Japanese bath, plunge bath, Russian bath, sauna, sauna bath, Scandinavian steam bath, steam room, sweat bath, Swedish bath, Turkish bath, whirlpool bath

steam iron clothes iron, electric iron, pressing iron

steam locomotive iron horse

steam shovel digger, excavator, navvy, power shovel

steel-collar worker robot
steel drum kettledrum, timpani
steel guitar acoustic guitar; Hawaiian guitar
steering committee council, executive committee, interlocking directorate, panel, quango, select committee
steering wheel helm, tiller, wheel
step aerobics stepping
stern sheets stern area
sticker price advertised price, list price, price tag, published price, ticket price
stick insect mantis, praying mantis, walking stick
stick-in-the-mud conservative, diehard, fuddy-duddy, obstinate person, unadventurous person
stick shift manual transmission, standard transmission
stick-to-itiveness endurance, grit, perseverance, persistence, stamina
sticky wicket difficult problem, difficult situation, embarrassing problem, embarrassing situation, hot seat, hot spot, jam, squeeze, tricky situation
stiletto heel spike heel, thin high heel
still life inanimate object picture, nature morte, study in still life
still photography unit photography
stink bomb odorous bomb, stink ball, stinkpot
stir-crazy confined, having cabin fever, restless
stirrup cup nightcap, one for the road, parting cup
stock car dragster, hot rod, racing car
stock certificate certificate of stock
stock exchange American Stock Exchange, Amex, Big Board, bourse, exchange, NASDAQ, New York Stock Exchange, OTC, over-the-counter, stock market, Wall Street
stocking cap knit cap
stock-in-trade available means, cash flow, funds, inventory, ready resources, resources, stock, supply
stock market American Stock Exchange, Amex, Big Board, board, bourse, New York Stock Exchange, stock exchange, the market, Wall Street
stomach acid hydrochloric acid
Stone Age Acheulean, Aurignacian, Azilian, Capsian, Chellean, Cro-Magnon, Eolithic, Magdalenian, Mousterian,

Neolithic, Oldowan, Olduvai, Paleolithic, prehistoric times, Solutrean

stone china ironstone, ironstone china

stone plant living stones

stone's throw close range, earshot, eyeshot, holler, near, next door, not far, short distance, shouting distance, spitting distance

stool pigeon agent provocateur, decoy, fink, informer, narc, nark, plant, police informer, rat, rat fink, shill, snitch, spy, squealer, stoolie, tattletale, whistle-blower

stop order order to buy, order to sell

stop payment block, freeze, refuse to pay, welsh, withhold payment

storage battery accumulator, dry battery, secondary battery, secondary cell, storage cell, storage device, wet battery

storm cellar bomb shelter, cyclone cellar, fallout shelter, storm cave, tornado shelter

storm cloud hard times, heavy weather, rain cloud, rainy day

storm trooper Nazi militia, shock trooper

storm window double-glazed window, secondary window, Thermopane™ window

stormy petrel bird of ill omen, harbinger, Mother Carey's chicken, omen, raven, rebel, red flag, storm petrel

stovepipe hat top hat, topper

straight and narrow honesty, integrity, moral integrity, morality, proper conduct, right conduct, righteousness

straight angle 180-degree angle

straight arrow good person, honest person, salt of the earth, square shooter, straight shooter, upright person

straight A's 4.0 grade point average, perfect report card

straight face deadpan, impassiveness, poker face

straight man feed, feeder, foil, second banana, sidekick, stooge, straight person

strange bedfellows cats and dogs, Montagues and Capulets

Strategic Defense Initiative nuclear deterrent, SDI, Star Wars

strawberry blond honey blond

strawberry mark birthmark, hemangioma, nevus, port-wine stain, vascular nevus

straw boss subforeman

straw in the wind harbinger, indication, indicator, omen, portent, sign, sign of the times, slight hint

straw man cover, empty suit, front, hollow man, man of straw, paper tiger

straw vote experimental sample, opinion poll, public opinion poll, random sample, straw poll, straw to show the wind, unofficial vote, voting poll

stream of consciousness apostrophe, aside, association of ideas, chain of thought, free association, inner monologue, interior monologue, train of thought, word association, word painting

street intersection crossing, stoplight, stop sign

street person bag lady, bag person, bum, derelict, displaced person, down-and-out, hobo, homeless person, shopping-bag person, tramp, vagrant

street-smart cunning, experienced, savvy, seasoned, shrewd, streetwise, worldly

street theater guerrilla theater, theater of cruelty

strep throat septic sore throat

stressed-out anxious, nervous, tensed, unnerved, worried

stress test cardiovascular test, treadmill test

stretch receptor baroreceptor

strike camp break camp, decamp, pull up stakes, strike tent

strike force attackers, storm troops

strike home hit where it hurts, hit where one lives, touch a nerve ending, touch a sore spot

strike zone kitchen, wheelhouse

striking distance close grips, close quarters, short distance

striking price exercise price

string bean green bean

string line balkline

strip mine open mine

strip search skin search

strobe light blinking light, searchlight, sodium light, strobe, stroboscope, stroboscopic light

stroke of luck blessing, fate, fluke, good break, good fortune, lucky break, lucky strike, one in a million, piece of good luck, run of luck

strong force strong interaction, strong nuclear force

strong force equation nuclear equation

strong suit forte, long suit, métier, strength, strong point

strong-willed decisive, iron-willed, obstinate, strong-minded, uncompromising

strontium 90 nuclear fallout

structural formula atom arrangement, bond arrangement, chemical formula arrangement

stuck-up arrogant, conceited, haughty, hoity-toity, snobbish, snooty, snotty, uppity

student body student population, students

student housing dorm, dormitory

student lamp reading lamp

student teacher intern teacher, practice teacher

studio apartment flat, garden apartment, one-room apartment, small apartment, studio

stud poker eight-card stud, five-card stud, seven-card stud, six-card stud

study group cram session, study hall

stuffed shirt blimp, bloated aristocrat, pompous ass, pompous person, twit

stumbling block barrier, catch, complication, deterrent, difficulty, discouragement, drawback, fly in the ointment, handicap, hindrance, hitch, hurdle, impediment, limitation, obstacle, obstruction, restraint, roadblock, snag, stone in one's path, stumbling stone

stump speaker campaigner, stump orator, stumper, whistle-stopper

Sturm und Drang ferment, storm and stress, turmoil

stylized art conventionalized art

styptic pencil alum, astringent bitters, medicated stick

subject matter category, contents, focus of attention, subject, subject of thought, text, theme, topic

subject to based on, conditional, contingent, contingent on, dependent, depending

subject to change conditional, not carved in stone, not firmed up, proposed, tentative, uncertain

submachine gun Bren gun, burp gun, machine pistol, subgun, Thompson submachine gun, tommy gun, Uzi™, Uzi™ submachine gun

submarine sandwich grinder, hero, hero sandwich, hoagie, poor boy, sub

subsistence farming crop farming, truck farming, undersoil

substance abuse addiction, alcohol abuse, alcoholism, chemical abuse, dipsomania, drug abuse, drug dependence, drug habit, drug use, narcotics abuse, solvent abuse
substantive right basic right
suction pump aspirator, extractor
sudden death deathblow, early death, premature death, stroke of death, unexplained death, untimely end; extra play, tiebreaker
sudden infant death syndrome cot death, crib death, SIDS
suede shoes Hush Puppies™
sugar cone brown cone
sugar daddy amoroso, cavaliere servente, gigolo, Robin Hood, Santa Claus
suit coat suit jacket, tailored coat
summa cum laude highest honors, with highest praise, with the greatest honor
summer cottage summer home
summer stock repertory theater, stock, strawhat, strawhat circuit, summer theater
summit meeting conference at the summit, high-level talk, summit, summit conference, summitry
Sunday clothes best bib and tucker, best clothes, dressy clothes, glad rags, Sunday best, Sunday-go-to-meeting clothes
Sunday funnies Sunday cartoons, Sunday comics, Sunday comic strips
Sunday punch destructive blow, knockout blow
Sunday school catechism class, church school, religious instruction
sun god Amaterasu, Amen-Ra, Apollo, Helios, Hyperion, Mithras, Phaëthon, Phoebus, Ra, Savitar, Shamash, Sol, Surya, Titan
sunk fence ha-ha
sunny-side up fried on one side
sun parlor conservatory, lounge, solarium, sun lounge, sunporch, sunroom
sun protection factor SPF, sunblock, suntan lotion, suntan oil
supergiant slalom super G
superiority complex overconfidence, psychological defense mechanism
supernatural being alien, deity, divineness, divinity, immortal, intelligence, spirit
supersonic transport Concorde, SST, supersonic jet
support group AA, Alcoholics

Anonymous, encounter group, family, friends, morale boosters, safety net, self-help group, support system, therapy, 12-step group, Weight Watchers™

Supreme Being Almighty, Alpha and Omega, Creator, Divine Being, God, King of Kings, Lord, Lord of Lords, Maker, the Diety

Supreme Court high court, highest federal court, United States Supreme Court

sure thing cert, certainty, cinch, dead certainty, destiny, foregone conclusion, open-and-shut case, safe bet, shoo-in

surface structure deep structure, shallow structure, underlying structure

surgeon general chief medical officer

surge protector surge suppressor

surgical gown scrubs, scrub suit

surgical needle suture needle

survival of the fittest adaptation, Darwinian, Darwinism, evolution, evolutionism, law of the jungle, natural law, natural selection, neo-Darwinism, organic evolution, phylogeny, punctuated equilibrium, social Darwinism, social evolution, theory of evolution

suspended animation cryonics, deep-freezing, freeze-drying, motionlessness, suspension

suspension bridge swing bridge

swaddling clothes swaddle, swaddling bands

swagger stick conductor's baton, swanking stick

swamp fever equine infectious anemia, leptospirosis, malaria

swamp gas marsh gas, poison gas

swan dive cannonball, gainer, jackknife, plunge, swallow dive

swan song coda, crowning achievement, dying words, envoi, epilogue, famous last words, farewell, farewell performance, final appearance, final gesture, final performance, good-bye, last hurrah, last shot, last words, parting song, peroration

SWAT team gestapo, posse, posse comitatus, special weapons and tactics, SWAT

swearing in enthronement, inauguration, induction, installation, investiture, solemn declaration, solemn promise, vow

sweat sock athletic sock

sweat suit athletic suit, exercise suit, gym suit, sweat clothes, sweats, warm-ups

sweetheart contract labor contract, sweetheart agreement, unethically favorable contract, union contract, yellow-dog contract

sweetie pie darling, dear, honey, sugar, sweetheart

sweetness and light hearts and flowers, love and peace

sweet talk blandishment, blarney, cajolery, fair words, flattery, honeyed words, incense, insincere flattery, nobbling, smooth talk, snow job, soft soap, sweet nothings

sweet tooth craving for sweets, fondness for sweets

swelled head big head, cockiness, immodesty, large hat size, stuck-upness, swelled-headedness

swim bladder air bladder

swimming hole pond, water hole, watering hole, water pocket

swimming pool natatorium, plunge bath, pool, swimming bath, swimming hole, wading pool

swimming suit bathing suit, beachwear, bikini, Jams™, maillot, one-piece suit, swimming trunks, swimsuit, swim trunks, swimwear, two-piece suit

swine fever African swine fever, hog cholera

swinging door revolving door

swing loan bridge loan, short-term loan

swing shift anchor watch, dog-watch, early evening shift, graveyard shift, night shift

Swiss Army knife knife, pocket tool, pocketknife, switchblade knife

switchblade knife pocketknife, Swiss Army knife, switch knife, switchblade

switch plate cover plate

swizzle stick drink stick

sworn statement affidavit, attestation, deposition, notarized statement, oath, statement under oath, sworn evidence, sworn testimony, testimony, written testimony

symbolic logic formal logic, mathematical logic

sympathetic magic chaos magic, sorcery

sympathy strike empathy, fellow feeling, joint action

symphonic poem tone poem

symphony orchestra chamber orchestra, large orchestra, philharmonic

synchronized swimming water ballet

synchronous motor synchronic motor, synchronous machine

synodic month lunar month

synthetic grass artificial turf, AstroTurf™

system crash computer failure

systems analysis feedback system engineering, system engineering, systems theory

systems engineer sysop, system operator, systems analyst

systems program command-line interpreter, disk operating system, I/O routine, memory-management routine, operating system, OS, system software, task scheduling, user interface

Tt

table d'hôte à la carte, communal table, ordinary, prix fixe

table linen felt, napery, napkins, place mat, tablecloth, table cover, table mat, table napkin, table pad, table runner

table salt common salt, saltshaker

table talk casual conversation, chitchat, idle chat, mealtime conversation, small talk, tea-table talk

table tennis Ping-Pong™

table wine unfortified wine

tabula rasa blank cartridge, blank mind, blank slate, blank tablet, clean slate, featureless mind, palimpsest, square one, untaught state

tack lifter tack puller

tail fin vertical stabilizer

tailor-made custom-built, custom-fit, custom-made, designer, made-to-order, made-to-measure, perfectly fitted, tailored

tail rotor antitorque rotor

tail section empennage, tail assembly

take advantage of exploit, impose upon, milk, step on, use, use for one's own ends

take-home pay net earnings, net income, net pay, net wages, pay after deductions, real wages, take-home, take-home income, taxable income, wages after taxes

take into account consider, think about

take into custody apprehend, arrest, bust, capture, collar, nab, pick up, put under arrest, run down, seize, take prisoner

taken with carried away with, enamored, enamored of, fond of, gaga over, hot for, infatuated, partial to, smitten, smitten with

takeover bid hostile takeover, leverage, leveraged buyout, takeover

talent scout body snatcher, critic, executive recruiter, flesh peddler, headhunter, reviewer, scout, talent agent

talking book book on tape, book recording, e-book

talking head announcer, broadcaster, commentator, newscaster, newsreader

talking point persuasive point

talk radio all-talk, audience-participation show, call-in show, interview show, phone-in show, talk show

talk show chat show

talk turkey get down to brass tacks, make no bones about it, mince no words

tall tale cock-and-bull story, exaggeration, fable, far-fetched story, fish story, flight of fancy, tall story, yarn

tandem bicycle bicycle built for two, two-seater bicycle

tank farming hydroponics, tray agriculture

tank suit maillot, one-piece suit

tank top sleeveless top

tank truck tank trailer

tap dance clog dance, step dance, toe dance

tape deck audiocassette player, cassette player, tape player, tape recorder

tape measure measuring tape, metal rule, meterstick, tape, tape line

tape recorder audiocassette recorder, cassette recorder

tapestry carpet Brussels carpet, tapestry Brussels

tap water Adam's ale, faucet water

tar and feather criticize severely, draw and quarter, excoriate, persecute, punish severely, torture

target date A-day, D day, deadline, H hour, target day, term, terminal date, time allotment, time frame, time limit, zero hour

target language object language

target market target audience

tarot reading fortune-telling

task force commando, squadron, task group

taste bud gustatory cell, lingua, palate, taste bulb, taste cell, taste goblet, taste hair, tongue

tau cross Saint Anthony's cross

taxi driver cabbie, cabby, cab driver, cabman, hack, hackman, hackie

tax rebate tax refund

tax return annual return, federal tax return, joint return, separate returns, state tax return, tax form

tax shelter tax haven

T-bar lift chairlift, poma, ski lift

tea ball steeper, tea filter

teachers college normal school

teaching fellowship graduate fellowship, internship, teacher's assistantship

teaching hospital university hospital

tea dance dansant, dinner dance, late-afternoon dance

tea garden tea plantation

team sport baseball, basketball, Canadian football, canoe polo, cricket, curling, cycle polo, field hockey, football, hurling, ice hockey, korfball, netball, polo, rugby, soccer, softball, speedball, team handball, ultimate Frisbee™, volleyball, water polo

tea party ceremonial ritual, chanoyu, tea and crumpets, tea ceremony

tear gas asphyxiant, lachrymatory gas, poison gas

tear sheet periodical page

tea service cups and saucers, tea caddy, tea cosy, tea cozy, tea set, tea table, tea things, tea tray, tea wagon

tea shop bistro, coffeehouse, coffee room, tea garden, teahouse, tearoom

tea table snack table

tea towel cleaning cloth, dish towel

tea tray service tray, tea caddy

tea wagon tea cart

technical adviser expert consultant

technical foul technical, unsportsmanlike conduct

technical knockout boxing victory, knockout, KO, TKO, win

technicolor yawn vomiting

teddy bear Beanie Baby™, stuffed animal, toy bear

tee shirt T-shirt

teething ring chewy toy, pacifier, rubber soother

telephone advertising telemarketing

telephone booth call box, coin telephone, pay phone, pay station, public telephone, telephone box, telephone kiosk

telephone call buzz, call, collect call, crank call, local call, long-distance call, person-to-person call, phone call, ring, station-to-station call, toll call, toll-free call, trunk call

telephone directory directory, phone book, telephone book, white pages, yellow pages

telephone number cell phone number, 800 number, fax number, phone number

telescopic sight scope, telescopic finder, telescopic range

television room entertainment center, TV room

television set boob tube, idiot box, small screen, television receiver, telly, tube, TV, TV set

Temperate Zone North Temperate Zone, South Temperate Zone

tempt fate ask for it, ask for trouble, bell the cat, court danger, court disaster, push one's luck, tempt the gods, try one's hand, try one's luck

tenant farmer crofter, métayer, peasant farmer, sharecropper

ten-cent store dime store, five-and-dime, five-and-ten, variety store

Ten Commandments Decalogue, Law of Moses, Mosaic Law, ten injunctions

ten-gallon hat cowboy hat, Stetson™

Tennessee walking horse Tennessee walker

tennis shoe athletic shoe, gym shoe, runners, sneaker, tennies

tensile strength load-bearing capacity, TS

terminal emulation ANSI, VT-52, VT-100, VT-200

terminally ill at death's door, critically ill, in critical condition, on one's deathbed, on the critical list

term paper discourse, monograph, research paper, study, theme

terra-cotta adobe, argil, ceramic clay

terra firma dry land, earth, firm ground, ground, ground covering, solid ground, sure ground, terra, terrain

terrestrial planet Earth, inner planet, major planet, Mars, Mercury, Venus

territorial waters coastal waters, continental shelf, inland waters, offshore rights, three-mile limit, twelve-mile limit

Tertiary period Cenozoic era, Eocene epoch, Lower Tertiary, Miocene epoch, Oligocene epoch, Paleocene epoch, Pliocene epoch, Upper Tertiary

test ban ban on testing, de-escalation

test case acid test, crucial test, experiment, first case, first occurrence, precedent

testing ground lab, laboratory, proving ground, testing room

test paper blue book, examination paper, written, written exam, written examination

test pattern adjustment chart, grid, scanning pattern

test pilot analyst, test driver, tester, tryer-out

test-tube baby in vitro fertilization, IVF

tête-à-tête confidential discussion, cozy chat, duologue, face-to-face chat, heads together, heart-to-heart talk, huddle, intimate discussion, mutual consultation, one-on-one, parley, powwow, private conversation

Texas leaguer bloop, blooper, can of corn, fly, looper, pop-up

Texas turkey armadillo

text edition school edition

text editor full-screen editor, word processor

text file ASCII file, data file, data set, file, text, word-processing file

textual criticism close reading, criticism, detailed analysis, literary criticism, lower criticism

thank you danke, gracias, merci, much obliged, thanks

theater of the absurd kitchen-sink drama, problem play, slice-of-life drama

theatrical makeup blackface, clown white, greasepaint, makeup

theme park adventure park, amusement park, carnival, safari park, water park

theme song signature song, signature tune

theological virtue cardinal virtue, charity, faith, goodness, hope, love, supernatural virtue

theory of everything grand unification theories, grand unified theory, superunified theory, TOE, unified field theory

theory of relativity continuum theory, $e=mc^2$, Einstein theory, energy-matter relationship, general theory of relativity, principle of equivalence, principle of relativity, relativity, special theory of relativity

thermal paper fax paper

thermal pollution heated water discharge

thermal printer nonimpact printer

thermal spring hot spring, thermae, warm spring

thermonuclear reaction atomic reaction, cold fusion, fission, fusion, fusion reaction, laser-induced fusion, nuclear fusion reaction, thermonuclear fusion

Thermos™ bottle insulated bottle, thermos, Thermos™ flask, vacuum flask

thick skin apathy, armor, callousness, elephant skin, formidable defenses, hard shell, imperviousness, numbness, rhinoceros hide, thick hide, thick shell, unfeelingness

thick-skinned callous, hardened, insensitive, obtuse, tough, unconcerned, unfeeling

think back live in the past, recollect, reminisce

thinking cap cerebration, considering cap, headwork, state of thinking

think piece background material, news analysis, personal opinion piece

think tank brain trust, ivory tower, workshop

thin-skinned easily hurt, easily offended, oversensitive, sensitive, ultrasensitive

third base hot corner, third, third bag, third sack

third class low standard

third degree cross-examination, cross-interrogation, cross-questioning, grilling, inquisition, interrogation, pressure

third-degree burn scorch

third dimension depth, distance through, thickness

third estate bourgeoisie, commonality, common man, everyman, everywoman, middle classes, vulgus

third eye clairvoyance, ESP, extrasensory perception, insight, intuition, the force; pineal eye

third eyelid nictitating membrane

Third International Comintern

third market over-the-counter market

Third Order laypeople, laypersons

third party arbiter, arbitrator, mediator, minor party, third force, unbiased observer

third rail electrified line, live rail, overhead wires, pantograph

Third World developing nations, minority groups, nonaligned nations, unaligned nations, underdeveloped countries, underdeveloped nations

thirty-second note demisemiquaver

thought-provoking allusive, challenging, interesting, provocative, stimulating

threatened species endangered species

three-base hit three-bagger, three-base shot, triple

three-card monte shell game, thimblerig

3-D thick, three-dimensional

three Graces Aglaia, Euphrosyne, Thalia

three-legged race potato sack race, sack race

three-mile limit offshore rights, territorial waters, twelve-mile limit

three-point landing normal landing, perfect landing

three R's arithmetic, reading, writing

throat lozenge cough drop

throw down the gauntlet ask for trouble, call out, challenge, confront, contest, cross swords, dare, defy, do something about it, invite to debate, invite to do battle, knock the chip off one's shoulder, meet face-to-face, provoke, stand up to, start something

throwing stick boomerang, harpoon, javelin, lance, spear, throwing spear

throw rug scatter rug, small rug

throw up barf, be sick, blow grits, blow lunch, disgorge, drive a truck, gag, heave, hurl, pray to the porcelain god, puke, ralph, regurgitate, retch, spew, spit up, toss one's cookies, upchuck, urp, vomit

thrust stage theater-in-the-round, three-quarter-round stage

thumb one's nose deride, disparage, ridicule, sneeze at, sniff at

thumb piano kalimba, mbira

thumbs-down disapproval, dissatisfaction, ostracism, red light, veto

thumbs-up approval, go-ahead, green light, rubber stamp, satisfaction, stamp of approval

thyroid hormone TH, thyroxine, triiodothyronine

ticker-tape parade hero's welcome, reception, red-carpet treatment

tickled pink amused, delighted, exhilarated, high as a kite, loving it, thrilled, tickled, tickled to death

tickler file aide-mémoire, memorandum, memory aid

tidal flat flat, intertidal zone, mudflat, salt marsh, tidal land, tidal pool, tideland, wetlands

tidal wave eagre, giant sea swell, giant wave, rogue wave, sea wave, seiche, seismic sea wave, surface wave, tidal bore, tsunami, white horses

tie clasp scarfpin, tie clip, tie tac, tie tack, tiepin

tie the knot become one, celebrate a marriage, get hitched, get married, get spliced, marry, tie the wedding knot, united in marriage, wed

tight-lipped closemouthed, loath to speak, mum, mute, quiet, secretive, silent

tightrope walking brinkmanship, funambulism, risk-taking, ropedancing, venturousness

tight ship efficient business, efficient household, efficient organization, well-managed business

till hell freezes over forever, till you're blue in the face, to a finish, to the end

tilt at windmills attack imaginary enemy, get nowhere, run in circles, waste one's effort

time after time ad infinitum, again and again, a thousand times, day after day, endlessly, repeatedly, time and again, year after year

time and a half double time, incentive pay, overtime

time bomb infernal machine, powder keg, time fuse

time exposure exposure, shutter speed

time frame interval, lapse of time, period, span, stretch, time span

time-honored age-old, classic, respected, traditional, venerable, vintage

time immemorial aeons ago, ages, eternity, long time, month of Sundays, remote ages, time long past, time out of mind

time killer dallier, dillydallier, time waster

time lag delay, interval, lagging, lapse of time, space, time gap, time warp

time limit deadline, term, time allotment, time frame

time off break, breathing spell, day off, downtime, furlough, holiday, leave of absence, leisure time, liberty, mental-health day, pause, recess, respite, sabbatical, shore leave, sick leave, vacation

time-out break, breather, breathing spell, halt, interlude, intermission, letup, lull, pause, recess, rest, short break, spell

time out of mind aeons ago, ages, auld lang syne, days beyond recall, long ago, long since, month of Sundays, remote ages, time immemorial

time payments installment buying, installment payments

time sheet daybook, log, time book

time signature key signature, measure signature, metered time

times sign multiplication sign, ×

time warp time distortion

time zone longitudinal division, time belt

tinea cruris jock itch

tin ear bad ear, music insensitivity, no ear, poor ear

tin god idol, little tin god, official, paper tiger, popular idol, sacred cow

tinker's damn damn, darn, fig, hoot, smallest amount, smallest degree

tin lizzie cheap car, crate, dilapidated car, heap, jalopy, rattletrap, wreck

Tin Pan Alley musical district

tit for tat equivalent, eye for an eye, like for like, measure for measure, quid pro quo, something for something, trade-off

title deed deed, instrument, muniments, security

title page front matter, half-title page, masthead

toaster pastry Pop-Tart™

to-do ado, bother, commotion, excitement, fuss, hoopla, hubbub, stir, uproar

toe dance ballet, step dance, tap dance

toe the line adhere to rules, come to heel, conform, fall in, fall in line, follow the book, obey the rules, stay in line, toe the mark

toggle bolt Molly™ bolt

toilet paper bathroom tissue, toilet roll, toilet tissue, TP

toilet training potty training

toilet water attar of roses, eau de toilette, lavender water, rose water, scented liquid

token payment down payment, earnest

toll call long-distance call, trunk call

toll road interstate, state highway, tollway, turnpike

Tom, Dick and Harry anybody at all, common man, everyman, everywoman, plain folks, ragtag and bobtail, rank and file

tommy gun .45 caliber submachine gun, Thompson submachine gun

Tom Thumb dwarf, homunculus, Lilliputian, midget, Thumbelina

tone poem symphonic poem

tone row dodecuple scale, tone block, tone cluster, twelve-tone row, twelve-tone scale

tongue-in-cheek crossed fingers, irony, kidding, lip service, playacting, pretense, sarcasm, unseriousness

tongue in cheek in fun, in jest, jokingly, kiddingly

tongue-lashing bawling-out, berating, castigation, diatribe, dressing-down, rating, reprimand, scolding, talking-to, upbraiding

tongue-tied at a loss for words, bashful, choked up, dumbfounded, dumbstruck, garbled, inarticulate, mute, shy, silent, speechless

tongue twister unpronounceable phrase

tonic accent pitch accent

tooth and nail bec et ongles, hammer and tongs, hog-wild, with every available resource

tooth decay caries, cariosity, dental caries

tooth powder cleanser, dentifrice, toothpaste

tooth shell scaphopod, tusk shell

top banana ace, big enchilada, bigwig, head honcho, head person, main comic, second to none, star, top dog

top curtain trimming, valance

top-drawer blue-chip, excellent, first-class, first-rate, the best, top-notch

Top 40 best-sellers, hit parade, hits, popular music, the charts, top of the charts, top twenty

top hat high hat, silk hat, stovepipe hat, topper

topic sentence main thought

top-level high-echelon, leading, top-ranking

top-notch A1, blue-chip, excellent, first-class, first-rate, supreme, the best, top-drawer

topographic map detailed map, topographical map

top quark truth quark

top secret classified, highly classified, hush-hush, supersecret, under security restrictions, under wraps

topsy-turvy backwards, chaotic, confused, inside out, jumbled, mixed up, upended, upside down, wrong side up

torch song sentimental love song

toreador pants matador pants

torn to pieces ragged, ripped, shredded, tattered

tossed salad garden salad, greens, mixed greens, vegetable salad

total eclipse occultation

total recall eidetic imagery, eidetic memory, exercise of memory, photographic memory, recollection, total memory

tote bag large handbag, shopping bag, shoulder bag

tote board totalizator, totalizer, tote

touch and go coin toss, even

chance, even odds, heads or tails, level playing field, toss-up

touch base chat, have a friendly chat, have a little talk, renew communication, talk tête-à-tête, visit

touchy-feely sensitive, tactile, tactual

tough-minded hard-nosed, realistic, resolute

tour de force accomplishment, achievement, chef d'oeuvre, exploit, feat, feat of strength, grand achievement, magnum opus, masterpiece, masterstroke, masterwork, pièce de résistance, spectacular achievement

touring bicycle all-terrain bike, folding bicycle, mountain bike, racer, touring bike, touring cycle

touring car grand touring car, GT, runabout

tourist class cheap seats, coach class, lowest class

tourist guide chaperon, cicerone, docent, escort, guide

tour of duty hitch, shift, spell, stint, tour, watch

tout de suite at once, immediately, in an instant, in a wink, now, pronto, right away, without delay

town clerk city clerk

town crier announcer, bellman, crier, proclaimer, publicizer, stentor

town hall city center, city government, city hall, courthouse, municipal building, municipal center, municipal government, town government, town house

town meeting comitia

tow truck tow car, wrecker

toxic waste atomic waste, contaminated materials, environmental pollutant, hazardous waste, industrial waste, nuclear waste, poison, pollution

trace element microelement, micronutrient, minor element, minute amount, trace mineral

trace fossil fossil footprint, fossil record, index fossil, zone fossil

track-and-field athletics, broad jump, cross-country running, dashes, discus throw, field events, hammer throw, high jump, hurdles, javelin throw, jumping, long jump, pole vault, running, running events, shot put, triple jump

tracking shot dolly shot

tracking station astronomical station, control center, mission control, radar tracking station, tower, visual tracking station

track lighting mounted lighting, mounted lights

track meet games, races, racing, running, running events, track-and-field competition

track record accomplishment, achievement, credentials, history, performance, performance history, record, record of performance, statistics, stats, track

tractor feed pin feed

tractor pull tug of war

trade acceptance acceptance bill, bank acceptance, bill of exchange

trade agency chamber of commerce, cooperative society, guild, trade association

trade agreement trade pact, trade treaty

trade balance balance of payments, balance of trade

trade ban exporting ban, export sanctions, trade embargo, trade injunction, trade prohibition, trade restrictions, trade sanctions, trading ban, trading sanctions, trafficking ban

trade book general edition, trade edition, trade paperback, trade title

trade deficit trade gap

trade discount discount on list price, time discount

trade language business language, creole, diplomatic language, jargon, language universal, lingua franca, linguistic universal, pidgin

trade name brand name, logo, logotype, registered trademark, service mark, technical name, trademark

trade route air lane, flight path, sea-lane, shipping lane, silk road, trader route, traffic lane

trade school vocational school

trade secret classified information, proprietary knowledge, secret device, secret formula, secret method

trade show multivendor sales event, trade conference, trade convention

trade union craft union, guild, industrial union, labor union, organized labor, trades union

trade winds prevailing winds, trades

trading post barter store, market, post, trading center

traffic circle circle, circular one-way road, rotary, roundabout

traffic island crosswalk, pedestrian crossing

traffic jam blockage, bottleneck, congestion, gridlock, jam, logjam, roadblock, rush hour, traffic congestion, traffic tie-up

traffic light amber light, caution light, go light, green light, pedestrian light, red light, stoplight, traffic control, traffic signal, yellow light

tragic flaw Achilles' heel, character flaw, chink in one's armor, fatal flaw, vulnerability, weak point

tragic irony dramatic irony

trail bike dirt bike, minibike, motorbike, motor scooter, scooter, scrambler, small motorcycle

trailer park bivouac, campsite, trailer camp, trailer court

trailing arbutus mayflower

trail mix gorp

training school Borstal institution, industrial school, reformatory, reform school, remand school, tech, training camp, training college, training ground, training ship

transcendental meditation Hindu meditation, mantra, TM

transmigration of souls metempsychosis, metempsychosis avatar, reembodiment, reincarnation, transanimation

transverse section cross section

transverse wave longitudinal wave

trash bag garbage bag

trash can ash can, compost heap, Dumpster™, dustbin, garbage bag, garbage can, litter basket, skip, trash bag, wastebasket, waste bin, wastepaper basket

trash compactor garbage compactor, garbage disposal, garbage grinder, waste disposal unit

travel agency holiday company, travel bureau

travel bag carry-on, garment bag, overnighter, satchel, suitcase, tote

traveler's check banker's check, traveler's cheque

traveling salesman commercial traveler, detail man, door-to-door salesman, knight of the road, road warrior, traveling agent

traverse rod curtain rod

tread the boards act, appear on stage, perform, playact, strut one's stuff

tread water bide, bide one's time, coast, float, mark time

treasure chest depository, storage, vault

treasure-house coffers, exchequer, treasure room, treasury

Treasury bill exchequer bill, T-bill

tree farm orangery, orchard, stand, timberland, tree nursery

tree hugger activist, conservationist, ecologist, environmentalist, Green Panther, nature lover, preservationist

tree line timberline, tree zone, upper reaches, upper slopes

tree of heaven ailanthus

tree of knowledge bodhi tree, forbidden fruit, Garden of Eden

trench coat Burberry™

trench mouth Vincent's angina, Vincent's infection

trench warfare guerrilla warfare, static warfare

trial and error analysis, cut and try, examination, experiment, hit and miss, hit or miss, probe, R and D, research, research and development, study, tentation, test

trial balloon ballon d'essai, barometer, feeler, fishing question, pilot balloon, test of public reaction, toe in the water

trial jury petit jury, petty jury

trial run bench test, dry run, dummy run, practical test, practice run, rehearsal, road test, spot check, taste test, test flight, trial, trials, tryout

Triassic period Mesozoic era

tried-and-true demonstrable, dependable, proved, proven, reliable, reputable, tested, tested and proved, tried, trustworthy

trifle bowl layered-dessert bowl

trigonometric function circular function

Triple Crown Belmont Stakes, Kentucky Derby, Preakness Stakes

triple jump high jump; hop; hop, stride and jump; long jump, step

triple play three putouts, triple killing

Trojan horse decoy, subversive device

trolley car streetcar, trolley

tropical cyclone cyclone, hurricane, tempest, tropical storm, typhoon, violent rainstorm

tropical fish aquarium fish, exotic fish

tropical storm cyclonic storm, hurricane, tempest, tropical cyclone, typhoon, violent rainstorm

trouble spot hornet's nest, hotbed, hot spot, plague spot, possible difficulty, source of trouble, time bomb, volatile situation, war zone

trouser suit pantsuit

truck farm fruit farm, vegetable farm

true bill accusation, arraignment, bill of indictment, claim, impeachment, indictment, justifiable charge

true-blue faithful, in good faith, loyal, steadfast, tried-and-true, trusty

true colors cards on the table, heart on one's sleeve, truth

true north magnetic north, true directions

trump card ace in the hole, ace up one's sleeve, card up one's sleeve, key resource, leg up, secret weapon, trump, upper hand, whip hand

trumped-up concocted, cooked-up, devised, fabricated, false, fraudulent, invented, made-up

trundle bed truckle bed

trunk hose ballooning breeches

trunk line direct line, main line, trunk

trust territory trusteeship, TT

truth serum Pentothal™, scopolamine, thiopental sodium, truth drug

try square straightedge, T square

T square carpenter's square, square, try square

tubal ligation tied tubes

tuckered out drained, exhausted, fatigued, pooped, spent, tired, wiped out, worn-out

tug of war contest of strength, tractor pull

tummy tuck abdominoplasty

Tuneful Nine Calliope, Clio, Erato, Euterpe, Melpomene, Muses, Nine, Pierides, Polyhymnia, sacred Nine, Terpsichore, Thalia, Urania

tuning fork diapason, tuning bar

tuning pipe pitch pipe

tunnel vision blinders, blind side, blind spot, constricted vision, fixation, monomania, myopia, narrow outlook, narrow-mindedness, obsession, one-track mind, shortsightedness

turbopropeller engine prop-jet, prop-jet engine, pulse-jet engine, ramjet engine, turboprop, turboprop engine

turbulent flow burble, burble point, eddies, turbidity, turbulence

turkey-cock male turkey

Turkish bath bagnio, hummum, sauna, steam bath, sweat bath

Turkish delight Turkish paste

turning point climax, crisis, critical juncture, critical mass, critical point, crossroads, crucial moment, crucial period, crunch, cusp, decisive moment, defining moment, emergency, high noon, hinge, kairotic moment, moment of truth, nexus, peripeteia, pivotal moment, point of no return, race against time, rising action, turn of the tide, when push comes to shove, zero hour

turn signal blinker, directional signal, indicator

turn tail desert under fire, make a U-turn, retreat, run scared, skedaddle, turn around, turn on a dime

turn turtle capsize, keel over, overturn, turn over, turn topsy-turvy

TV dinner frozen dinner, frozen entrée, frozen prepared meal, precooked frozen meal

TV evangelism telepreaching, televangelism, television evangelism

TV set boob tube, idiot box, television receiver, television set, telly, TV

Twelfth Day Epiphany

Twelfth Night Carnival, Epiphany eve, January 5

twelve-step program AA, Alcoholics Anonymous, Narcotics Anonymous, self-help group, 12-step

twenty questions quiz

twenty-twenty clear-sighted, normal vision, normal visual acuity, perfect vision

twiddle one's thumbs do nothing, not lift a finger, sit it out, sit on one's hands

Twilight of the Gods Götterdämmerung, Ragnarok

twilight zone borderline case, dreamworld, gray area, hallucinatory state, nightmare world

twin bed single bed

twin bill double feature, doubleheader

twist of fate reversal of one's fortune, wild card

twist tie coated wire

two-base hit double, two-bagger, two-base shot

two-bit a dime a dozen, cheap, inferior, piddling, second-rate, small-time

two bits a quarter, petty sum, quarter, twenty-five cents, $0.25, 25 cents

two cents worth broad hint, comment, flea in the ear, observation, remark, say, tip, unsolicited opinion

two-faced back-stabbing, deceitful, dishonest, disingenuous, disloyal, double-dealing, double-faced, fake, insincere, phony, shifty, slippery, underhanded, ungenuine

two-time back-stab, be disloyal, betray, be unfaithful, cheat, deceive

two-timing adultery, cheating, disloyalty, unfaithfulness

two-way radio two-way communication, walkie-talkie

tympanic membrane eardrum, membrana tympana, tympanum

type A aggressive personality, hostile personality

type B relaxed personality

type genus family representative

type species genus representative

type specimen embodiment, individual specimen, representation, specimen, type species, typification

Typhoid Mary carrier, vector, walking time bomb

typographical error clerical error, erratum, misprint, mistake in printing, mistake in typing, printer's error, typing mistake, typist's error, typo

Uu

U-boat German submarine, sub, submarine

ugly duckling fright, homely person, no beauty, rough diamond

un-American activity unconstitutional act

uncalled-for inappropriate, needless, nonessential, pointless, unasked-for, undeserved, uninvited, unnecessary, unrequired, unwanted, unwarranted, unwelcome

uncertainty principle Heisenberg principle, indeterminacy principle, principle of indeterminacy, quantum mechanics, statistical mechanics

Uncle Sam Brother Jonathan, U.S. government, Washington

uncollectable debt worthless asset, write-off

unconditional surrender capitulation, white flag, yielding

under fire on the hit list, under attack

undergraduate degree baccalaureate, bachelor's degree

underground railroad secret cooperative network, subway, underground railway, underground route

under one's breath between the teeth, in an undertone, lower one's voice, sotto voce, whisper

under one's hat buttoned up, confidential, private, secret, under wraps

under-the-counter bootleg, illicit

under the gun at gunpoint, at knifepoint, in a hurry, pressured, under duress, under pressure, under threat

under the influence crocked, drunk, inebriated, intoxicated, loaded, pickled, tipsy, under the table, wasted

under the weather ailing, bedridden, below par, diseased, ill, out of sorts, run-down, sick, sickly, unhealthy, unwell

under the wire at the eleventh hour, at the last minute, just in the nick of time, without a minute to spare

under wraps buttoned up, classified, covert, hidden away, hush-hush, kept concealed, restricted, top secret, with a lid on

undreamed-of inconceivable, unexpected, unforeseen, unimagined

unearned increment invalid claim

unemployment benefit unemployment compensation, unemployment insurance, welfare

unheard-of exceptional, new, novel, unique, unknown, unprecedented, unusual

unidentified flying object extraterrestrial spacecraft, flying saucer, spacecraft, spaceship, UFO

unified field theory grand unified theory, relativity theory, superunified theory

Union Jack U.K. flag, Union flag

Union of Soviet Socialist Republics Russia, Soviet Union, U.S.S.R.

union shop closed shop, preferential shop

union suit long johns, long underwear

United Kingdom Albion, Blighty, Britain, Britannia, British Empire, Commonwealth of Nations, England, Great Britain, Land of the Rose, Limeyland, U.K., United Kingdom of Great Britain and Northern Ireland

United Nations League of Nations, UN

United States America, Columbia, Land of Liberty, land of opportunity, New World, the States, United States of America, U.S., U.S.A., U.S. of A.

universal agreement agreement of all, common consent, consensus, consensus gentium, consensus of opinion, consensus omnium, universal accord, universal testimony

universal concept universal, universal conception

universal coupling universal joint

universal donor type O

universal language universal tongue, world language

Universal Product Code bar code, UPC

universal truth axiom, general truth, home truth, intrinsic truth, obvious truth, postulate, self-evident truth, truism, truth

universe of discourse framework, intellectual frame of reference, universe, world of discourse

university hospital health center, teaching hospital

university press academic press, university publishing house

unsaturated fatty acid polyunsaturated fatty acid

unskilled labor common labor, dirty work, grunt work, manual labor, manual work, physical work, unskilled work

untimed service flat-rate service

unwritten law convention, natural law, protocol

up-and-coming promising, rising, succeeding

up-front direct, frank, open

up front in advance

up in arms at odds, at swords' points, at war, hostile, in an uproar, indignant, in the midst of battle, prepared for war, provoked, wrought up

up in the air chancy, debatable, doubtful, iffy, pending, questionable, tentative, uncertain, undecided, undetermined, unfinished, unresolved, unsettled

uphill struggle difficult task, hard work, tall order, tough assignment, uphill battle

upper class aristocracy, beau monde, beautiful people, better sort, cream, cream of society, crème de la crème, cultured class, elite, gentry, haut monde, high life, high society, jet set, privileged, privileged class, second estate, smart set, society, the better sorts, the Four Hundred, the privileged, upper crust

upper hand advantage, a leg up, authority, control, dominance, driver's seat, lead, leverage, rule, trump hand, whip hand

upper house House of Lords, House of Peers, U.S. Senate

upright piano cottage piano, upright

ups and downs ebb and flow, good and bad times, highs and lows, peaks and valleys, systole and diastole, wax and wane

upset price lowest auction price

upset the applecart dislocate, disorder, make waves, sink, upset someone's applecart

upside down backwards, bottom up, inside out, inverted, orderless, overturned, topsy-turvy, vice versa, without order, wrong side out

up-to-date au courant, contemporary, current, cutting edge, fashionable, happening, in vogue, modern, new, state-of-the-art, stylish, trendy, up-to-the-minute, with-it

upwardly mobile likely to advance, socially mobile

upward mobility advancement, climbing the corporate ladder, social climbing, social mobility, status seeking, vertical mobility

urban legend urban myth, widely distributed untruth

urban renewal face-lifting, overhauling, refurbishment, rehabilitation, renovation, slum clearance, urban redevelopment

urban sprawl built-up area, spread city, uncontrolled development, urban corridor, urban spread

used to acclimated, accustomed to, familiar with

user-friendly convenient, easy to understand, easy to use, practical, untroublesome

user interface command-line interface, graphical user interface, menu-driven interface, UI

user's manual instruction book, instruction manual

utility player backup, bench, bench jockey, benchwarmer, replacement, secondary, second string, sub, substitute, succedaneum

utility pole telegraph pole, telephone pole

utility program file recovery, maintenance program, resource editor

utility room laundry room, sewing room

Vv

vacuum bag dust bag
vacuum bottle Thermos™
vacuum cleaner carpet sweeper, Hoover™, vacuum sweeper
vacuum tube electron tube, thermionic tube, VT
vaginal condom vaginal pouch
Valentine's Day February 14, Saint Valentine's Day
valet parking attendant parking
valley glacier alpine glacier
Valley of the Kings Valley of the Tombs
value-added tax estimated market value tax, sales tax, VAT
value judgment bias, ethics, evaluative criticism, intuition, morals, stocktaking, subjective evaluation, valuation
vanishing point convergence point, convergent view, far horizon, mathematical point, meeting point, nothingness, pinpoint, point of convergence, where earth meets sky
vanity case compact, makeup bag, makeup kit, toilet kit, toiletries case, vanity bag, vanity box
vanity fair beau monde, world of fashion
vanity plate customized license plate, custom license plate
vanity press author-published book, self-published book, small press, vanity publisher
vantage point angle, perspective, point of vantage, point of view, position, slant, vantage, vantage ground, viewpoint, where one stands
vapor pressure vapor tension
vapor trail condensation trail, contrail, vortex, wake, wash
variable resistor potentiometer
variable star Cepheid variable
variety meat brains, chitlins, chitterlings, giblets, gizzard, heart, kidneys, liver, marrow, mountain oyster, pancreas, prairie oyster, stomach, sweetbread, testis, thymus, tongue, tripe
variety show extravaganza, revue, stage show
variety store dime store, general store, retail store, variety shop
vector product cross product

V-E Day May 8, Victory in Europe Day

vegetable kingdom botany, flora, flowerage, greenery, green plants, herbage, plant kingdom, plant life, plants, vegetable life, vegetation, verdure

vegetable shortening Crisco™

veg out lie dormant, relax, relax slothfully, stagnate, vegetate

vending machine Automat, candy machine, cigarette machine, coin machine, coin-operated machine, soda machine, vendor

venereal disease crabs, gonorrhea, herpes, pox, sexually transmitted disease, social disease, STD, syphilis, the clap, VD

venetian blind jalousie, miniblind, window covering

Venetian window Palladian window

venial sin impropriety, indiscretion, lapse, minor wrong, misstep, peccadillo, slight, slight transgression, slip, vice

venture capital backing, equity capital, risk capital, support, VC, working capital

vermiform appendix appendix, vermiform process

vernal equinox spring, springtide, springtime

vernier caliper vernier micrometer

vertical file file cabinet, ready reference file

vertically challenged short

vertical union industrial union

very important person big shot, celebrity, dignitary, VIP

Very lights beacon, lighthouse, stormy petrel, warning lights

vestal virgin nun, vestal

vested interest absolute interest, beneficial interest, contingent interest, dominant interest, equitable interest, lobby, pressure group, special interest

Veterans Day Armistice Day, November 11, Remembrance Day

veterinary medicine animal medicine

vicar apostolic titular bishop

Vicar of Christ pope, Vicar of Jesus Christ

vice squad gambling police, prostitution police

vice versa backwards, contrarily, contrariwise, conversely, inversely, mutatis mutandis, reversed, the opposite way, upside down

Vichy water sparkling mineral water

vicious circle catch-22, causal nexus, chain of circumstances, chain reaction, circularity, concatenation of events, domino effect, endless loop, eternal return, impasse, vicious cycle

videocassette recorder tape machine, VCR, videorecorder, videotape recorder

video display terminal cathode-ray tube, CRT, display, graphics terminal, monitor, screen, VDT, VDU, video display unit, video terminal

video game computer game, computerized game, electronic game, Game Boy™, Nintendo™, PlayStation™

video jockey veejay, VJ

videotape format Beta, VHS

videotape recorder camcorder, recording instrument, VTR

view graph transparency

vigilance committee neighborhood watch, vigilantes, watch committee

vin ordinaire red table wine

vintage year special year, year of achievement

VIP bigwig, person of note, very important person

virgin birth immaculate conception, parthenogenesis

Virginia fence snake fence, Virginia rail fence, worm fence, zigzag fence

Virgin Mary Blessed Virgin Mary, Holy Mother, Madonna, Mater Dolorosa, Mother of God, Mother of Jesus, Our Lady

virtual image virtual screen

virtual reality artificial intelligence, computer simulation, cyberspace, simulated 3-D environment, VR

vis-à-vis eyeball-to-eyeball, face-to-face, facing, frontal, opposite to

visiting card business card, calling card, card, carte de visite

visiting fireman important visitor

visual acuity acute sight, keen sight, perspicacity, perspicuity, sharp sight, twenty-twenty vision, 20/20 vision

visual arts arts, beaux arts, ceramics, design, drawing, fine arts, graphic arts, painting, photography, sculpture

visual field field of vision, horizon, ken, purview, range, scope, sweep, VF

vital force animating force, élan vital, force of life, life force, living force, soul, spirit, vis vitae, vis vitalis, vital energy, vitality, vital principle

vital signs pulse rate, respiratory rate, temperature

vital statistics birth statistics, death statistics, immigration statistics, marriage statistics

vitamin C ascorbic acid

V-J Day August 15, Victory in Japan Day

vocal cords Adam's apple, larynx, throat, vocal bands, vocal folds, vocal organs, vocal processes, voice, voice box

voice box larynx

voice mail answering machine, autoattendant, telephone message storage

voice vote aye, nay, show of hands, viva voce vote, yea, yeas and nays

volcanic glass obsidian, perlite, pitchstone

volte-face about-face, contraposition, tergiversation, U-turn

voting machine ballot box, polling booth, polling place

vouch for assert under oath, attest, guarantee, swear to, vouch

vox populi general voice, one accord, popular belief, popular opinion, popular sentiment, public opinion, single voice, unison, vox pop

Vulgar Latin ancient Roman speech, VL

Ww

wading pool kiddie pool, shallow pool, swimming pool
waffle cloth honeycomb
wage earner breadwinner, employee, income producer, jobholder, one who brings home the bacon, salaried worker, staffer, staff member, wage slave, wageworker
Wailing Wall Western Wall
wait and see bide one's time, lie low, play a waiting game, tread water, watch and wait
waiting game cat and mouse, lying low, wait-and-see attitude, wait-and-see policy, waiting it out, watchful waiting, watching and waiting
waiting list short list, standby
waiting room antechamber, anteroom, foyer, lobby, reception room, salle d'attente, vestibule
walkie-talkie intercom, pager, two-way radio
walking-around money pocket money
walking dead corpse, living dead, revived corpse, zombie
walking papers discharge notice, dismissal, dismissal notice, heave-ho, marching orders, pink slip, the boot, the sack, walking ticket
walking stick alpenstock, cane, crutch, handstaff, shillelagh, stick, walking aid
walk of life calling, chosen career, life's work, lifework, line of business, line of work, mission, occupation, practice, profession, trade, vocation
walk-on part bit part, extra, stand-in, understudy, walking part
walk out on abandon, dump, jilt, leave, leave high and dry, leave in a lurch, reject
wall anchor beam anchor
wall hanging map, tapestry
wall socket electrical receptacle
Wall Street financial district, stock exchange, stock market, world of commerce
wall unit wall system
walrus mustache drooping mustache, handlebar mustache
Walter Mitty daydreamer, woolgatherer
want ad classified ad, classified advertisement, classifieds

War Between the States American Civil War, Civil War

war bride GI bride

war correspondent foreign correspondent, special correspondent

war crime crime against humanity, genocide, holocaust

war cry banzai, battle cry, call to arms, rallying cry, rebel yell, war dance, war song, war whoop

ward heeler camp follower, hanger-on, hatchet man, heeler, henchman, partisan, party hack, sectary, supporter, votary

ward off avert, block, defend, deflect, fend off, keep at bay, turn aside

warehouse store cooperative, discount house, discount store, megastore, outlet store, superstore, warehouse, wholesale house

war game dry run, kriegspiel, maneuvers

war hawk militarist, war dog, war hound, warmonger

warm front dog days, heat wave, hot spell, hot wave

warm reception hero's welcome, red carpet, red-carpet treatment, ticker-tape parade

warm-up suit sweats, sweat suit

warning track fences, outfield

war of independence internecine war, revolution, revolutionary war, war of revolution

war of nerves browbeating, demoralization, intimidation, psychological conflict, psychological warfare, saber rattling

war paint cosmetics, drugstore complexion, makeup

war party hard-liners, hawks, patriotic political party

warp speed escape velocity, flash, greased lightning, lightning speed, terminal velocity

war zone battle zone, combat area, combat zone, hot spot, seat of war, theater, theater of operations, theater of war, trouble spot

wash-and-wear dry goods, no-iron clothes, off-the-rack clothes, permanent press clothes, ready-to-wear, store-bought clothes

wash drawing aquarelle, wash, water, watercolor

washed-up done, done for, finished, kaput, over the hill, through

washing machine washer

wasp waist hourglass, hourglass figure, nipped waist, slender waist

wastepaper basket dustbin, garbage can, litter basket, litter bin, trash can, wastebasket, waste bin

waste time burn daylight, dally, dawdle, delay, dillydally, fiddle about, fritter away time, goof off, idle away time, kill time, linger, loiter, lollygag, lose time, pass the time, piddle, procrastinate, shilly-shally, take one's own sweet time, take one's time, tarry, while away the time

watch and ward guard, vigil, ward, wardenship, wardship, watch

watch fire balefire, beacon, beacon fire, fire kept burning, flare, signal beacon, signal fire, smoke signal, warning light

watching one's weight calorie counting, dieting, fasting, food abstinence, regimen, watching one's calories, weight watching

watch night New Year's Eve, watch meeting, watch-night service

water ballet synchronized swimming

water-based paint watercolor

water boy bheesty, water bearer, water carrier

water clock clepsydra

water closet bathroom, latrine, outhouse, toilet, WC

water dog bluejacket, sailor, Seabee, sea dog, shipman

water down dilute, reduce, thin, weaken

water fountain drinking fountain, faucet, watercooler

water gap gap, notch, pass, transverse cleft

water gate culvert, floodgate, water carrier, water channel, waterway

water gauge fluviograph, fluviometer

water glass drinking glass, goblet

water hammer banging pipes

watering can sprinkling can, watering pot

watering hole bar, tavern, watering place, watering spot

watering place baths, health resort, spa, springs, swimming hole, water hole

water level mean sea level, sea level, water table

water main main, plumbing, principal pipe, water line

water moccasin cottonmouth, semiaquatic pit viper

water nymph kelpie, limniad, mermaid, naiad, Nereid, nix, Oceanid, ocean nymph, river nymph, sea nymph, water elf, water spirit, water sprite

water of crystallization water of hydration

water pill diuretic pill

water pipe hookah, hubble-bubble, kalian, narghile, nargileh; conduit, main, plumbing, sluice, steam pipe, water conduit, water main

water pistol squirt gun, water gun

waterproof covering moisture-proof covering, tarp, tarpaulin

water supply available water, water system, waterworks

water table aquifer, artesian basin, artesian spring, sinkhole, water level

water tower reservoir, standpipe

water under the bridge bygones, days gone by, past, times past, yesterday

water vapor cloud, steam

water wave gravity wave

water wings swimmies

water witch dowser, water diviner

watery-eyed blubbering, crying, misty-eyed, sniveling, sobbing, tearful, teary, wailing, weepy

wave number wavelength reciprocal

wax museum waxworks

ways and means means, means to an end, methods and means, methods and resources, ways, wherewithal

way station halfway station

way with words articulateness, articulation, command of language, elocution, eloquence, expressiveness, facility of speech, fluency, gift of gab, oratory, silver tongue, word power

weak interaction weak force

weak-minded feebleminded, foolish, indecisive, irresolute, silly, spineless, wishy-washy

weak sister chicken, gutless wonder, hothouse plant, invertebrate, jellyfish, meek soul, softy, weakling, weak soul

weak spot chink in one's armor, fatal flaw, vulnerable point, weak link, weakness, weak point, weak side

wear and tear ablation, attrition,

consumption, decrement, depletion, depreciation, dissipation, erosion, hard wear, overuse, ravages of time, wearing away, weathering

weasel word confusing statement, confusing word, dodge, equivocal saying, evasion, misleading statement, misleading word, suppressio veri, waffling

weather deck open ship's deck, weather bow

weather eye eagle eye, hawk-eyed, nautical experience, peeled eye, sharp eye, watchful eye, X-ray eye

weather forecast five-day forecast, forecast, general outlook, local forecast, long-term forecast, regional forecast, small-craft advisory, storm warning, storm watch, weather prediction, weather report

weather map isobar, isobaric line, isopiestic line, meteorological map

weather station anemometer, barometer, meteorological station, weather bureau

weather vane cock, vane, weathercock, wind sock, wind vane

Web site home page, HTML documents, Web page, World Wide Web documents

wedding apparel bridal gown, bridal outfit, trousseau, tuxedo, wedding attire, wedding clothes, wedding dress

wedding ring engagement ring, wedding band

wedge heel platform heel

weed whacker edger, weed cutter, Weed Eater™

weekend bag carry-on bag, duffel, duffle, small suitcase, weekender

weigh anchor bring the anchor home, cast off, loose for sea, put to sea, unmoor, up-anchor

weigh down burden, encumber, load, saddle

weight training bodybuilding, free weights, iron pumping, Olympic lifting, power lifting, pumping iron, weight lifting, weight work, working out

Weird Sisters Atropos, Clotho, coven, Fatal Sisters, Fates, Lachesis, Moirai, Weirds, witches' coven

welfare state social democracy, social services, welfare statism

welfare work casework, social service, social welfare, social work

well-advised intelligent, judicious, prudent, smart, wise

well-appointed well-equipped, well-furnished

well-balanced prudent, rational, reasonable, sensible, sound

well-being comfort, contentment, happiness, health, prosperity, success, welfare

well-bred civil, courteous, courtly, cultivated, finished, genteel, gentlemanly, good-mannered, gracious, groomed, ladylike, mannerly, polished, polite, refined, sophisticated, well-mannered

well-defined clear, clear-cut, distinct, sharp, unambiguous

well-founded based on hard data, based on hard facts, factual, proven, rock-solid, solid, substantiated

well-informed aware, schooled, trained, versed, with-it

Wellington boot tall boot

well-known celebrated, famed, famous, illustrious, notable, prominent, renowned

well-mannered accommodating, affable, benevolent, charitable, considerate, cordial, courteous, cultivated, friendly, good-mannered, gracious, hospitable, kind, mannerly, polite, well-behaved, well-bred

well-off prosperous, rich, wealthy, well-to-do

well-read bookish, educated, literate, scholarly, versed, widely read

well-to-do prosperous, rich, wealthy, well-off

Western Hemisphere Central America, North America, Occident, South America, West

western movie cowboy picture, cowboy story, horse opera, oater, shoot-'em-up, spaghetti western, western, western story

Western saddle stock saddle

Western Wall Wailing Wall

wet blanket cold water, damper, downer, drag, grinch, grouch, killjoy, malcontent, marplot, party pooper, poor sport, proser, sourpuss, spoilsport

wet dream erotic dream, nocturnal emission

wet nurse feeder, hired breast-feeder

wet suit rubber suit

wetting agent humidifier, liquidizer, moisturizer, wetting-out agent

wet vac Shop Vac™, wet-and-dry vac

whatever will be will be fatalism, predestination, resignation, submission to fate

what's what fact, truth of the matter, where it's at, whole story

wheat flour buckwheat flour, ground wheat

wheel and deal finagle, lobby, plot, scheme, wire-pull

wheel cover hubcap

wheeler-dealer big-time operator, gamesman, horse trader, operator, strategist, Yankee horse trader

wheel lock flintlock, matchlock

wheel of fortune big six wheel, fortune's wheel, gambling wheel, raffle wheel, roulette wheel, wheel of chance

wheel of life circuition, life cycle

whipping boy chopping block, fall guy, goat, patsy, scapegoat

whipping cream Devonshire cream, heavy cream

whirlpool bath contrast bath, hot tub, Jacuzzi™, spa

whispering campaign character assassination, innuendo, insinuation, negative campaign, slander, sly suggestion, smear campaign

whistle-stop tour campaigning, campaign trail, candidature, canvassing, door-to-door, grassroots campaign, politicking, stump, stump excursion, stumping, stumping tour

white blood cell leukocyte, white blood corpuscle, white cell, white corpuscle

white book government publication

white bread light bread

white-collar worker career woman, clerical worker, management, nonmanual worker, office worker, professional worker, salaried workers, skilled worker

whited sepulcher hypocrite, paper tiger, sham

white elephant albatross, ball and chain, burden, burthen, more trouble than it's worth, onus

white feather cold feet, cowardice, jellyfish, lily-livered, weak knees, yellow belly, yellow streak

white flag backing down, capitulation, caving in, flag of truce, giving in, retreat, submission, throwing in the towel, truce flag, unconditional surrender

white gasoline unleaded gasoline

white glue Elmer's™ glue

white gold gold nickel alloy, white metal

white goods linens, napery, yard goods

white heat extreme heat, high temperature, intense heat, oppressive heat, sweltering heat, torrid heat, tropical heat

white hole active galactic nucleus

White House executive branch, executive mansion, official residence, presidential mansion, presidential palace

white knight knight, paladin, savior

white lie exaggeration, half-truth, harmless untruth, little white lie, mental dishonesty, near truth, partial truth, slight stretch, suggestio falsi, trivial untruth, untruth, well-intentioned untruth

white lightning bathtub gin, bootleg, bootleg liquor, home brew, hooch, moonshine, mountain dew, rotgut, sheep-dip, stump liquor, tiger milk, white mule

white magic good magic, theurgy

white meat breast meat, light-colored meat, viande blanche, wing meat {compare *dark meat*}

white night insomnia, insomnolence, night without sleep, sleeplessness, tossing and turning

white noise acoustical noise, broadcasting noise, electrical noise, hiss, hissing, hum, moan, purl, siss, sissing, white sound

white pages residential listings, telephone directory, telephone listings

white paper command paper, position paper, state paper, technical paper, white book

white sale clearance sale, January sale

white slave streetwalker, unwilling prostitute

white-tie dress clothes, evening wear, full dress, man's formal dress, tails

white trash poor white people, poor white person

white water breakers, lather, rapid, rapids, soapsuds, spindrift, spoondrift, spray, suds, surf, wild water

white whale beluga, sea canary

white wine Asti Spumante, Chablis, chardonnay, chenin blanc, gewürztraminer, liebfraumilch, Moselle, Orvieto, Rhine, Riesling

whiz kid boy wonder, child prodigy, comer, genius, gifted child, gifted student, girl wonder, phenom, polymath, prodigy, quiz kid, sensation, talented child, wonder, wunderkind

whole blood arterial blood, blood, lifeblood, venous blood

whole caboodle all of it, full measure, full monty, kit and caboodle, limit, whole ball of wax, whole bit, whole deal, whole hog, whole kit and boodle, whole kit and caboodle, whole mess, whole nine yards, whole shebang, whole shooting match, whole show, whole shtick, whole works, works

whole hog all out, full measure, fullest extent, whole nine yards, whole way

whole note semibreve

whole number integer

whole rest breve rest, semibreve rest

whole step major second, whole tone

whooping cough pertussis

who's who blue book, directory, social register

wide-awake alert, bright-eyed and bushy-tailed, on one's toes, on the ball, sharp, vigilant, watchful, wide-eyed

wide of the mark beside the point, far afield, nihil ad rem, off course, off target, off the subject, wide

wide receiver pass receiver, primary receiver, receiver, wideout

widow's peak cowlick, fetlock, forelock, quiff

widow's walk captain's walk

widow's weeds black, crape, crepe, mourning garments, weeds, weepers

wife-to-be bride-to-be, fiancée, future mate

wig out blow a gasket, flip out, get into a tizzy, go ape, lose one's cool, pop one's cork

wildcat strike mutiny, outlaw strike, strike, unofficial strike, work stoppage

wilderness area national forest, national park, wilderness preserve

Wilderness Road migration route

wild-goose chase bootless errand, fool's errand, hopeless case, lost cause, merry chase, red herring, snipe hunt, vain attempt, wasted effort, wasted labor, waste of time

wild pitch erratic pitch, erratic throw, wild throw

wild rice basmati rice, brown rice, long-grain rice, orzo, pilaf, unpolished rice

windchill factor algidity, chill factor

wind chimes wind-bells

wind gauge anemograph, anemometer, wind cone, wind sleeve, wind sock

winding-sheet cerecloth, cerement, cerements, corpse wrapping, grave clothes, shroud

window box flowerpot, planter

window dressing decorative exhibition, false front, facade, front, showmanship, store window display, varnish, window display

window seat window bench

window shade blind, jalousie, venetian blind

window-shopping browsing, comparison shopping, grazing, just looking

window unit room air conditioner

wind rose barometric wind rose, dynamic wind rose, humidity wind rose, hyetal wind rose, rain wind rose, temperature wind rose, wind direction diagram

wind shear microburst, slant of wind, sudden downdraft, veering wind, wind shift

wind sleeve wind cone, wind direction indicator, wind sock

wind sprint dash, extremely fast run, sprint run

wind tunnel proving ground, test bed

wine and dine cook for, feast, feed, fete, have to dinner, mess, regale

wine cellar larder, wine stock, wine storage

wine cooler wine spritzer

wine steward sommelier, wine waiter

wing case elytron

wing it ad-lib, improvise

wing nut butterfly nut, thumb nut

wire glass safety glass

wireless telephony radiotelegraphy, wireless telegraphy

wire rack cooling rack

wire rope cable, locked-wire rope

wire service AP, Associated Press, news agency, news service, news-gathering organization, news wire, press agency, press association, Reuters, TASS, the press, United Press International, UPI

wisdom tooth rearmost molar

wise man intellectual, oracle,

philosopher, religious sage, sage, sapient, thinker, wise woman

wise saying adage, aphorism, apophthegm, apothegm, dictum, gnome, maxim, moral, precept, proverb, saw, saying, witticism, words of wisdom

wish for covet, crave, fancy, hanker for, hunger for, long for, lust after, thirst after, want, yearn for

wish fulfillment dream come true, dream vision, ignis fatuus, will-o'-the-wisp, wish-fulfillment fantasy, wishful thinking

wishful thinking mistaken belief, self-deception, sophistry

wishing well wish fountain

wish list laundry list, shopping list, things wanted, want list

wishy-washy blowing hot and cold, indecisive, irresolute, spineless, undecided, vacillating, weak

witch doctor alternative practitioner, faith healer, isangoma, medicine man, mundunugu, obeah doctor, shaman, voodoo, wangateur

witches' brew concoction, hell-broth, witches' cauldron

witches' Sabbath witches' coven, witches' meeting

witch-hunt fishing expedition, inquisition, persecution, treasure hunt

witching hour black mass, dead of night, hush of night, midnight, midnight hours, twelve o'clock, wee small hours

without question certain, doubtless, incontestable, indisputable, irrefutable, sure, unmistakable, unquestionable, without doubt

witness stand dock, testimony box, witness-box

wolf in sheep's clothing four-flusher, fraud, impostor, mountebank, poser, pretender, ringer

wolf whistle love call, mating call, two-note whistle

woman of letters bookwoman, scholar, woman of learning

woman of the house head of household, lady of the house, primary woman

woman of the streets call girl, hooker, hustler, lady of the evening, lady of the night, prostitute, slut, streetwalker, whore, woman of easy virtue, woman of the town, working girl

woman of the world clubwoman, cosmopolitan, fashionable woman, mondaine, socialite, sophisticated woman, woman about town

woman suffrage right of representation, suffragettism, suffragism, women's right to vote

women's liberation equal rights, feminism, rights of women, sisterhood, womanism, women's lib, women's liberation movement, women's movement, women's rights movement, women's studies, women's suffrage

women's room girls' room, ladies' room, little girls' room, powder room, women's restroom

women's studies women's history

wonder drug miracle drug, synthetic drug

wood alcohol methanol

wood engraving block print, lignography, woodblock, woodcut, wood print, xylography

wooden Indian cigar-store Indian

wood nymph dryad, hamadryad, tree nymph

wood pulp paper pulp, papier-mâché, pulp, pulpwood, rag paper, rag pulp

word blindness alexia

word class part of speech

word for word according to the letter, faithfully, in the same words, ipsissima verba, literally, literatim, strictly, to the letter, verbally, verbatim, verbatim ac litteratim, word by word, word for word and letter for letter, word-perfectly

word list glossary, gradus, index, lexicon, thesaurus, vocabulary, wordbook

word of honor assurance, commitment, faith, gentlemen's agreement, guarantee, oath, pledge, plight, promise, solemn declaration, solemn oath, solemn promise, solemn word, swearing, troth, verbal agreement, vow, warrant, warranty

word of mouth oral communication, orally, oral message, parol, personal account, speech, spoken communication, spoken word, verbal evidence, viva voce

word on the street gossip, grapevine talk, hearsay, rumor, scoop

word order structure, syntactic arrangement, syntactics, syntactic structure, syntax, word arrangement

word processing data processing, text editing

word processor data processor, editor, text editor, word processing program

word square acrostic

word stress accent, emphasis, pronunciation, stress

word to the wise advice, good word, recommendation, suggestion, word in the ear

work both sides of the street have one's cake and eat it too, play both ends against the middle

work camp prison camp

workers' compensation workers' compensation insurance, workman's compensation, workmen's compensation, workmen's compensation insurance

working capital business assets, equity capital, fixed capital, risk capital, venture capital, working asset

working class blue-collar workers, common laborer, common laborers, factory laborer, factory laborers, grass roots, laboring class, plebeians, proles, proletariat, rank and file, the other half, unskilled laborer, unskilled laborers, wage earners, workers, workfolk, working people, working stiff, working stiffs, workpeople

working day daily grind, grind, nine-to-five, workday

working girl career woman, workgirl, working woman

working hypothesis hypothesis, theorem, theory, working proposition

working order good condition, trim

work of art art object, artwork, composition, object of art, objet d'art, piece, study

work stoppage lockout, sit-down strike, strike, walkout, work cessation

World Bank International Bank for Reconstruction and Development

world beyond afterlife, great beyond, hereafter, next world, unknown, world to come

World Council of Churches ecumenical council

World Court International Court of Justice

World Cup international soccer tournament

worldly-wise cosmopolitan, experienced, knowing, learned, sophisticated, worldly

world power dominion, imperium, lordship, powerful nation, sovereignty, superpower

world's fair global exposition

world spirit anima mundi, animating force, infinite spirit, Logos, oversoul, universal ego, universal life force, world principle, world reason, world self, world soul

world war global war, great war, major war, War of the Nations, World War I, World War II

World Wide Web cyberspace, hypertext documents, information server, information superhighway, Internet, Net, the Net, Web, WWW

world without end forever, time without end, whole wide world, wide world

worm fence snake fence, Virginia fence, Virginia rail fence, zigzag fence

worm's-eye view bird's-eye view, fly on the wall

worn-out battered, broken down, crumbling, decaying, decrepit, deteriorated, dilapidated, falling apart, falling down, in disrepair, in ruins, ramshackle, run-down, the worse for wear

wrapped up in oneself conceited, egocentric, egotistic, narcissistic, self-absorbed, self-admiring, self-centered, self-important, selfish, self-obsessed, smug, vainglorious

wrapping paper decorative wrap, gift wrap

wreak havoc cause destruction, create chaos, desolate, despoil, destroy, devastate, lay waste, play mischief with, ravage, ruin, wreck

wrest pin tuning pin

wrist pin gudgeon pin

write off charge off, depreciate, reduce

writer's cramp carpal tunnel syndrome, graphospasm, hand spasm, writer's palsy, writer's spasm

writing desk desk, escritoire, rolltop desk, secrétaire, secretary

writing on the wall fair warning, fate, foretaste, hunch, omen, ominous indication, portent, sign of the times

writing paper notepaper, recycled paper, stationery, wove paper

writing utensil pen, pencil

writ of summons subpoena, summons, warrant

wrought iron decorative iron

Xx Yy Zz

Xerox™ copier, copy machine, duplicator, photocopier, Photostat™ machine

X-rated dirty, hard-core, obscene, pornographic, raunchy, sexual

yard goods dry goods, linens, piece goods, soft goods, textiles, white goods

yard sale flea market, garage sale, moving sale, rummage sale, tag sale, white elephant sale

yellow apple Golden Delicious, Golden Harvest, Yellow Transparent

yellow-dog contract labor contract, sweetheart contract, union contract

yellow fever jaundice, yellow jack

yellow jacket social wasp

yellow journalism exploitative journalism, sensationalism, sensational journalism, shock reporting, tabloid journalism, yellow press

yellow pages business directory, phone book, telephone directory

yellow spot macula lutea

yellow streak chicken liver, cold feet, faint heart, gutlessness, weak knees, white feather

yes-man apple-polisher, assenter, bootlicker, brown-nose, flatterer, flunky, groveler, lackey, pawn, stooge, sycophant, toady, underling

yin and yang male and female

Yom Kippur Day of Atonement, Ninth of Ab, Ninth of Av, Tishah-b'Ab

young adult adolescent, junior, juvenile, minor, pubescent, teenager, teenybopper, young person, youngster

young turk bright young man, comer, progressive youngster

youth hostel youth hotel

Yule log backlog, Christmas log, log

yuppie flu chronic fatigue syndrome

zebra crossing crossing, crosswalk, crossway, pedestrian crosswalk, zebra

zero hour A-day, appointed hour, climax, crisis point, crossroads, crunch time,

D day, deadline, H hour, moment of truth, pivotal moment, start time, target day, turning point

zero population growth dying race, falling birthrate, population decrease, ZPG

ZIP code postal code, postcode, zip, zip plus four

zip fastener Velcro™, zipper

zip gun homemade pistol, repeater

zodiacal light counterglow, gegenschein, glow, heavens, streamers

zoological garden marine park, menagerie, sea zoo, Tiergarten, zoo, zoological park

zoom lens telephoto lens, wide-angle lens

zoot suit flamboyant suit, leisure suit

ADDENDUM

PHRASE MAKER

Here is a list of words that can be used with certain synonyms interchangeably. For example, in the first entry, both "reckless" and "wild" can be paired with "abandon": reckless abandon and wild abandon. The semicolon in an entry indicates that there is more than one meaning. For example: 1) exceptional ability, great ability, remarkable ability; 2) genuine ability, innate ability, natural ability.

Aa

abandon : reckless, wild

ability : exceptional, great, outstanding, remarkable; genuine, innate, natural

abortion : criminal, illegal

abstinence : complete, total

abuse : shower of, stream of, torrent of; alcohol, drug, substance

accent : heavy, noticeable, pronounced, strong, thick

acceptance : general, universal, widespread

access : easy, free, unlimited, unrestricted

accident : automobile, car, road, traffic; railroad, railway, train

account : newspaper, press

accountant : certified public, chartered

ace : air, flying

achievement : brilliant, crowning, dazzling, epic, glorious, great, lasting, magnificent, major, memorable, monumental, notable, outstanding, phenomenal, remarkable, signal, staggering, superb, wonderful

acid : corrosive, strong

acknowledgment : frank, open

acquaintance : slight, superficial; casual, nodding, passing, slight

acquiescence : complete, total

act : foolish, impulsive, irresponsible, rash; friendly, humane, kind, thoughtful; variety, vaudeville

action : concerted, united; decisive, firm; direct, immediate, prompt, swift

activity : business, economic; leisure, recreational

ad : classified, small

addiction : chronic, hopeless

address : eloquent, moving, stirring

adherence : close, strict

adjuster : claims, insurance

adventure : breathtaking, exciting, real, thrilling

adventurer : bold, dauntless, intrepid
adversary : formidable, powerful
affair : clandestine, secret; extramarital, illicit; passionate, tempestuous, torrid; sinister, sordid, ugly
affairs : domestic, home
affection : deep, great, strong, warm
affiliation : party, political
age : early, tender, young; atomic, nuclear
agent : secret, undercover
aggression : brazen, flagrant, naked, outright, stark, unprovoked; deep-rooted, deep-seated, hidden
agreement : armistice, cease-fire, peace; arms control, nonproliferation; complete, full, solid, total, unanimous
aid : economic, financial
alcohol : ethyl, grain; methyl, wood; pure, unadulterated
alibi : airtight, cast-iron, foolproof, unassailable
allegation : unproved, unsubstantiated, unsupported
allegiance : true, unfailing, unswerving
alteration : minor, slight
ambition : boundless, unbridled; burning, consuming, devouring
amount : negligible, paltry, small
analysis : careful, painstaking, thorough
anger : blind, burning, deep, profound, seething, unbridled; mounting, rising
animal : carnivorous, flesh-eating, meat-eating; herbivorous, plant-eating
animosity : bitter, burning, deep, seething
answer : clear, definite, straight, straightforward; blunt, brusque, curt; affirmative, positive; incorrect, wrong
antagonism : bitter, deep, deep-rooted, deep-seated, profound, strong
anxiety : deep, grave, great, high; gnawing, unrelieved
appeal : eloquent, irresistible, moving, ringing, stirring
appetite : good, healthy, hearty; huge, ravenous, voracious
approach : creative, innovative; fresh, new, novel
approval : limited, qualified
aptitude : inborn, innate, natural
architecture : contemporary, modern
area : metropolitan, urban; assembly, staging
argument : animated, lively; tenuous, weak

aroma : delicate, delightful, fragrant, pleasant, pleasing

assault : indecent, sexual

assistance : considerable, great, invaluable; economic, financial

assumption : erroneous, false, mistaken

atmosphere : congenial, convivial; informal, relaxed; stifling, stultifying

atrocity : dreadful, grisly, gruesome, heinous, horrible, horrid, monstrous, revolting, vile

attack : all-out, concerted, full-scale; sneak, surprise

attempt : all-out, concerted, last-ditch; brave, valiant; feeble, halfhearted, weak; abortive, fruitless, futile, vain; ill-fated, unsuccessful

attendance : low, poor

attitude : condescending, patronizing; bad, belligerent, defiant, surly; inflexible, rigid, uncompromising

attraction : physical, sexual

audience : appreciative, attentive, enthusiastic, receptive, responsive; cold, passive, unresponsive; large, wide

audit : annual, yearly

author : established, famous, noted, recognized, well-known

authorities : civil, civilian

authority : absolute, complete, full, supreme, unquestioned; appropriate, competent, reliable

aversion : deep, deep-rooted, distinct, marked

awakening : rude, sudden

awareness : growing, heightened

Bb

back : far, way

background : rich, well-rounded; deprived, disadvantaged; academic, educational

bank : national, people's, state

banquet : elaborate, lavish, sumptuous

banter : good-natured, light

barbarism : outright, unmitigated, utter

bargain : good, real

barrier : sonic, sound

base : advanced, forward

basis : firm, solid, sound

basket : laundry, linen

bath : steam, Turkish

battle : fierce, pitched, raging

beard : bushy, heavy, rough, thick; light, sparse

bearing : proud, regal, royal

beating : bad, brutal, good, merciless, savage, severe, vicious

beauty : dazzling, raving, striking, wholesome
bedfellow : odd, strange, unlikely
beginner : absolute, complete, rank
beginning : auspicious, promising; fresh, new
belief : ardent, firm, sincere, strong, unshakable; erroneous, false, mistaken
believer : ardent, firm, great, sincere, staunch, strong
belt : lap, safety, seat, shoulder
beneficiary : chief, main, principal
best : next, second
bet : good, safe, sure
bias : deep-rooted, strong
bicycle : exercise, stationary
bigot : fanatical, narrow-minded, vicious
bigotry : fanatical, ingrained, narrow-minded, vicious
bill : hospital, medical
binoculars : high-powered, powerful
bleeding : heavy, profuse, uncontrollable
bliss : complete, pure, sheer, total, utter
blood pressure : elevated, high
blow : crippling, crushing, decisive, hard, heavy, knockout, powerful, resounding, severe, staggering, telling, terrible; bitter, cruel, devastating; fatal, mortal; glancing, light
blunder : awful, colossal, costly, egregious, fatal, glaring, grave, monumental, serious, stupid, terrible
boast : empty, idle, vain
body : celestial, heavenly
bomb : atom, atomic, fission, nuclear
bombing : pinpoint, precision
bond : close, firm, strong
bonfire : blazing, roaring
boom : business, economic
booth : phone, telephone; polling, voting
bore : crashing, frightful, insufferable, utter
boredom : complete, sheer, utter
boss : absolute, undisputed
bottle : disposable, no-deposit, no-return; returnable, reusable
bottom : double, false
box : safe-deposit, safety-deposit; music, musical
boycott : economic, trade
bracket : angle, broken
brawl : barroom, drunken
breach : egregious, flagrant
breakdown : emotional, mental, nervous
breakthrough : dramatic, major, significant

breath : out of, short of
breathing : heavy, labored, noisy; regular, steady
breeder : cattle, livestock
breeding : cattle, livestock
breeze : balmy, fresh, gentle, light, soft
brogue : heavy, incomprehensible, thick
brother : big, elder, older; little, younger
brutality : demonstrate, display, exhibit
buddy : bosom, good, great
budget : family, household
buff : film, movie
building : dilapidated, gutted, ramshackle, tumbledown
buildup : arms, military
bun : cinnamon, sticky
burden : crushing, heavy, onerous
bureaucracy : bloated, overgrown, swollen
burn : mild, minor, superficial
butter : sweet, unsalted

Cc

cable : electric, power
cake : piece of, slice of
calamity : crushing, dire, grave, great
calendar : crowded, full
calm : dead, perfect
camel : Arabian, one-humped; Bactrian, two-humped
camera : motion-picture, movie; television, TV
camp : prisoner-of-war, POW, PW; displaced-persons, DP
campaign : active, aggressive, all-out, hard-fought, relentless, vigorous; feeble, weak; publicity, public relations; election, political; national, nationwide
campus : college, university
can : ash, garbage, trash
canard : absurd, preposterous
capacity : intellectual, mental; full, peak
capital : circulating, working; fixed, permanent
car : patrol, police, prowl, squad; secondhand, used
card : business, calling, visiting
cards : deck of, pack of
care : great, meticulous, painstaking, scrupulous, utmost; antenatal, antepartal, prenatal; postnatal, postpartum
career : brilliant, distinguished
caricature : bold, striking
carrier : letter, mail; common, public
case : airtight, ironclad, open-and-shut, watertight; clear, convincing, prima facie; benchmark, landmark; extreme, flagrant

cash : cold, hard
cast : all-star, star-studded
casualties : heavy, serious
catalog : college, school, university
category : main, major
cause : good, just, noble, righteous, worthwhile, worthy; deep-rooted, root, underlying; leading, major
celebrity : film, Hollywood, movie
cell : jail, prison
censure : bitter, strong
center : birthing, childbearing; business, commercial
cereal : cooked, hot
ceremony : marriage, wedding
certainty : absolute, dead
certitude : absolute, complete, utter
chagrin : deep, profound
challenge : formidable, real, serious
challenger : formidable, strong
chance : even, fifty-fifty; faint, fat, outside, poor, slight, slim, small
change : abrupt, quick, sudden; complete, dramatic, drastic, great, major, marked, momentous, profound, radical, significant, striking, sweeping; discernible, visible; long-overdue, needed, welcome; little, minor, slight
changeover : complete, radical, thorough, total
channels : regular, usual
chaos : complete, total, utter
chap : decent, fine, good, nice
chapel : interdenominational, nondenominational
chaplain : college, university
chapter : introductory, opening
character : excellent, fine, good; impeccable, irreproachable, stainless, unblemished; firm, strong; bad, disreputable, unsavory; leading, main, major, principal; minor, supporting; curious, strange, weird; seedy, shady
characteristic : distinctive, marked; distinguishing, identifying; dominant, outstanding
charge : baseless, fabricated, false, trumped-up
charm : good-luck, lucky; great, irresistible; particular, special
chasm : gaping, yawning
chat : friendly, nice, pleasant
chatter : constant, endless, idle, incessant
check : safety, security
cheek : burning, flushed; chubby, full, rounded; hollow, sunken
cheekbones : high, prominent
cheeks : red, rosy, ruddy

cheer : loud, resounding, ringing, rousing
child : pampered, spoiled; good, well-behaved; bright, gifted, intelligent; abused, mistreated
choice : good, happy, intelligent, judicious, wise; bad, poor, sorry, unwise, wrong
chord : responsive, sensitive, sympathetic
chores : domestic, household
circle : business, financial; exclusive, select; close, closed, inner, intimate, narrow
circulation : enormous, large, wide; general, unrestricted; national, nationwide; limited, restricted, small; good, healthy, normal
circumstances : adverse, difficult, trying; reduced, straitened; extenuating, mitigating; exceptional, special
citizen : eminent, leading, prominent; respectable, solid, upright, upstanding
claim : excessive, extravagant, unreasonable; unsubstantiated, unsupported; competing, conflicting, rival
clarification : additional, further
clause : dependent, subordinate; independent, main
clientele : exclusive, fashionable, select
cliff : sheer, steep
climate : friendly, hospitable; hostile, inhospitable; arctic, cold, frigid; mild, moderate, temperate
climb : arduous, difficult; rough, rugged
clinic : antenatal, prenatal
clipping : newspaper, press
clothes : elegant, fashionable; secondhand, used
clothing : custom-made, tailor-made; secondhand, used
cloud : rain, storm
clue : important, key, vital
coal : anthracite, hard; bituminous, soft
coalition : broad-based, broadly based, umbrella
coast : forbidding, inhospitable
coastline : broken, irregular, jagged
code : criminal, penal; ethical, moral
coincidence : mere, pure, sheer; odd, strange
cold : biting, bitter, extreme, intense, severe; bad, severe
collapse : emotional, mental, nervous; complete, total, utter
color : bright, brilliant; garish, gaudy, loud
column : social, society

combat : close, hand-to-hand; deadly, fierce, mortal

combination : fixed, recurrent

comfort : cold, little

command : high, supreme

comment : appropriate, fitting; perceptive, shrewd; caustic, critical, derogatory, sarcastic, scathing, unfavorable; nasty, vicious

commentary : play-by-play, running

commitment : all-out, total; deep, passionate

community : academic, college, university

company : bad, fast; engine, hose, ladder

compassion : deep, great, profound, strong

compensation : adequate, appropriate

competition : bitter, close, fierce, formidable, heavy, intense, keen, stiff, strong, tough; cutthroat, unfair, unscrupulous; free, unfettered

competitor : formidable, keen, strong

complaint : bitter, loud, vociferous; formal, official

compliment : backhanded, dubious, left-handed; nice, pretty

component : basic, essential, key, main, principal

compromise : acceptable, reasonable

conceit : insufferable, overwhelming

concern : deep, grave, serious; considerable, utmost

conclusion : reasonable, tenable, valid; inescapable, inevitable; erroneous, false, invalid, wrong

concurrence : complete, full, unanimous

condemnation : bitter, harsh, scathing, strong; sweeping, universal; unfair, unjust

condition : bad, poor, terrible; excellent, good, mint, peak, perfect, tip-top; operating, running; fair, satisfactory; bad, critical, poor

conditions : deplorable, pitiful, squalid

condolences : heartfelt, sincere

conduct : inappropriate, unbecoming

confederation : loose, weak

conference : news, press

confidence : absolute, every, perfect, supreme; buoyant, unbounded

conflict : armed, military

confrontation : armed, military

confusion : complete, general, mass, total, utter

congestion : lung, pulmonary

congratulations : deepest, heartiest, hearty, sincere, warm, warmest

connection : loose, tenuous

consequences : dire, disastrous; far-reaching, fateful

conservative : die-hard, dyed-in-the-wool

consonant : double, geminate

constitution : feeble, frail; iron, rugged, strong

construction : solid, sturdy

contact : close, intimate

contempt : bitter, deep, profound, total, unmitigated, utter

contender : formidable, leading, main, serious, strong

contest : bitter, hard-fought

contract : legal, valid; oral, verbal

contradiction : flat, outright

contrast : harsh, sharp, stark, startling; marked, striking, vivid

contribution : big, generous, large; small, token; brilliant, great, notable, outstanding, remarkable; invaluable, key; major, significant, substantial

control : lax, loose

controller : air traffic, flight

controversy : bitter, fierce, furious, heated, lively

conversation : animated, lively; boring, dull

conviction : burning, deep, firm, strong, unshakable

cook : chief, head

correspondence : business, commercial

costume : folk, national, traditional

cotton : 100 percent, pure

cough : bad, heavy, nasty; hacking, persistent

count : accurate, correct; final, last

countenance : forbidding, stern; radiant, shining

courage : dauntless, great, immense, indomitable, sheer

course : demanding, difficult, rigorous; easy, gut; beginning, elementary, introductory

court : domestic relations, family

coverage : comprehensive, full; complete, extensive, full, wide

coward : abject, dirty

cowardice : abject, rank

crack : dirty, nasty

crash : loud, resounding

craving : powerful, strong

credentials : excellent, impeccable, sound

crime : atrocious, brutal, heinous, horrendous, horrible, infamous, outrageous, unspeakable, vicious, violent; minor, petty

criminal : habitual, hardened, inveterate, vicious; infamous, notorious
crisis : acute, grave, serious; economic, financial, fiscal
criterion : reliable, valid
critic : harsh, severe, unkind; impartial, unbiased; drama, theater
criticism : nitpicking, petty; adverse, biting, damaging, devastating, harsh, hostile, scathing, severe, sharp, strong, sweeping, unsparing, withering
crop : bountiful, bumper, fine, record
crowd : angry, hostile, unfriendly; cheering, friendly; enormous, huge, tremendous
cruelty : consummate, deliberate, wanton
cruise : round-the-world, world; extended, long
cry : battle, war
cure : certain, known, sure
currency : convertible, hard; nonconvertible, soft, weak; stable, strong
current : powerful, strong
curriculum : basic, core
curtain : stage, theater
curve : hairpin, horseshoe; bell, bell-shaped, normal distribution
custom : ancient, old; time-honored, traditional
customer : regular, steady
cut : personnel, staff

Dd

damage : grave, great, extensive, heavy, incalculable, irreparable, serious, severe; lasting, permanent; light, slight
damages : exemplary, punitive
dance : circle, round
dancing : ballroom, social; circle, round
danger : acute, deadly, extreme, grave, mortal; immediate, imminent, impending
darkness : complete, pitch, total
dash : frantic, mad
day : bright, sunny; chilly, cool; clear, fine, nice; dreary, gloomy; hot, stifling; eventful, field, memorable, red-letter
deal : fair, square; raw, rotten, rough; good, great
death : certain, sure; instant, instantaneous; sudden, unexpected
debate : acrimonious, bitter, heated, sharp, stormy; lively, spirited
debt : outstanding, unsettled

decay : dental, tooth; inner-city, urban

deception : by, through

decision : big, momentous; good, sensible, wise; collective, joint; irreversible, irrevocable; agonizing, difficult; hasty, rash, snap; bad, poor, unwise; unfair, unjust

deck : aft

dedication : complete, great, total

deed : brave, daring, heroic; good, kind; great, illustrious, noble, praiseworthy; evil, foul, wicked

defeat : crushing, decisive, disastrous, humiliating, overwhelming, resounding, total, utter; ignominious, shameful

defect : birth, congenital

defense : airtight, impenetrable; inadequate, weak; strong, vigorous

deficiency : major, serious; minor, slight

degree : college, university; advanced, graduate, postgraduate; great, high, large; greater, higher; lesser, lower; low, slight

delay : interminable, long; unexpected, unforeseen

delicacy : extreme, great

delight : great, intense, sheer

demand : excessive, exorbitant, unrealistic; moderate, modest, reasonable; brisk, enormous, great, heavy, strong; growing, increased, increasing

demeanor : cheerful, friendly

demonstration : disorderly, violent; nonviolent, orderly, peaceful

denial : categorical, emphatic; strenuous, strong, vehement

denture : complete, full

denunciation : angry, bitter, scathing, strong, vehement

depression : major, severe; deep, total; postnatal, postpartum

descendant : direct, lineal

description : accurate, correct, exact; clear, graphic; matter-of-fact, objective; lively, picturcsquc, vivid; detailed, full, lengthy, thorough; brief, short

desire : ardent, blind, burning, deep, earnest, fervent, insatiable, intense, keen, overwhelming, passionate, strong

desolation : complete, utter

despair : bitter, deep, sheer, total, utter

destruction : complete, mass, total, utter

detail : essential, important; mere, minor; gory, graphic, grisly, gruesome, harrowing, lurid, revolting, sordid, unsavory; meticulous, microscopic, minute

determination : dogged, fierce, firm, great, grim, iron, sheer, unflinching, unyielding

deterrent : effective, powerful

devastation : complete, total, utter, widespread

development : dramatic, exciting; new, recent

deviation : marked, sharp

devotion : absolute, blind, complete, deep, great, selfless, slavish, thorough, undying, unflagging, unstinting, unswerving, utter

dialect : local, regional

dialogue : constructive, fruitful, meaningful

diamond : flawless, perfect

dictionary : abridged, desk; college, collegiate; combinatorial, combinatory; general-use, general-purpose; orthographic, spelling

diet : balanced, healthy, well-balanced; vegan, vegetarian

difference : considerable, great, huge, marked, striking, vast; essential, fundamental; noticeable, perceptible; insignificant, little, minor, slight

difficulty : grave, great, insurmountable, serious, severe; economic, financial

dilemma : ethical, moral

dinner : at, during

diplomat : career, professional

directions : explicit, precise, specific

disability : serious, severe

disagreement : bitter, marked, serious, sharp

disappointment : bitter, cruel, deep, great, keen, profound

disarmament : general, universal

disarray : complete, sheer, total, utter

disaster : major, terrible, tragic, unmitigated, unqualified

disbelief : complete, total, utter

disciple : ardent, devoted

discipline : firm, harsh, iron, rigid, severe, stern, strict; lax, loose, slack

discord : domestic, family, marital

discovery : exciting, startling, world-shaking

discrepancy : glaring, striking, wide

discretion : complete, full, wide

discussion : animated, brisk, heated, lively, spirited; candid, frank, open, lengthy, long; quiet, peaceful

disease : debilitating, wasting; incurable, untreatable; communicable, contagious, infectious; sexually transmitted, social, venereal; industrial, occupational; foot-and-mouth, hoof-and-mouth

disgust : complete, deep, great, utter

dislike : active, cordial, deep, hearty, strong, violent

dismissal : abrupt, curt

disparity : considerable, great, wide

display : dazzling, imposing, impressive; lavish, ostentatious, spectacular

disposition : buoyant, cheerful, genial, happy, lively, pleasant, sunny; sour, unpleasant

dispute : acrimonious, bitter, heated, sharp; industrial, labor

disregard : blatant, callous, complete, flagrant, total

disrespect : deep, profound

disruption : complete, total

dissatisfaction : deep, keen, profound

distance : good, great, long, vast; braking, stopping

distinction : doubtful, dubious

distortion : crude, gross, grotesque

distress : deep, great, profound; economic, financial; emotional, mental, psychological

distribution : equitable, fair; inequitable, unfair

divergence : marked, sharp, wide

dividend : share, stock; handsome, large

dock : dry, floating

documentation : adequate, appropriate, proper; inadequate, insufficient, weak

dog : mad, rabid; guide, Seeing Eye™

donation : big, generous, large, sizable

door : front, main

dose : fatal, lethal; heavy, massive, strong; light, small, weak

doubt : deep, serious, strong

draft : final, polished; first, preliminary, rough

dress : casual, informal; evening, formal; native, traditional

drink : cold, cool; potent, stiff, strong

drinker : hard, heavy; light, moderate

drinking : hard, heavy

driver : drunk, drunken; careful, cautious, defensive, safe

driving : careful, defensive, safe; careless, reckless

drop : abrupt, sudden

drug : dangerous, toxic; potent, powerful, strong; nonprescription, over-the-counter; miracle, wonder

drugs : illegal, illicit

dues : annual, yearly

dust : fine, powdery

duty : ethical, moral; painful, unpleasant

Ee

earnings : annual, yearly; net, take-home

earphones : pair of, set of

earthquake : devastating, destructive; strong, severe

eater : big, heavy; fussy, picky

eclipse : full, total

ecology : human, social

economy : capitalist, free-market; ailing, shaky, weak; sound, stable, strong

ecstasy : pure, sheer

edge : jagged, ragged

education : elementary, primary; college, university; adult, continuing, further; broad, general

effect : beneficial, good, salutary; net overall; limited, marginal; adverse, bad, deleterious, harmful; crippling, damaging, deadening, disastrous

efficiency : maximum, peak

effort : all-out, bold, concerted, conscious, furious, gallant, great, Herculean, heroic, massive, maximum, painstaking, sincere, strenuous, studious, superhuman, valiant; collaborative, joint, united; useless, vain; ceaseless, unceasing; unsparing, untiring

egg : addled, bad, rotten

ego : enormous, inflated, overbearing

election : close, hotly contested

element : basic, essential, key, vital; extremist, radical; rowdy, unruly

embankment : high, steep; railroad, railway

embrace : loving, tender, warm

emergency : grave, serious

emotion : deep, sincere; conflicting, mixed

encounter : brief, fleeting

enemy : avowed, bitter, deadly, implacable, insidious, irreconcilable, mortal, relentless, sworn, vicious; formidable, powerful; common, mutual

enforcement : rigid, strict, stringent

engagement : previous, prior

enjoyment : full, great

enrollment : heavy, large; light, small

enthusiasm : boundless, contagious, great, infectious, unbounded, unbridled, unflagging, wild

entrance : dramatic, grand, triumphal

environment : clean, healthy; polluted, unhealthy; friendly, pleasant; hostile, unfriendly

episode : funny, humorous

epithet : harsh, offensive, vicious, vile

equinox : autumn, autumnal; spring, vernal

erosion : gradual, slow

error : cardinal, costly, egregious, flagrant, glaring, grievous, gross, major, serious; minor, slight; printer's, typographical

escape : daring, dramatic; hairbreadth, narrow

estimate : approximate, rough

evaluation : fair, objective

event : earthshaking, earthshattering

evidence : ample, strong, substantial; clear, cogent, compelling, convincing; concrete, hard; incontestable, indisputable, irrefutable, undeniable, unquestionable; reliable, trustworthy

examination : difficult, stiff; careful, close, complete, in-depth, thorough; cursory, perfunctory, superficial

example : glaring, striking; prime, shining

exchange : angry, heated

excitement : considerable, great, intense

excuse : acceptable, good, satisfactory, valid; feeble, flimsy, lame, poor, unacceptable, unsatisfactory, weak

exercise : hard, strenuous, vigorous

exercises : commencement, graduation

existence : drab, miserable; hand-to-mouth, precarious

expanse : broad, vast, wide

expectations : great, high

experience : broad, extensive, wide; direct, firsthand; educational, learning; bitter, painful, terrible, traumatic, unpleasant; frightening, hair-raising, harrowing, terrifying, unnerving; enlightening, ennobling, rewarding; memorable, unforgettable

expert : acknowledged, recognized

explanation : brief, concise, simple, succinct; clear, lucid

explosion : deafening, loud

export : chief, leading, major

exposition : international, world

expression : hackneyed, trite; silly, vacuous; puzzled, quizzical; grave, serious

exterior : forbidding, stern

extermination : complete, total

eye : bright, clear; good, strong; sharp, watchful, weather; curious, prying; good, keen; artificial, glass

eyebrow : bushy, thick

eyesight : failing, poor, weak

Ff

fabrication : complete, outright, total

face : beautiful, lovely, pretty; poker, straight

facilities : dining, eating

fact : accepted, demonstrable, established; cold, dry, hard, incontestable, incontrovertible, indisputable, irrefutable, proven, undeniable, unquestionable; basic, essential, pertinent

factor : critical, crucial, deciding, determining, essential, important, key, major

fad : latest, newest

failure : abject, complete, dismal, hopeless, ignominious, miserable, outright

faith : abiding, enduring, steadfast; deep, strong, unshakable

fall : bad, nasty; sharp, steep

falsehood : absolute, downright, utter

family : close, immediate

fan : ardent, avid

fashion : contemporary, current

fatalities : highway, motorway, traffic

fate : bitter, cruel; blind, inexorable; quirk of, stroke of, twist of

fatigue : battle, combat

favorite : heavy, strong

fear : grave, mortal, strong

feast : royal, sumptuous

feat : brave, heroic; brilliant, notable, noteworthy, outstanding, remarkable; no mean, small

feature : characteristic, distinctive, distinguishing; noteworthy, salient

fee : fat, large; admission, entrance

feeling : deep, strong; eerie, strange; friendly, tender, warm; gloomy, sad; delicate, sensitive

fellow : fine, good; nice, regular

fellowship : graduate, postgraduate; close, strong, warm

feminist : ardent, dedicated

feud : bitter, deadly, internecine

fiasco : complete, total, utter

fiber : artificial, synthetic
field : flying, landing
fight : bitter, desperate, fierce, hard, stubborn; clean, fair; dirty, unfair; championship, title
fighting : bitter, fierce, hard, heavy
figure : conspicuous, dashing, fine, handsome, imposing, striking, trim; ridiculous, sorry; familiar, key, leading; prominent, well-known; approximate, ballpark, round
filling : broken, cracked
film : adult, blue, erotic, porno, pornographic, X-rated
fine : big, heavy, hefty, stiff
finger : index
fit : snug, tight
flight : bumpy, rough; full, headlong
flop : complete, total
fog : dense, heavy, thick
follower : devoted, faithful
following : devoted, faithful, loyal
food : appetizing, delicious, tasty; nourishing, nutritious, wholesome
footing : firm, secure, solid, sure
force : enemy, hostile; armed, military; labor
forest : dense, thick
form : abridged, condensed; convenient, handy; excellent, good, superb
fortress : impenetrable, impregnable
fortune : enormous, large, vast
forum : open, public
foundation : firm, solid, sound, strong
fountain : drinking, water
fox : arctic, white
fraction : complex, compound; simple, vulgar
freeze : deep, hard
frequency : great, high
friend : bosom, close, good, intimate, old; faithful, fast, loyal, staunch, strong, true
friendship : close, firm, intimate, lasting, strong, warm
front : bold, brave, brazen
frost : bitter, hard, heavy, severe; light, slight
fruit : candied, glazed
fun : clean, good, harmless
fund : contingency, emergency
furniture : garden, lawn, outdoor, patio; secondhand, used
fury : savage, unbridled
future : bright, promising, rosy

Gg

gain : considerable, enormous, notable, substantial, tremendous; economic, financial

gale : heavy, raging, severe, strong
gambler : compulsive, inveterate
gap : unbridgeable, wide, yawning
garb : formal, official
gas : poison, toxic
gash : deep, nasty
gasoline : lead-free, unleaded
gauge : broad, wide
gaze : intense, rapt, steady, unblinking; penetrating, piercing
generality : broad, sweeping
generalization : broad, sweeping
generation : coming, future, next
generosity : great, lavish, magnanimous, unstinting
gentleman : complete, perfect, real, true
geography : dialect, linguistic
gesture : empty, meaningless; haughty, imperious; humane, kind; glorious, grand, grandiose, magnificent, noble
ghetto : inner-city, urban
gift : extravagant, lavish
gimmick : advertising, promotional
glance : casual, cursory, fleeting, passing; meaningful, significant; penetrating, probing, searching; stolen, surreptitious; disapproving, indignant
glass : clear, translucent; pane, sheet; piece of, sliver of, splinter of
glimmer : faint, pale, slight, weak
glimpse : brief, fleeting
gloom : all-pervading, deep, unrelieved
glory : eternal, everlasting
goal : long-range, long-term; short-range, short-term
gossip : malicious, vicious
government : authoritarian, autocratic
grade : excellent, high
graduate : college, university
grass : high, tall
gratification : deep, profound
gratitude : deep, profound, sincere, undying; eternal, everlasting
grave : common, mass
greeting : cordial, friendly, sincere, warm
greetings : cordial, friendly, sincere, warm, warmest
grief : bitter, deep, inconsolable, overwhelming, profound
grievance : justified, legitimate, valid
grin : contagious, infectious; foolish, silly
grip : firm, iron, strong, tight, viselike; loose, weak

ground : firm, hard, solid; hallowed, holy

group : ethnic, minority

growth : benign, noncancerous, nonmalignant; cancerous, malignant

grumbler : chronic, constant

grumbling : chronic, constant

guess : educated, informed, shrewd; random, wild

gulf : wide, yawning

gunfire : heavy, murderous

guy : great, nice, regular

Hh

habit : entrenched, fixed, ingrained

hair : braided, plaited; bobbed, short; unmanageable, unruly

hall : city, town

halt : grinding, screeching

hand : good, strong

handling : careless, inept

handshake : cordial, friendly, warm

handwriting : clear, legible

hardship : severe, unrelieved

harm : considerable, grave, great, immeasurable, irreparable, severe

harvest : abundant, bountiful, bumper, rich

hat : cowboy, Stetson™, ten-gallon

hatred : abiding, bitter, blind, deep, deep-rooted, implacable, intense, profound, violent, virulent

head : cool, level

headache : bad, racking, severe, splitting

health : bad, broken, delicate, deteriorating, failing, feeble, fragile, frail, ill, poor; community, public

hearing : acute, keen; defective, impaired; fair, impartial

heart : bad, weak; good, healthy, strong; cold, cruel, hard; good, kind, soft, tender, warm

heat : blistering, extreme, great, intense, oppressive, scorching, stifling, sweltering, unbearable

heels : high, stiletto

height : dizzy, precipitous, vertiginous

hell : sheer, unmitigated, unspeakable

helmet : crash, safety

help : great, invaluable, tremendous

hemorrhage : brain, cerebral

heritage : priceless, proud, rich

hero : military, war

hesitation : momentary, slight

hint : broad, obvious; delicate, gentle, subtle

hold : firm, strong, tight

hole : gaping, yawning

holiday : bank, legal, public

hope : ardent, fervent, fond; realistic, reasonable; dim, faint, slender, slight; false, idle, illusory, vain; unrealistic, unreasonable

horror : indescribable, unspeakable, sheer

hospital : city, municipal; community, nonprofit; private, proprietary

host : congenial, gracious

hostility : bitter, deep, profound

hotel : deluxe, five-star, luxury

hour : business, office, working

house : dilapidated, ramshackle

housing : low-cost, low-income

hovel : miserable, wretched

hug : affectionate, loving

humor : bitter, caustic; deadpan, dry, straight; sly, wry

husband : philandering, unfaithful

Ii

idea : bright, brilliant, clever, good, great, ingenious; fresh, new, novel; approximate, rough; faintest, slightest; old, outmoded, stale, warmed-over; absurd, bad, crackpot, crazy, fantastic, far-fetched, foolish, wild; silly, simplistic, stupid

idiot : blithering, blooming, blundering, confounded, driveling; local, village

ignorance : abysmal, appalling, blatant, complete, crass, profound, total

illness : grave, major, serious; incurable, untreatable

imagination : active, fertile, lively, vivid

impact : considerable, strong

impetus : powerful, strong

implication : derogatory, negative

importance : considerable, great, overriding, paramount, primary, prime, utmost, vital; minor, secondary

impression : deep, indelible, lasting, profound, strong, vivid; excellent, favorable, good; erroneous, false, inaccurate, wrong; bad, unfavorable

improvement : considerable, decided, definite, distinct, great, marked, noticeable, significant, substantial; gradual, slow; minor, slight

incentive : powerful, strong

incident : amusing, funny, humorous; nasty, painful, ugly, unpleasant

income : annual, yearly; good, high, sizable

increase : considerable, dramatic, large, sharp, significant, sizable, substantial

index : consumer-price, cost-of-living

industry : basic, key

infection : minor, slight, superficial; serious, severe

inferno : blazing, raging, roaring

infidelity : conjugal, marital

inflation : galloping, high, rampant, runaway, uncontrolled

influence : bad, baleful, baneful, negative; beneficial, good, positive, salutary; powerful, profound, strong

information : classified, confidential

ingredients : basic, essential

injury : minor, slight; serious, severe

injustice : blatant, gross, rank

inn : roadside, wayside

inquiry : exhaustive, thorough

inquisition : cruel, senseless

insanity : outright, pure, sheer

insight : deep, profound

insistence : dogged, firm, stubborn

inspection : careful, close, thorough; cursory, perfunctory, superficial

instruction : beginning, elementary

instructions : clear, explicit, precise

insult : nasty, vicious

insurance : life, term life, whole life; auto, automobile, car

intellect : keen, sharp, superior

intelligence : great, high, keen; outstanding, remarkable; native, natural

intention : bad, evil

interest : burning, consuming, deep, great, intense, keen, lively, profound, serious, strong; broad, wide; common, mutual; universal, widespread

interval : brief, short

intervention : armed, military

invention : brilliant, ingenious

investigation : cursory, perfunctory; full, painstaking, thorough

investment : good, lucrative, profitable; solid, sound; bad, poor

invitation : cordial, kind; open, standing

island : desert, uninhabited

issue : collateral, side; contentious, controversial, debatable, thorny

Jj

jargon : professional, technical, trade

jealousy : bitter, blind; groundless, unfounded

job : difficult, hard; cushy, easy, soft

joke : old, stale; blue, coarse, crude, dirty, obscene, off-color, smutty

journal : learned, professional, scholarly

joy : boundless, deep, great, indescribable, ineffable, overwhelming, pure, sheer, unbounded

judge : fair, impartial; harsh, severe

judgment : bad, poor; good, sound

juice : digestive, gastric

jungle : asphalt, concrete

Kk

kick : nasty, vicious

killer : multiple, serial

kiss : fervent, passionate; loving, tender

knife : blunt, dull

knowledge : slight, superficial; inside, intimate

Ll

label : adhesive, gummed

labor : manual, physical; difficult, prolonged, protracted

laceration : minor, superficial

landowner : big, large

landscape : beautiful, magnificent, picturesque; bleak, gloomy

language : colloquial, informal; dead, extinct; everyday, plain, simple; bad, coarse, crude, dirty, foul, nasty, obscene, offensive, street, unprintable, vile, vulgar; blunt, explicit; rough, strong, vituperative; computer, machine, programming

lapse : momentary, temporary

larder : full, well-stocked

laugh : hearty, loud

laughter : contagious, infectious; hearty, loud, raucous, uproarious

law : fair, just; business, commercial; family, marriage

leader : born, natural; decisive, firm, strong

league : big, major; bush, minor

leap : giant, great

left : extreme, far, radical; hard, stiff

leg : artificial, wooden

lens : telephoto, telescopic

letter : capital, large, uppercase; lowercase, small

liar : abject, compulsive, congenital, consummate, incorrigible, inveterate, outright, pathological

liberty : individual, personal

library : free, municipal, public

lie : bald-faced, barefaced, blatant, brazen, deliberate, downright, monstrous, outright, transparent, whopping

life : peaceful, quiet, serene; ascetic, austere; difficult, hard, miserable, tough; lonely, solitary; dissipated, dissolute; stormy, turbulent; daily, everyday; country, rural

lifestyle : alternate, alternative

light : bright, strong; dim, dull, faint

lightning : heat, sheet

likeness : striking, uncanny

limitations : budgetary, financial

limp : decided, marked, pronounced

line : solid, unbroken; fine, thin; heavy, thick; complete, full; firm, hard; assembly, production

liquor : hard, strong

listener : good, sympathetic

literature : extensive, voluminous

load : capacity, maximum, peak

logic : false, specious, spurious

look : close, hard; curious, inquiring, searching; eloquent, meaningful; pensive, thoughtful; come-hither, inviting; blank, distant, faraway, vacant; anxious, worried; bemused, puzzled, quizzical; disapproving, stern; dirty, nasty, vicious; furtive, shifty, sinister

loser : bad, poor

loss : irredeemable, irreparable, irreplaceable, irretrievable

lot : hard, sorry, unhappy

love : deep, profound, sincere, true

loyalty : deep-rooted, steadfast, strong, unquestioned, unshakable, unswerving

luck : pure, sheer; bad, hard, tough

lull : momentary, temporary

lunch : business, working

lust : insatiable, unquenchable

luxury : pure, sheer

Mm

machine : adding, calculating; cash, money; access; composing, linotype, typesetting; copy, copying, duplicating, Xerox™

magic : pure, sheer
magnitude : considerable, great
majority : great, large; overwhelming, vast; bare, narrow, slender, slim, small
malarkey : pure, sheer
malevolence : pure, sheer
man : betting, gambling; con, confidence
management : senior, top
maneuver : brilliant, clever
manner : cheerful, lively; gentle, mild; courteous, polite; elegant, grand, polished, suave; casual, hit-or-miss, offhand, relaxed; stern, unsmiling; slipshod, sloppy; ingratiating, servile, unctuous; abrupt, brusque; arrogant, cavalier, imperious, overbearing; coarse, crude, rude, uncouth; sullen, surly
march : lively, rousing, stirring
mare : brood, stock
margin : comfortable, decisive, handsome, large, wide
marina : municipal, public
mark : accent, stress
market : free, open
marksman/markswoman : crack, expert, skilled
marriage : good, happy, stable; bad, unhappy
matter : complex, complicated; important, pressing, serious, weighty; petty, trifling, trivial; no easy, no laughing
mattress : double, full; single, twin
meal : big, heavy; decent, hearty, solid, square; light, small
measures : stopgap, temporary; precautionary, preventive, prophylactic; safety, security; drastic, harsh, stern, stringent, tough; extreme, radical
mechanic : auto, automobile, car
medication : potent, strong
medicine : aerospace, space; community, social; industrial, occupational
meditation : deep, profound
meeting : clandestine, secret
membership : agency, institutional
memorandum : confidential, secret
memory : bad, poor; dim, vague; happy, pleasant; haunting, poignant; painful, sad, unpleasant
merchandise : first-class, high-quality; defective, inferior, shoddy
mess : complete, terrible, unsightly, utter
message : cryptic, secret
method : antiquated, obsolete; infallible, sure; modern, up-to-date; orthodox, traditional; refined, sophisticated

microphone : concealed, hidden

might : armed, military

mile : land, statute; nautical, sea

military service : compulsory, universal

milk : curdled, sour

mind : analytical, brilliant, disciplined, keen, logical, nimble, quick, sharp; clear, sound, uncluttered; inquiring, inquisitive, open, scientific; closed, narrow, one-track; deranged, dirty, sick, twisted, unbalanced, unsound, warped

mining : open-pit, strip

miscalculation : bad, glaring, serious

misconception : general, popular

misery : abject, acute, deep; sheer, untold

missile : air-to-ground, air-to-surface; antiaircraft, ground-to-air, surface-to-air; ground-to-ground, surface-to-surface; intermediate-range, medium-range; short-range, tactical

mist : dense, heavy, thick; fine, thin

mistake : bad, big, costly, dreadful, ghastly, glaring, serious, terrible, tragic

mistrust : deep, profound

mixer : cement, concrete

moan : barely audible, feeble, weak

mob : undisciplined, unruly, wild

mobilization : full, general

moment : appropriate, suitable; auspicious, opportune; critical, crucial; embarrassing, inappropriate, inopportune

money : pin, pocket, spending

monopoly : government, state

monument : historic, historical

mood : festive, holiday; genial, good, happy, jovial, joyful; solemn, somber; bad, foul

morals : lax, loose

morsel : choice, juicy, tasty

mother : biological, birth, natural

motive : base, dishonorable, sinister

mountain : snowcapped, snow-clad, snow-covered

move : brilliant, clever, shrewd, smart, wise; stupid, wrong

movement : feminist, women's; deft, dexterous

murder : brutal, cold-blooded, grisly, heinous, savage, vicious, wanton; multiple, serial

murderer : cold-blooded, vicious

music : canned, piped; incidental; soft, sweet; country, hillbilly

Nn

name : bad, dirty; brand, proprietary, trade; common, vernacular

nasal passages : blocked, congested
nation : belligerent, warring
necessity : absolute, dire
neckline : low, plunging
need : acute, compulsive, crying, desperate, dire, pressing, urgent; basic, fundamental; emotional, psychological
neglect : complete, gross, total; child, parental
negotiations : high-level, top-level; marathon, round-the-clock; fruitless, unsuccessful
neighborhood : good, nice, pleasant; bad, rough, tough
nerves : frayed, frazzled, jangled
news : good, welcome, wonderful; earthshaking, earth-shattering, sensational, shocking, startling, world-shaking; bad, devastating, grim
night : dark, murky; restless, sleepless; first, opening
nightmare : horrible, terrible
nipples : sore, tender
nonsense : complete, outright, perfect, pure, sheer, total, utter
nose : aquiline, Roman; pug, snub, turned-up; blocked-up, stuffed-up; running, runny
notes : copious, detailed
notion : abstract; concrete; foggy, hazy, vague; odd, strange
noun : mass, uncountable
nuance : delicate, fine, subtle
nuisance : confounded, damned, dreadful
number : considerable, goodly, large; enormous, great, untold; approximate, round
nurse : community-health, public-health; geriatric, gerontological; industrial-health, occupational-health
nursing : geriatric, gerontological; industrial-health, occupational-health
nutrients : basic, essential

Oo

oath : sacred, solemn
obedience : blind, strict, unquestioning
objection : serious, strenuous, strong, violent, vociferous
objective : major, primary
observance : solemn, strict
observation : astute, keen, penetrating, shrewd
observer : keen, perceptive
obstacle : formidable, great, huge
occasion : festive, gala; happy, joyful, joyous
occurrence : common, daily, everyday, regular, usual; rare, unusual

odds : considerable, formidable, great, heavy, hopeless, insurmountable, long, overwhelming

odor : pungent, strong; faint, slight; bad, fetid, foul, rank, unpleasant

offense : minor, petty, trivial

offer : attractive, generous

official : high, high-ranking, senior, top-ranking

operator : slick, smooth

opinion : candid, frank, honest; prevailing, prevalent; contrary, dissenting

opponent : formidable, strong

opportunity : lost, missed; golden, once-in-a-lifetime

opposite : direct, polar

opposition : bitter, determined, fierce, stiff, strong, unbending, unyielding, vehement; growing, mounting

optimism : cautious, guarded; eternal, incurable, unflagging

optimist : eternal, incurable

oratory : eloquent, persuasive, powerful; inflammatory, rabble-rousing

ordeal : dreadful, terrible, terrifying, trying

order : apple-pie, good, shipshape

ordinance : city, municipal

organ : reproductive, sex, sexual; sense, sensory

organization : charitable, philanthropic; civic, community; nonprofit, not-for-profit

outline : broad, general

outlook : cheerful, optimistic, positive; negative, pessimistic; bleak, dark, dim, dismal, dreary, gloomy; long-range, long-term; short-range, short-term

ovation : thunderous, tremendous

overdose : fatal, lethal

Pp

pace : even, steady; blistering, brisk, fast, rapid; dizzy, frantic, hectic; grueling, killing; slack, slow, sluggish

paddle : Ping-Pong™, table-tennis

pain : acute, agonizing, excruciating, great, intense, severe, sharp, unbearable; burning, searing; chronic, constant, gnawing, intractable, lingering, nagging, persistent, steady; abdominal, stomach

panel : control, instrument; blue-ribbon, expert

panic : sheer, total, utter

paper : exam, examination, test

parent : biological, natural

part : leading, major; important, significant; insignificant, minor, small; component, constituent, integral

participant : reluctant, unwilling

party : garden, lawn; pajama, slumber

passion : all-consuming, burning, deep, smoldering; animal, frenzied, wild

past : colorful, glorious

patience : endless, inexhaustible, infinite

patriot : ardent, fervent, staunch

patriotism : ardent, fervent, staunch, strong

pause : long, prolonged

pay : annual, yearly

peace : durable, lasting, permanent

pedal : accelerator, gas

penalty : heavy, severe, stiff, strict; light, mild

pencil : cosmetic, eyebrow

people : average, common, little, ordinary, plain

performance : breathtaking, brilliant, electrifying, inspired, outstanding, remarkable, spellbinding, superb, wonderful; listless, mediocre, run-of-the-mill

personality : charismatic, charming, dynamic, forceful, magnetic, striking; dual, split

personnel : qualified, skilled

perspiration : excessive, profuse

phase : closing, final, last; critical, crucial; first, initial, new, opening

phoneme : independent, separate

phrase : hackneyed, stock, trite; nominal, noun

physics : high-energy, particle

physique : burly, magnificent, muscular, powerful

picture : motion, moving; gloomy, grim

pie : cottage, shepherd's

pigeon : carrier, homing

pilot : airline, commercial

plain : broad, vast

plan : brilliant, ingenious; complicated, elaborate; grandiose, sweeping; floor, seating; pension, retirement

planning : long-range, long-term; short-range, short-term

plea : ardent, emotional, fervent, impassioned, moving, passionate, tearful

pleasure : genuine, great, real

pledge : campaign, election

ploy : clever, ingenious

poem : epic, heroic

poetry : epic, heroic

point of view : optimistic, positive; negative, pessimistic

poison : deadly, lethal

police : city, municipal

policy : clear, clear-cut; sound, wise; established, firm, set; long-range, long-term; short-range, short-term; financial, fiscal, monetary; government, public

politician : astute, shrewd; crafty, crooked, cunning, scheming, wily

politics : partisan, party

poll : national, nationwide

pollution : noise, sound

popularity : growing, increasing

population : decreasing, shrinking; excess, overflow; expanding, growing, increasing, rising

pores : blocked, clogged, closed

pornography : explicit, hard-core; soft, soft-core

position : awkward, uncomfortable; powerful, strong; untenable, vulnerable, weak; high, leading, prominent

posture : erect, upright

poverty : abject, dire, extreme, grinding, severe

power : curative, healing

practice : common, normal, standard, usual; universal, widespread; law, legal; family, general; sharp, unethical, unfair, unscrupulous

practitioner : family, general

praise : fulsome, unctuous; glowing, high, lavish, strong, unrestrained, unstinting

prank : cruel, mean, wanton

prayer : devout, fervent, solemn

precision : great, utmost; unerring, unfailing

prediction : dire, gloomy, unfavorable

prejudice : blind, deep, deep-rooted, deep-seated, ingrained, strong; race, racial

preparations : careful, elaborate, thorough

president : former, past

pressure : enormous, great, heavy, inexorable, intense, maximum, relentless, severe, strong, unrelieved

prestige : great, high; little, low

price : attractive, fair, moderate, popular, reasonable; bargain, low, reduced; exorbitant, high, inflated, outrageous, prohibitive, steep, stiff; buying, purchase

pride : fierce, great, strong; injured, wounded

principle : basic, fundamental
print : fine, small
priority : first, number one, top
probe : exhaustive, thorough
problem : acute, daunting, difficult, grave, major, pressing, serious; insoluble, insurmountable; complex, complicated, involved, knotty, perplexing, thorny; delicate, ticklish; minor, petty
procedure : correct, proper; normal, regular, standard; complex, complicated
proceedings : judicial, legal
production : stage, theatrical
professor : college, university
profit : handsome, juicy, large, tidy; marginal, small; excess, exorbitant, windfall
prognosis : gloomy, unfavorable
program : graduate, postgraduate
progress : amazing, considerable, good, great; material, significant
projector : film, motion-picture
promise : empty, false, hollow; sacred, solemn; great, real
proof : ample, clear, conclusive, concrete, convincing, definite, incontestable, incontrovertible, indisputable, irrefutable, living, positive, tangible, undeniable, unquestionable
proportions : astronomical, huge
prospect : bright, rosy; bleak, grim
protest : strong, vehement, vigorous
protocol : court, palace, royal
provocation : extreme, gross, severe
publicity : enormous, extensive, wide; adverse, bad; favorable, good
pulse : erratic, irregular, unsteady; regular, steady
punishment : cruel, cruel and unusual; harsh, severe, unjust; light, mild
purpose : lofty, worthy
pursuit : dogged, relentless

Qq

qualifications : excellent, fine, outstanding, strong
quality : excellent, sterling, superb, superior; fine, good, high; inferior, low, poor
quantity : considerable, huge, large, vast; negligible, small
quarrel : bitter, furious, violent; domestic, family
question : academic, hypothetical, rhetorical; debatable, moot; blunt, direct; awkward, embarrassing, sticky, ticklish; loaded, tricky

Rr

race : close, even, hotly contested, tight; governor's, gubernatorial

racism : blatant, out-and-out; vicious, virulent

racketeer : big-time, notorious

rage : blind, towering, ungovernable, violent

rain : drenching, driving, heavy, pouring, soaking, torrential

rainfall : annual, yearly

range : close, short

rape : acquaintance, date

rapport : close, good

rapture : complete, total, utter

reaction : favorable, positive; immediate, instantaneous, quick, spontaneous; instinctive, knee-jerk; natural, normal; adverse, negative; angry, hostile

reactionary : die-hard, dyed-in-the-wool

reactor : atomic, nuclear

reader : avid, omnivorous, voracious

realist : down-to-earth, hardheaded

reason : cogent, compelling, convincing, good, important, plausible, solid, sound, strong, urgent

reasoning : cogent, logical, plausible, solid, sound

rebuke : scathing, sharp, stern, stinging

reception : cordial, friendly, warm; chilly, cold, cool; good, strong; poor, weak

recession : business, economic

recluse : aging, elderly

recognition : general, universal; international, worldwide

recollection : dim, hazy, vague

record : clean, impeccable, spotless, unblemished; brilliant, distinguished, outstanding; mediocre, spotty; criminal, police

recorder : video, videocassette

recovery : quick, rapid, speedy

reference : indirect, oblique; good, positive, satisfactory

reform : radical, sweeping; agrarian, land; penal, prison

refueling : in-flight, midair

refusal : adamant, brusque, categorical, curt, flat, out-and-out, outright, point-blank, unyielding

regard : little, scant

regards : best, cordial, friendly, kind, kindest, sincere, warm, warmest

regime : authoritarian, dictatorial, totalitarian

regret : bitter, deep, great, keen, sincere

regulation : safety, security

rehearsal : dress, final

rejection : complete, flat, outright, total

relapse : complete, total

relations : close, intimate; cordial, friendly, harmonious; strained, troubled; business, commercial, economic, trade; industrial, labor

relationship : stormy, tempestuous

relief : great, immense

religion : established, organized

reluctance : extreme, great

remark : biting, catty, caustic, cutting, nasty, sarcastic, scathing, snide; cruel, unkind; disparaging, insulting, offensive, rude

remedy : certain, reliable, sure; effective, efficacious

remorse : bitter, deep, profound

renown : great, wide; international, worldwide

repair : extensive, major

repast : light, meager

repentance : genuine, sincere

reply : immediate, prompt; brusque, curt, gruff

report : detailed, exhaustive, full; favorable, positive; impartial, objective; biased, slanted; negative, unfavorable

reporting : impartial, objective; biased, slanted

reprimand : severe, sharp, stern; oral, verbal

reproach : above, beyond

repugnance : deep, profound

reputation : enviable, excellent, fine, good, impeccable, spotless, unblemished, unsullied, untainted, untarnished; tainted, tarnished, unenviable; international, worldwide

repute : ill, low

request : moderate, modest; desperate, urgent

requirement : admission, entrance

rescue : daring, heroic

research : detailed, diligent, laborious, painstaking, solid, thorough

resemblance : close, strong; faint, remote, slight

resentment : bitter, deep, profound, sullen

reservations : deep, strong

reserves : limited, meager; limitless, unlimited

resistance : determined, fierce, stiff, strong, stubborn, valiant; nonviolent, passive

resources : limited, meager; limitless, unlimited
respect : deep, great, profound, sincere, utmost
response : affirmative, positive
responsibility : awesome, grave, great, heavy, terrible
restaurant : elegant, first-class
result : end, final
retirement : compulsory, forced
retort : sharp, stinging
retreat : hasty, precipitate
retrieval : data, information
revelation : amazing, astonishing, astounding, startling, stunning, surprising
reverence : deep, profound
review : complimentary, favorable, glowing, positive, rave; negative, unfavorable
revulsion : deep, utmost, utter
reward : ample, handsome
rhetoric : impassioned, passionate
riches : great, untold, vast
ride : bumpy, rough
ridicule : draw, incur
right : exclusive, sole; extreme, far, radical; hard, stiff
ring : false, hollow
rise : sharp, steep; dramatic, sharp
rival : arch, bitter, keen
rivalry : bitter, deep, fierce, intense, keen, strong
river : broad, wide
road : paved, surfaced; back, country; deserted, lonely
roar : deep, thunderous
rope : loose, slack
rout : complete, total, utter
route : alternate, alternative
routine : daily, ordinary
rug : scatter, throw
ruin : complete, utter
ruins : charred, smoking
rule : firm, hard-and-fast, inflexible, ironclad, strict
ruler : absolute, authoritarian, despotic, dictatorial, tyrannical
ruling : fair, just; unfair, unjust
rumor : baseless, unconfirmed, unfounded; idle, vague
run : dry, dummy, trial
rung : bottom, lowest
runner : distance, long-distance
ruse : clever, subtle

Ss

sacrifice : supreme, ultimate
saddle : stock, western
sadness : deep, profound
salary : annual, yearly; big, handsome, high; decent, good; low, meager, poor, small
sale : garage, tag, yard
salt : common, table
salute : smart, snappy

sanctions : economic, trade
sarcasm : biting, devastating, keen, piercing, scathing, withering; mild
satire : biting, scathing
satisfaction : deep, great, profound
save : brilliant, spectacular
saw : buzz, circular, carpenter's
saying : common, old, popular, wise
scale : pay, salary, wage; enormous, grand, large
scandal : juicy, sensational
scar : emotional, psychological; hideous, ugly; noticeable, prominent
scene : disgraceful, shameful
scenery : beautiful, majestic, picturesque
scheme : preposterous, wild-eyed
scholarship : solid, sound, thorough
school : elementary, grade, grammar, primary; high, secondary
science : computer, information
scorn : bitter, withering
scowl : permanent, perpetual
scream : bloodcurdling, loud, shrill
screen : big, silver; television, TV
scrutiny : close, intense, strict, thorough
seaman : able, able-bodied
seaport : bustling, busy
search : careful, exhaustive, painstaking, systematic, thorough; body, strip; door-to-door, house-to-house
seas : calm, smooth
season : breeding, mating, rutting
secret : dark, deep, ugly; closely guarded
seizure : cardiac, heart
self-control : admirable, complete, great, total
self-discipline : great, tremendous
self-examination : frank, honest
sense : common, good, horse; literal, narrow, strict
sentence : harsh, heavy, severe, stiff; jail, prison; indefinite, indeterminate
sentimentality : cloying, maudlin, mawkish
servant : civil, public; faithful, loyal, trusted
service : burial, funeral; midday, noontime; intelligence, secret
serving : generous, large, liberal
session : bull, rap
settlement : fair, reasonable
sex : good, great; kinky, perverse
shack : dilapidated, run-down
shade : delicate, pale, pastel, soft
shame : awful, crying, dirty

shape : excellent, fine, tip-top; bad, poor
share : large, major
shelling : constant, round-the-clock
shelter : air-raid, bomb, underground
shirt : sport, sports
shock : mild, slight; deep, great, nasty, profound, severe, terrible; rude, sudden
shot : crack, good; dunk, stuff
show : one-man, one-person, one-woman
shrine : holy, sacred
sickness : altitude, mountain; motion, travel
side : dark, gloomy
sigh : deep, profound
sight : into, within; comical, funny; horrendous, horrible
sign : sure, telltale, unmistakable
signal : clear, unmistakable; danger, distress
significance : deep, great
silence : absolute, complete, perfect, total, utter; deep, profound; respectful, reverent
silk : artificial, synthetic
silver : pure, sterling
sin : unforgivable, unpardonable
sister : big, elder, older; kid, little, younger
site : building, construction
situation : ticklish, touchy; complex, complicated; crisis, emergency; grave, serious; hopeless, no-win; fluid, unstable
size : enormous, tremendous
skill : consummate, great; management, managerial
skin : sensitive, tender; coarse, rough
sky : blue, clear, cloudless, fair; dull, gray, overcast, sullen
slaughter : indiscriminate, mass, wanton, wholesale
slave : fugitive, runaway
sleep : deep, heavy, profound, sound
sleeper : heavy, sound
slope : gentle, gradual
slump : business, economic
slums : festering, squalid; inner-city, urban
slur : ethnic, racial
smell : delicious, good; faint, slight; bad, dirty, disagreeable, foul, putrid, rank
smile : beautiful, pretty; beguiling, intriguing; cheerful, happy; disarming, engaging
smoke : heavy, thick
smoker : habitual, heavy, inveterate
snake : poisonous, venomous
snore : heavy, loud

snow : driving, heavy; coating of, dusting of
soap : bar of, cake of
sock : ankle, ankle-length
solitude : complete, utter
something : certain, indefinable, indescribable, intangible
sonnet : Italian, Petrarchan
sorrow : deep, great, inexpressible, keen, profound
source : impeccable, unimpeachable; informed, well-informed; reliable, reputable, trustworthy; undisclosed, unnamed; original, primary
space : blank, empty
span : brief, short
speaker : effective, good
spectrum : broad, wide
speech : rousing, stirring; brief, short; impromptu, unrehearsed
speed : breakneck, breathtaking, high, lightning; full, top
spirit : dauntless, hardy
sport : bad, poor; strenuous, vigorous
sports : aquatic, water
spot : isolated, secluded
spring : hot, thermal
stage : beginning, elementary; closing, final, last; critical, crucial
staircase : circular, spiral
stakes : big, high
stand : firm, resolute, strong
standard : rigorous, strict; academic, scholastic
standstill : complete, total
star : falling, shooting; film, movie
stare : cold, icy
start : flying, running
state : bad, poor
statement : brief, short
station : subway, tube, underground; filling, gas, gasoline, petrol, service
stench : dreadful, horrible, unbearable
step : even, steady; careful, prudent; rash, risky
stimulation : erotic, sexual
stimulus : powerful, strong
stop : abrupt, sudden; comfort, rest; regular, scheduled
store : liquor, package; five-and-dime, five-and-ten-cent
storm : fierce, heavy, raging, severe, violent
story : amusing, funny, humorous; likely, plausible; complicated, involved; cock-and-bull, far-fetched; dirty, off-color, risqué; bedtime, children's, fairy
strain : considerable, great; terrible, tremendous; emotional, mental; strong, virulent; attenuated, weak

straits : desperate, dire
stranger : complete, perfect, total, utter
strategy : grand, long-range, long-term; campaign, political; defense, military; economic, financial
streak : mean, nasty, vindictive
street : bustling, busy; deserted, lonely
strength : brute, great; full, maximum
stress : emotional, mental, psychological
stride : considerable, giant, great, tremendous
stroke : crippling, massive, severe
struggle : bitter, desperate, fierce, frantic, violent; ceaseless, unending, unrelenting
student : excellent, outstanding; good, strong; poor, weak; college, university; graduate, postgraduate
studies : graduate, postgraduate
study : careful, detailed, exhaustive, in-depth, intensive, rigorous, thorough; classic, classical
style : classic, classical; flowery, ornate
subject : appropriate, suitable; everyday, mundane; controversial, thorny; delicate, ticklish
submarine : nuclear, nuclear-powered
subsidy : government, public, state
subsistence : bare, hand-to-mouth
success : brilliant, dazzling, great, howling, huge, resounding, roaring, rousing, signal, spectacular, thorough, total, tremendous, unequivocal, unqualified; instant, overnight
suffering : great, incalculable, intense, untold
suggestion : preposterous, ridiculous
suit : custom-made, made-to-measure, made-to-order; off-the-peg, off-the-rack, ready-made
sum : considerable, large, substantial, tidy
sunlight : bright, brilliant, glaring, strong
sunshine : bright, dazzling
supervision : close, strict; lax, slack
supply : abundant, liberal, plentiful
support : ardent, complete, enthusiastic, firm, full, solid, strong, unflagging, unqualified, unstinting, unwavering, wholehearted; lukewarm, qualified; emotional, psychological; government, state; popular, public

supporter : ardent, enthusiastic, fervent, firm, loyal, stalwart, staunch, steady, strong

surface : bumpy, rough, uneven; even, smooth; below the, beneath the, underneath the, under the

surgery : corrective, remedial

surveillance : around-the-clock, constant, round-the-clock

suspicion : groundless, unfounded; lingering, lurking; slight, sneaking

sword : double-edged, two-edged

sympathy : deep, deepest, great, heartfelt, profound, strong

system : highway, motorway, road; rail, railroad, railway; education, school

Tt

table : bargaining, conference, negotiating

tact : considerable, exemplary, great

tale : absorbing, exciting, fascinating, gripping, incredible; hair-raising, harrowing, shocking

talk : blunt, plain; idle, small

talker : fast, glib, smooth

talks : candid, frank; arms-control, arms-limitation

tape : adhesive, sticky

task : delicate, ticklish; fruitless, hopeless

taskmaster : hard, rigid, severe, stern

taste : excellent, exquisite, impeccable; bad, poor; bad, foul; nice, pleasant, sweet

tax : death, estate, inheritance

teacher : practice, student

teaching : practice, student

team : opposing, rival; track, track-and-field

technology : advanced, latest, modern, state-of-the-art

temper : bad, explosive, foul, hot, nasty, quick, uncontrollable, ungovernable, violent; calm, even, mild

temperament : calm, even, mild, quiet

temptation : irresistible, strong

tenet : basic, fundamental

term : concrete, specific

terms : equal, even; familiar, intimate; friendly, good

terrain : harsh, rough, rugged

terror : blind, mortal, sheer, stark

test : demanding, difficult; lie-detector, polygraph; acid, demanding, exacting, litmus, rigorous, severe; exhaustive, extensive, thorough

texture : delicate, fine

theme : central, dominant, main
thesis : doctoral, Ph.D.
thief : common, petty
thinker : deep, profound
thoroughfare : busy, crowded
thought : disconcerting, upsetting
threat : dire, grave, serious
throat : inflamed, red, sore
thunder : clap of, crash of, peal of, roll of
ticket : complimentary, free
time : appropriate, suitable; free, leisure, spare; delightful, good, great, lovely, pleasant, wonderful; bad, hard, miserable, rough, tough, unpleasant
timing : flawless, perfect
tip : big, generous, handsome
tirade : blistering, lengthy
toil : arduous, backbreaking, unremitting
tone : dulcet, sweet; condescending, patronizing; angry, querulous
tongue : caustic, foul, nasty, sharp
tooth : baby, milk
torrent : angry, raging
torture : plain, sheer
touch : gentle, light, soft, soothing
tour : lecture, speaking; conducted, guided
town : jerkwater, one-horse, provincial, sleepy, small
trade : brisk, lively, thriving; foreign, international, overseas
trading : slow, sluggish
tradition : ancient, old; deep-rooted, deep-seated, established
traffic : bumper-to-bumper, heavy; brisk, lively; illegal, illicit
training : in-service, on-the-job
trait : genetic, hereditary
transaction : business, financial
transformation : complete, radical, total; dative-movement, indirect-object
translation : close, literal, word-for-word; free, loose, rough
transportation : ground, surface
trap : radar, speed
travel : foreign, international
traveler : experienced, seasoned
treatment : equal, equitable; atrocious, barbarous, brutal, cruel, harsh, inhumane; exhaustive, lengthy
treaty : bilateral, bipartite; commercial, trade
tree : family, genealogical
trend : discernible, noticeable
tribe : nomadic, wandering
tribute : moving, touching
trick : cheap, contemptible, dirty, low, mean, nasty, shabby, sneaky

trip : extended, long

triumph : glorious, splendid

trouble : deep, real, serious

truck : delivery, panel; garbage, trash

trust : blind, unquestioning

truth : absolute, basic, fundamental, gospel, naked, plain, unvarnished, whole

tumble : bad, nasty

turnout : big, enormous; light, poor, small

turnover : brisk, quick, rapid

twist : bizarre, strange, unusual

type : bold, boldface, boldfaced

tyranny : cruel, merciless

tyrant : cruel, merciless

Uu

ulcer : gastric, stomach

uncertainty : grave, great

undergraduate : college, university

undergrowth : dense, heavy

understanding : complete, full

unemployment : mounting, rising

uniform : dress, full-dress

union : currency, monetary

unit : basic, primary; crack, elite; mechanized, motorized

university : free, open

untruth : blatant, deliberate, transparent

upheaval : big, great

upturn : modest, slight

urge : irrepressible, irresistible, uncontrollable

urgency : great, utmost

utensils : cooking, kitchen

Vv

vacation : extended, long

value : great, high; symbolic, token; religious, spiritual

vegetation : dense, lush, rank

veneration : deep, profound

venture : business, commercial; collaborative, cooperative, joint

verb : auxiliary, helping; copulative, linking

verdict : fair, just; unfair, unjust; adverse, unfavorable

version : abridged, condensed; unabridged, uncut; accepted, authorized, official; different, differing; unauthorized, unofficial; film, movie

viability : commercial, financial

victory : clear, clear-cut, decisive, outright, signal; landslide, overwhelming, resounding, stunning, sweeping

view : cheerful, favorable, optimistic, rosy; grave, grim, pessimistic; contrary, unfavorable; liberal, progressive; beautiful, breathtaking, magnificent, majestic, marvelous, superb, wonderful; clear, unhampered, unimpaired

village : agricultural, farming

villain : arch, consummate

violation : brazen, flagrant, gross

violence : eruption of, flare-up of, outbreak of, outburst of

visibility : clear, good; limited, poor

visit : brief, flying, short; extended, lengthy, long

vocabulary : extensive, huge, large, rich; limited, meager, restricted, small

vocation : genuine, real

voice : friendly, gentle, good, kind, pleasant, soft; mellifluous, melodious, sweet; firm, steady; high, high-pitched; low, low-pitched; quaking, quivering, shaking, shaky, trembling; gruff, harsh, raucous

volcano : active, live; dead, extinct; dormant, inactive

vow : formal, solemn

Ww

wage : decent, living; annual, yearly

waist : slender, slim

war : all-out, full-scale, total; global, world; limited, local; hot, shooting; atomic, nuclear, thermonuclear

ward : maternity, obstetrics

warfare : atomic, nuclear, thermonuclear; bacteriological, germ

waste : complete, sheer, total, utter

wasteland : barren, desolate

water : carbonated, fizzy, sparkling; salt; contaminated, polluted

wave : high, tall

wealth : enormous, fabulous, great, untold

weapon : atomic, nuclear, thermonuclear

weather : clear, fair; fine, good, nice, pleasant; atrocious, bad, beastly, bleak, dismal, dreary, foul, gloomy, inclement, nasty, stormy; cloudy, overcast; humid, muggy

web : intricate, tangled

welcome : cordial, effusive, enthusiastic, hearty, rousing, royal, warm; chilly, cool

while : good, long, little
wife : abused, battered
willpower : great, sheer
wind : balmy, gentle, light; fair, favorable; brisk, heavy, high, stiff, strong; biting, cold, cutting, icy
window : shop, store; back, rear
winter : cold, cruel, hard, harsh, severe, terrible
wiring : defective, faulty
wisdom : folk, homespun
wish : fervent, strong
wit : keen, penetrating, sharp; quick, ready; acerbic, acid, biting, caustic, cutting, mordant, trenchant
woman : attractive, beautiful, pretty
word : archaic, obsolete; dialectal, regional; dirty, four-letter, obscene
words : angry, cross, sharp; heated, hot; hollow, hypocritical
work : meticulous, precise; backbreaking, hard, heavy; exhausting, tiring; dirty, scut; shoddy, slipshod, sloppy; clerical, office
worker : diligent, efficient, good, hard, indefatigable
workmanship : conscientious, meticulous, sound; delicate, exquisite, fine; poor, shoddy
worry : deep, serious
wound : fatal, mortal; serious, severe; bullet, gunshot
wrangling : constant, incessant
wretch : miserable, poor

Yy

year : banner, good; peak, record; bad, lean; financial, fiscal

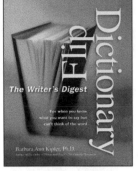

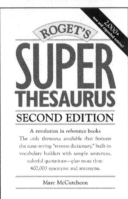

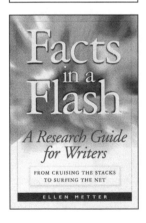

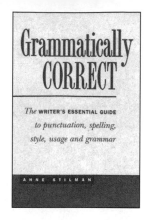

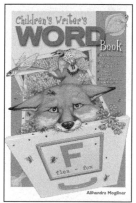

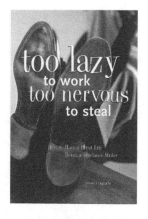

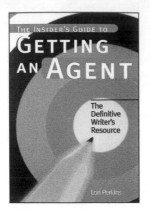

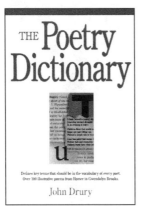

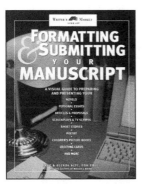